EUROPE'S STEPPE FRONTIER

WILLIAM H. McNEILL

EUROPE'S
STEPPE FRONTIER

1500-1800

THE UNIVERSITY OF CHICAGO PRESS
CHICAGO AND LONDON

The University of Chicago Press, Chicago 60637
The University of Chicago Press, Ltd., London
© 1964 by The University of Chicago
All rights reserved. Published 1964.
Paperback edition 1975

PRINTED IN THE UNITED STATES OF AMERICA

20 19 18 17 16 15 14 13 12 11   3 4 5 6 7

ISBN-13: 978-0-226-56152-3 (paper)
ISBN-10: 0-226-56152-6 (paper)

Library of Congress Catalog Card Number: 64-22248

♾ This paper meets the requirements of ANSI/NISO Z39.48-1992
(Permanence of Paper).

PREFACE

THE HISTORIOGRAPHY of Danubian and Pontic Europe has
been heavily colored by the nationality collisions of the nineteenth and twentieth centuries which so bitterly distracted
the last days of the Hapsburg, Russian, and Ottoman empires. Formidable linguistic obstacles have usually inhibited
outsiders from attempting to thread a path between the
claims of rival national patriotisms. In addition, the traditional compartmentalization of learning, which has assigned
the study of Ottoman history to Islamists for whom all too
often anything subsequent to the sack of Baghdad by the
Mongols in 1258 is anticlimax, has encouraged a neglect of
the Ottoman side of the balance. Stubborn and often quite
unexamined biases that reflect the fear and hostility with
which Christian Europe long regarded the Turks have also
clouded Western scholars' minds, even in quite recent times
and among men for whom the original religious basis of dislike had long since been forgotten.

Since World War II, however, the intensity of the nationality conflicts of eastern and Balkan Europe has begun
unmistakably to fade, while the progress of Islamic and Ottoman studies begins to make possible a more balanced understanding of what transpired in the borderlands between the
Hapsburg, Russian, and Ottoman states. It is in hope of ex-
ploiting these newly opening possibilities that this essay has
been written. Mastery of the primary sources upon which
scholarship must ultimately rest is beyond me; but it is only
when linguistically well-prepared scholars come at their material with well-formulated questions in mind that fruitful
and intellectually satisfying history is likely to result. The
role of this essay, therefore, is to present a new viewpoint on
the tangled tale of Danubian and Pontic Europe's past, in the
hope that better equipped scholars may in the future use
their skills to correct what must at this stage inevitably be
fumbling and imperfect initial formulations.

This essay was started during the academic year 1963 as an

experiment in bringing seminar work and active historianship together. Distractions allowed only the achievement of a rough draft of the first two chapters before the summer, when temporary liberation from other concerns permitted completion of the whole.

The general point of view here set forth was developed through a course of lectures to graduate students at the University of Chicago, repeated four times during a period of some seven years. Their patient but not uncritical attention was very helpful in compelling me to give definition to my thoughts. Far more active was the contribution of John Renaldo, Frederick Young, and Humberto Nelli, members of my seminar in 1963, whose bibliographical energies and informed criticism was brought to bear on the rough draft of the first two chapters. In addition, the completed manuscript has been read by my colleagues Richard Chambers, Arcadius Kahan, and Donald Lach, and by Marc Raeff of Columbia University. Their suggestions saved me from some errors and confirmed my hope that even so thinly informed an essay as this inevitably remains might be worth putting into print.

WILLIAM H. MCNEILL
January 30, 1964

INTRODUCTION

D ANUBIAN AND Pontic Europe comprises the western-most portion of the Eurasian steppe. Before men altered the landscape by their agricultural and other activities, this broad ribbon of grass snaked its way across most of the Eurasian continent, extending from Manchuria in the east to the Hungarian plain in the west. To the north lay the forests; to the south through most of its length, the steppe grasslands shaded off into desert. The pattern broke up in the European portion of the steppe. A more abundant rainfall meant both a richer growth of grass and the possibility that topographic irregularities, by creating local water catchments, might increase ground moisture to a point at which trees could flourish. Hence in Danubian and Pontic Europe wooded hills and mountain slopes intersected the grasslands, and in the valley bottoms watercourses usually flowed through ribbons of forested land.

This more variegated natural landscape arose from the fact that Danubian and Pontic Europe is a region where the Eurasian steppe intersects the main mountain system of the earth — a system that runs from the Pyrenees and Alps, via the mountains of Asia Minor, Iran, and Tibet all the way to the Pacific coast and then sweeps in a great arc around the entire Pacific basin to Tierra del Fuego. To be sure, Europe's principal ranges run south of the Hungarian, Rumanian, and Ukrainian plains; but the spume of mountains thrown off to the north, constituting the Carpathians (together with their westerly extensions into Bohemia) and the similar spur that rises out of the Black Sea to constitute the mountains of the Crimea, differentiated our region from the wider steppe lands further east.

The mountain ranges are so arranged that, together with the Black Sea, they break up the region into a number of distinct plains, divided from one another by high and forested ground, and linked by waterways. Thus, if one follows the Danube from its Alpine sources downstream, through most of its length the plains it traverses are almost completely ringed round by mountains. Only after bursting through the Carpathian barrier at the Iron Gates does wider and more open country, characteristic of the Eurasian steppe, begin. Yet even here there is an anomaly, for the Danube flows into a sea which empties through still another narrow water gap that cuts southward through the earth's main mountain barrier — the straits of the Bosphorus and Dardanelles. The lengthy and, for the most part, slow-moving rivers that flow into the Black Sea from the forested zones of the north, together with the Danube itself, offered ready-made roadways for the transport of goods and men, and made possible trade and river-raiding, even across long distances, in early as in more recent times.

Movement along the major rivers cut across the width of the steppe. But the grass sea was itself a broad and almost undifferentiated highway for those who had mastered the arts of horse nomadry. Nomads could move to and fro at will, either peaceably in search of pasture for their flocks or with other purposes in view: flight, plunder, or trading, as the case might be. The general axis of this sort of movement was east-west, for horsemen had always to move within regions where adequate forage for their mounts could be found, i.e., had to stay within range of the natural grasslands of the steppe. Hence Danubian and Pontic Europe may also be defined as a region where the transcontinental gallop intersected the interregional river boat (in winter, sleigh).

These natural features gave Danubian and Pontic Europe its own unique character. Such an environment offered men a variety of possibilities. Pastoral parasitism on flocks and herds — the usual human adjustment to steppe conditions — could be supplemented (eventually even supplanted) by agriculture, since land well enough watered to sustain a thick cover of grass was also capable of producing excellent crops of grain. In the mountains, mining — the Carpathians became an important producer of silver in the fourteenth and fifteenth centuries — and the extraction or collection of forest products was a third possibility. Transhumance between high mountain pastures and the bottom lands offered yet another pattern of human life well attuned to the local differences of landscape. Trade, warfare, and varying forms of political mastery and subjugation linked these economic communities to one another in complex and persistently unstable fashion; but until 1500, a rough if fluctuating balance between the different elements in the human and animal population of the region maintained itself.

This balance was in part sustained by the comparatively weak and inefficient agricultural tools then known in Danubian and Pontic Europe. Deep-rooted sod offers stout resistance to a plow, and unless the turf can be effectively turned over and buried deeply enough to smother the native vegetation entirely, grass roots will send up fresh shoots in the spring to crowd out the young grain. By contrast, deciduous woodland was easy to cultivate with very simple tools. Girdling the bark with an ax sufficed to kill the trees. This let sunlight through to the ground, where, once the leaf mould had been scraped away or turned under, unencumbered soil awaited the seed. After a few years of such cultivation, fertility could be renewed by burning the dead trees and scattering their ashes on the soil.

This style of slash-and-burn agriculture was very ancient, dating back to neolithic times. As long as virgin forest land remained available, it constituted an effective mode of exploitation of the environment. The fact that stumps and tree roots cumbered such fields did not hamper operations seriously, for the plow was small and light and merely broke the surface (like a modern disk plow) without turning a furrow (as does a modern mouldboard plow). Hence there was no great difficulty in plowing around and between the tree trunks in a soil that, as anyone who has ever walked through a forest knows, was already soft and loosely compacted.

But the sort of plow suited for forest use was completely inadequate to the much heavier work of breaking sod. Only a mouldboard plow, capable of turning a deep furrow completely over, was equal to that task; and to pull a heavy mouldboard plow through tough, matted grass roots required a force several times as great as did the small scratch plows of the forest fields. Thus the agricultural techniques of the mountain woodland were quite unsuited to large-scale cultivation of the grassy plains.

Plows technically capable of penetrating the grasslands were not unknown in Pontic and Danubian Europe. In the thirteenth century, for example, pioneers from western Europe who settled in Transylvania, mainly in the mining districts of the Carpathians, brought the mouldboard plow into the region. But the long acres and open fields of the Saxon towns of Transylvania remained exceptional. Magyars, Slavs, and Rumanians found no compelling reason to imitate the German settlers' far more expensive implements, particularly when altered field shapes, new property concepts, and much larger plow teams had to be found if the new agricultural technology were to be put into operation. Since arable or potentially arable land was not yet critically short, such an enlarged capital outlay scarcely made sense.

Nevertheless, virgin forest land was not infinite, and the traditional modes of tillage in Danubian Europe used up the forests rather rapidly. Whenever they could, slash-and-burn farmers shifted their scene of operations every few years, for repeated cropping with grain rapidly reduced the initial fertility of their woodland plots. Whenever suitable virgin woodland could no longer be found, it became necessary to return (and at gradually shortened intervals) to land which had already been cropped to exhaustion and then abandoned. As thicker populations formed, therefore, a more settled type of agriculture, based upon fallowing (i.e., a cyclical return to once exhausted fields) established itself. Periodically renewed cultivation held back the forest and eventually led to the disappearance of old stumps, which simply rotted. The repeated action of the plow tended also to smooth out small irregularities in the surface of the ground. Hence, in the course of a single human generation, the tidy, leveled fields which we so firmly associate with the cultivation of grain could develop where primeval forest formerly had stood. Until quite modern times, no comparably simple technique for taming grasslands to agriculture lay at hand, though men could always make grain grow in the steppe if they weeded out competing grasses diligently enough. But this required careful work with hoe and hand, and tended to keep grassland grain fields to the proportion of gardens.

These limitations of traditional agricultural techniques were powerfully reinforced by the military superiority nomad herdsmen enjoyed over scattered agriculturalists. Nomads had horses and could raid and run over long distances with small risk, since their mobility allowed them either to concentrate superior forces at one spot, more or less at will, or to flee to safety if unexpected opposition developed. Cultivators, on the contrary, were strongly tempted to disperse whatever force they brought together in time of emergency, for each man was always eager and anxious to see what had happened to his own family, house, and fields. Hence only a professional military force could successfully cope with the nomad danger; but given the primitive character of agriculture in Danubian and Pontic Europe, both before and after 1500 A.D., the costs of such an establishment were a very heavy burden for the peasantry to bear. Herein lay the principal reason for the weakness of the medieval kingdom of Hungary, demonstrated so spectacularly on the field of Mohacz in 1526.

The defeat of Magyar chivalry at Mohacz was not the first such peripety in the history of the Hungarian, Rumanian, and Ukrainian plans. Cimmerians, Scythians, Sarmatians, Goths, Huns, Gepids, Avars, and Petchenegs had also in their time met disastrous defeat after varying periods of political dominion; and their empires, which had once looked most impressive on the map, each time dissolved almost at a blow into dispersed bodies of desperate fugitives. A formidable fragility was inherent in all steppe empires. Built, characteristically, on the strength of some great war captain's successes, they were capable of almost instantaneous fragmentation into the ultimate units of pastoral life: the small, dispersed, patriarchal kindreds whose flocks and herds pastured together the year round.

We may perhaps detect a natural ecological cycle in the political history of Danubian Europe between the eighth-seventh centuries B.C., when men first fully mastered the arts of steppe nomadry, and the sixteenth-seventeenth centuries A.D., when firearms, standing armies, and the supporting elements of modern civilized warfare reversed the age-old balance between steppe and sown and drove the nomads into permanent retreat. Prior to this reversal in roles — whose more detailed analysis will be the theme of this essay — a pastoral conqueror was likely to celebrate his victories by brutal harassment of any pre-existing human inhabitants who were so imprudent as to await his coming. Most of whatever agricultural population might have crept out into the plains under an earlier regime was thereby uprooted. Refugees crowded into the mountain valleys or fled northward to take cover in forested ground where nomad arrows and horsemen lost most of their effectiveness.

In the course of time, however, relations between hunter and hunted tended to stabilize themselves. Nomad conquerors badly needed agricultural products to supplement the yield of their flocks and herds, and found ways to acquire grain and other such commodities — sometimes by trade, but more usually by a successful transfer of nomadic parasitism from animal herds to human population. As this occurred, descendants of nomad conquerors became a species of landlord, exacting goods and services from an alien peasantry. But since farmland and granaries were as immobile for a noble lord as they were for a poor peasant, in proportion as the heirs of conquerors settled down to dependence on agriculture, they lost their mobility. They tended also to lose habits of prowess. Wealthy masters of a sullen peasantry were less eager to leave their estates for distant military adventure than their nomadic ancestors had been. Hence war-band discipline and cohesion tended also to disintegrate until the effective military strength of the ruling community waned to such a point that some fresh body of invading warriors could burst like a sudden storm upon the land and start the whole cycle over again.

After 1000 A.D., two factors complicated the operation of this cycle. Political weakness in the civilized regions of central Asia and northern India deflected the main thrust of nomad expansion southward, thus substantially reducing the pressure from the east on Danubian Europe. Simultaneously, the rise of western Europe as a center of a very vigorous and formidable civilization supplied the masters of the Hungarian plain with a new cultural model. The conversion of the Magyar monarch, St. Stephen, to Christianity in 1000 A.D. aptly symbolizes the new power Latin and German Europe had begun to exercise; and the subsequent dynastic history of the Kingdom of Hungary, which brought scions of the house of Anjou to the throne, enlarged the cultural connections of the Magyar aristocracy to encompass French as well as German and Italian Europe.

Another factor, whose importance cannot be satisfactorily determined, was the fluctuation of population density resulting from epidemic diseases. Dramatic and thoroughly drastic consequences could and sometimes certainly did result when a previously isolated community, among whose members no inherited or acquired immunities to a particular strain of disease germs existed, was for the first time exposed to a new infection. In a world composed of such isolated communities, unusual movements of large numbers of human beings were likely to trigger sudden and disastrous outbreaks of epidemic; and a general churning of peoples like that which accompanied the Mongol conquests of the thirteenth century may well have provoked outbreaks of plagues of different kinds in different places.

No satisfactory record of the virulence of really drastic epidemics can be expected, since in a time of general disruption, chroniclers are likely to be among the first to disappear. Hence, for example, the depopulation of the Ukraine after the breakdown of Kievan hegemony may have resulted less from the immediate rapine and bloodshed of conquest by the Polovtsi than from epidemics incident to such conquests. Since the rivers and open steppe of the Ukraine were peculiarly suited to long-distance communication, disease may have struck communities there much harder than happened further west, where secluded mountain valleys, bypassed alike by disease germs and by plundering conquerors and tax collectors, continued to sustain agricultural populations from which, in times of peace and in the absence of epidemic, repopulation of the plains could and did occur.

The consequences of these (and no doubt of other) factors was to create a distinct, cultural gradient within Danubian and Pontic Europe. In 1500, for example, a plain like the Marchfeld, where Vienna is located, belonged fully within the circle of western Christendom. The plain sustained peasant, noble, and burgher classes, united by governmental and ecclesiastical institutions and sharing all the other traits of European civilization. The Little Alföld, whose natural capital is called Pressburg by Germans, Pozsony by Magyars, and Bratislava by Slovaks, was less fully developed, but also clearly belonged to the circle of west European society.

The next plain, the Great Alföld, was transitional. The land was thinly occupied by Magyar lords and a peasantry partly Magyar, partly Slavic, partly Rumanian. Towns were less developed than in western Europe and were inhabited mainly by foreigners, mostly Germans. Spring flooding created extensive marshes along the rivers and streams, so that the ground could only be used for summer pastures. These marshes obstructed access to the rivers so severely that the value of the natural waterways for transport was practically nil except in winter, when the ice made movement to and along the riverways comparatively easy. Relations between nobles and commoners were unstable. Aristocrats' efforts to squeeze more money, goods, and services from the peasantry met with limited and local successes, but also inflamed hostilities between the two classes to a point seldom equaled in western Europe.

There were good reasons for this. On the one hand, peasants were aware of the free (or almost free) life of wandering slash-and-burn forest cultivators. Reversion to this pattern of life remained a practical possibility, which the nobles held in check only by the constant exertion of their superior military force. The nobles, for their part, recalled with pride their Magyar origin as conquerors from the east. Basing their claims on right of conquest, they recognized no binding limit upon their demands against the subjugated peasantry. Such a society, therefore, resembled the societies of western Europe in some outward aspects but remained structurally distinct. It was, in fact, transitional to the still nakedly predatory relation between mutually alien communities of cultivators and nomads (strictly, in most cases, of ex-nomads) that was then still characteristic of Pontic Europe.

The northern fringes of the Great Alföld were, however, more thickly settled by peasants who had emerged from the sheltering valleys of the Carpathians. Particularly in Transylvania, protected as it was by the crook of the Carpathian range and blessed with a fertile, well-drained soil, metalliferous rock outcroppings, and a more complex social structure than that prevailing in the open plain, the landscape attained a far more European aspect. From the twelfth century, German settlers had built a series of towns, modeled closely after those of their homeland; and German miners and farmers had also transplanted the full technical apparatus of western Europe to remote valleys of Transylvania. Free peasant warriors known as Szeklers constituted another distinctive element in the Transylvanian population. The Szeklers were descendants of a tribe of nomads, speaking a language closely related to the Magyar tongue. They had been established in the Kingdom of Hungary from the twelfth century and enjoyed special immunities from taxes and rents in return for frontier guard. Saxons had settled the region from the same period; but the major development of German town life occurred in the fourteenth and fifteenth centuries, when German miners made the silver mines of Transylvania into a major source of precious metal for all Europe. As a result, the polarity between Magyar magnates and poverty-stricken peasants, which was characteristic of the Great Alföld, was modified in Transylvania by the existence of substantial interstitial groups: privileged burghers, miners, and artificers, together with a noble gentry, great and small, which tailed off into families whose claim to noble status dignified what in fact amounted to the life of a free peasant, owning no master, but nonetheless compelled by poverty to work in the fields like any ordinary cultivator.

On both sides of the Carpathians, in Moldavia and Wallachia as well as in Transylvania, Rumanian-speaking Vlach populations preserved a semi-migratory style of life: some pasturing flocks high in the mountain uplands in summer and descending to protected lowlands in winter; others engaged in shifting slash-and-burn agriculture; still others descending to the plains to help with the harvest or with any other enterprise requiring manual labor paid by wages in kind.

Here a simpler style of social organization survived, though by 1500 its survival was clearly precarious. The critical problem was military defense. The rude, semitribal political organization of the Vlachs was sometimes effective in repelling an invader. In 1475, for example, Stephen the Great, Prince of Moldavia, won a remarkable victory over the field forces of the Turkish empire by summoning all his boyars with their followers, down to the last youngster strong enough to draw a bowstring. This ill-trained force lay in wait for the Turks in sheltering forest land, where forage for the invading host could not be found. Yet Stephen's great victory was not won without help from Polish and Hungarian detachments of a more professional type of warrior; and both these neighbors — as well as the Turks — regarded the Vlach provinces of Moldavia and Wallachia as a legitimate prey.

Moreover, the aristocratic, militarized life of a Polish or Magyar noble was attractive to the ambitions of the Vlach chieftains, or boyars. The conversion of traditional dues into rents, of followers into serfs, of leadership into lordship, opened fascinating possibilities. Wealth and culture both beckoned the boyars along such a path; but the further they progressed in that direction, the more impossible it became to rally the manpower of the entire community for common defense against an outside invader. Embittered followers and reluctant rent payers were not likely to fight bravely and well at the command of the men who were oppressing them.

For a while in the fifteenth century, a third path seemed possible. By holding key river and Black Sea ports and taxing trade heavily, Stephen the Great secured a significant income with which he was able to maintain a professional armed following. This, supplemented by the traditional levy of the whole people, made him a formidable force in local wars; but the commercial base was tenuous, and Moldavian boyars could not be prevented from eroding the strength of the national levy by trying to increase their own incomes at the expense of the commoners. Hence on his deathbed, Stephen instructed his son to come to terms with the neighboring power least likely to disturb the traditional social order of Moldavia — i.e., with the Turks, whose religious tolerance and more egalitarian polity threatened the Orthodoxy and patriarchal tribalism of Moldavia less than Catholic and aristocratic Poland or Hungary would have done.

The vast Pontic steppe, bordering the Black Sea on the west and north, was very thinly populated in 1500. Some settlers clung to the river courses, where bottom land offered easy tillage and the open grass sustained scattered herdsmen. But no well-ordered nomadism survived; still less did any considerable agricultural population. Instead, the heirs of nomad conquerors, concentrated for the most part in the natural bastion of the Crimean peninsula, had discovered that the heroic life of the raiding horseman, supplemented occasionally by more peaceable exchanges of goods, offered a more attractive existence than did the hard life of a steppe nomad. As a result, a long series of annual raids, directed against the bordering agricultural populations far to the north and west, had pushed the fringes of agricultural settlement back within the tree line and (perhaps helped by pestilence) had produced something approaching a desert across the entire Pontic steppe.

The Crimea itself, like Transylvania to the west, constituted a sort of islanded community, where the gains of raiding and trading across the whole Pontic region tended to concentrate. These gains sufficed to sustain a few towns, in which significant artisan and mercantile communities flourished. The politically dominant culture of the Crimea was Islamic, with ties both eastward into central Asia (the khans of Crim Tartary traced descent from the great Genghis himself) and southward to the still rising Ottoman Empire of the Balkans and Asia Minor. If Transylvania is properly described as a partially isolated offshoot of the west European style of society, the Crimea may be appropriately regarded as its Moslem parallel: a peripheral participant in the Ottoman style of civilization.

In retrospect, it is clear that the progress of civilized armament had already by 1500 doomed the cavalry raiding of the Crim Tartars to extinction. But it was a long time before this was definitively demonstrated on the spot. Decisive exercise of the military power of agricultural states depended in some measure upon the slower, surer advances of agricultural organization and technique, which by the latter part of the seventeenth century allowed men to tame the open steppe successfully to large-scale tillage. This possibility made conquest and protection of the empty steppe lands definitely worth while, since settlers could be brought in, rents and taxes collected, and new wealth created by whoever held the steppe securely in his power. Realization of this fact by the rulers of all the neighboring states resulted in very rapid advance of settlement, until by 1800 all of Danubian and Pontic Europe had been enfolded into one or other of the three great agricultural empires — Hapsburg, Russian, and Ottoman — bordering upon the region.

Until after the middle of the seventeenth century, however, things were not nearly so clear as such a statement suggests. Desperate confusion, intrigue, violence, with sudden reversals of fortune and continual brutal chicanery, characterized the political life of the region. The progress of agriculture was achieved for the most part by means of a more and more ruthless resort to compulsion against humble peasants, whose labor, being in short supply, was also in fierce demand. Nor was it sure that the centers around which Danubian and Pontic Europe was to organize a civilized style of life would lie outside the region's limits. Transylvania, the Rumanian principalities, the Zaporozhian Cossacks, and the Crim Tartars each made bids for independent sovereignty. Each failed; but only after a time of uncertainty, when the upshot appeared to hang in the balance. Nor, in 1500, was it obvious that the empires that would divide the steppe lands were to center in Vienna, Constantinople, and Moscow; for Warsaw and Prague were then still in the running as alternative foci of imperial rule.

CHAPTER
TWO

OTTOMAN ADVANCE
TO 1570

THE DEATH OF Matthias Corvinus, king of Hungary, in 1490 allowed the Magyar nobility to assert its interests very effectively against the aspiring absolutism of the crown. King Matthias' overgrown bodyguard — the "Black Troop" of mercenaries, sustained by ruthless taxation and unending plunder — was at once disbanded. The new king, Ladislas of Bohemia, promised the nobles who elected him to the Hungarian throne that he would utterly eschew his predecessor's subversive and expensive military policy. In the thirty-six years that followed, first Ladislas (1490–1516) and then his son, Louis (1516–1526) adhered faithfully to that promise. Consequently, the power of the Hungarian monarchy, which for a few brief decades had loomed large indeed on the map of southeastern Europe, abruptly evaporated. Unscrupulous intrigues among the magnate families at the top of the social pyramid were matched by bitter and brutal collisions between subordinate social classes; and the outlying dependencies which Matthias and his father John Hunyadi had grouped around the Hungarian kingdom — Silesia, Moravia, Austria, Moldavia, Wallachia, Serbia — all fell away.

Confusion and violence came to a crisis in 1514 when what started as a crusade against the Turks turned into a peasant rebellion, cruelly put down by the armed nobility of the land. The task of suppressing this rebellion did not fall primarily upon the great magnates, each of whom ruled thousands of acres and whose habit of life already aped the courtly manners of German and Italian aristocrats. Instead, the ruder and far more numerous petty nobles bore the brunt of the struggle. But the bloody work of hunting down runaway peasants and killing contumacious serfs accorded well with the outlook and tastes of the Magyar gentry who still retained a goodly share of the harsh military virtues of their nomad ancestors. The military leader of the victorious gentry was John Zapolya, Voivod of Transylvania,[1] who before King

---

[1] Literally, "war leader" of Transylvania, an office comparable to the

Louis' birth had openly aspired to be elected king of Hungary and still nourished his ambitions in private.

Zapolya's political past made him too controversial to be effective in framing the legal settlement that followed the suppression of the peasant rebellion. His initiative was automatically suspect by all those (including the entire circle of magnates and officeholders around King Louis) who had opposed his candidacy for the throne. Hence not Zapolya, but his agent and ally, a skilled lawyer and political orator, Stephen Verböczi, took the lead in redefining the constitutional laws of the kingdom. First the Diet enacted a series of punitive measures against the peasantry, reducing them to permanent servitude and specifically depriving them of their earlier right to change masters by moving away to a new place. Goods, services, and money payments that peasants had to render to the noble landowners were also defined afresh and to the peasants' disadvantage, for obligations which had before been sporadic, local, or exceptional were declared general, normal, and perpetual.

In the same year (1514), Verböczi reduced the customs of the Kingdom of Hungary to writing, in a document familiarly known as the *Tripartitum*. The *Tripartitum* was never enacted into law by the Diet. Custom stood on its own feet as the law of the land, and needed no such enhancement of its authority. The importance of the *Tripartitum* lay in the fact that it put into a form easily accessible to every Hungarian nobleman a definition of all the rights and immunities claimed by the nobility against the king and his agents. In particular, the *Tripartitum* stated that nobles enjoyed immunity from arrest without prior legal judgment, were subject only to a legally crowned king, paid no taxes whatsoever, and could be required to render military service only for the defense of the realm. Finally, the right of rebellion was guaranteed against any king who infringed upon the rights of the nobility in any way.

Such a statement of their rights and immunities suited

Lords Marchers of English medieval history, endowed with special powers to protect an exposed frontier region of the kingdom.

well enough the wishes of the old-fashioned Magyar cavalry-men, who constituted the bulk of the gentry class. They were free men and warriors who lorded it over a few poverty-stricken serfs, recognizing no master and obeying — whether in war or peace — only those captains whom they themselves chose to follow. But the *Tripartitum* fell far short of satisfying the needs of the country as a whole. By far the most critical defect of the constitutional settlement enshrined in the *Tripartitum* was the disruption it brought to the defense of the kingdom. For the nobles' effort to hedge in the monarch and check his power meant that effective military defense against any major foreign assault could no longer be organized. Moreover, at home the factionalism of the Magyar nobility itself prevented the attainment of a reasonable level of peace and order in the countryside. Noble habits of violence were partly controlled, partly unleashed at local county assemblies where such important matters as tax rates for peasantry and townsmen, lawsuits between nobles, military levies, and elections to the central Diet all were settled, sometimes by talk and sometimes by threat or actual resort to force.

The result, therefore, was that Hungary suffered from a mounting scale of local violence in the half century after 1514. Chronic local disorder was accentuated from time to time by border raids issuing from Turkish territory to the south. Then, in 1521, the sultan's field forces appeared on Hungarian territory for the first time since John Hunyadi had driven Mohammed the Conqueror back from Belgrade (1456). Thereafter, a series of full-scale Turkish campaigns, ending only with the death of the Sultan Suleiman the Law-giver in 1566, added an ultimate dimension to the disintegration of the public peace in Hungary.

Under such conditions, Danubian Europe tended to revert toward older and more primitive patterns of society. Herding gained ground at the expense of cultivation, population decreased, and a general impoverishment maintained or even sharpened the collisions among the social classes. On the eve of Hungary's great military disaster at Mohacz

- ▬ ▬ ▬ Ottoman Frontier *ca.* 1570
- ⊓⊓⊓⊓⊓ Kingdom of Hungary
- ············ Hapsburg Hereditary Lands *ca.* 1570
- ------- Kingdom of Poland-Lithuania

(1526), where the flower of Magyar chivalry was cut down by Turkish cannon, and even the pretense of central royal government ended when King Louis lost his life fleeing from the scene of the disaster, the papal nuncio described the state of the kingdom as follows:

> Everything needed for war is lacking. Among the Estates reign hate and need. And the subjects would, if the Sultan promises them freedom, raise an even more gruesome revolt against the nobles than in the time of the crusade [i.e., 1514]. But if the King gives them freedom, then he will alienate the nobility.[2]

Such devolution, however, simply enlarged the scope for the rough and ready Magyar cavalrymen who constituted the gentry class. Their ancestral way of life was, after all, tolerably well adapted to just such precarious conditions. Serf owners, of course, suffered unpalatable economic losses whenever a village was burnt and its population dispersed; and violent death in raid and counterraid very likely reduced the numbers of the Magyar nobility more or less in proportion to the general depopulation of the Hungarian plain. The point is merely that amid such local ruin and repeated disaster, the free and masterless fighting man on his horse had a better chance of survival than had any more elaborate military or governmental structure. The man of prowess was in a position to round up any stray serfs who had survived the latest disturbance and compel the wretches to work for him until another major unheaval dissolved and disorganized such local arrangements once more, whereupon the cycle merely started over again. Hence disorder, impoverishment, the retreat of cultivation, and depopulation tended always to confirm the predominance of the gentry within the Magyar body politic and thereby preserved the constitutional settlement enshrined in the *Tripartitum*, whose gross defects, ironically and to Hungary's great cost, were thus its greatest strength.

A little further east in Pontic Europe, a similar, and in

[2] Translated from Wilhelm Fraknoi, *Ungarn vor der Schlacht bei Mohacz, 1524–26* (Budapest: Lauffer, 1886), p. 231.

the end even more drastic, social devolution set in from the last quarter of the fifteenth century. The capture of Constantinople in 1453 by Mehmed the Conqueror put the Black Sea trade at the mercy of the new master of the straits; and since that trade had been mainly in Italian, especially Genoese, hands, Mehmed had no compunction in cutting it off. The Genoese had, after all, offered the only important foreign help the Byzantines had received in their death agony. Moreover, control of the narrow seas, particularly of the Black Sea and of the Aegean, was vital to the security and prosperity of Constantinople. Quite apart from such political-military considerations, the sultan was concerned to assure the provisioning of his new capital. Hence, like the Romans and Byzantines of old, he required all ships passing through the straits to submit to inspection and entirely prohibited the export of such strategic materials as grain, horses, leather, lead, gunpowder, and weapons.[3]

These regulations were particularly damaging to the fish and grain trade of Pontic Europe, which had assumed substantial scale in the fourteenth and fifteenth centuries. Instead of being able to direct their ships to any part of the Mediterranean where local harvest shortages had raised food prices, the merchants of Pontic Europe now had to offer their fish and grain preferentially to a single market, Constantinople, where prices were kept low by official regulation. At first, the Genoese attempted to escape such regulations by opening land and river routes through Moldavia and Poland, by running the Straits despite Turkish cannon on the shores, and by offering the sultan terms whereby, in return for allowing their ships to carry a definite quantity of grain through the Straits, the returning vessels would bring back specified items of commerce of which the Turks stood in need. But all in vain. Geography put the trade of the Black Sea inescapably under the control of any strong ruler of

[3] G. I. Bratianu, "Études sur l'approvisionnement de Constantinople, et le monopole du blé a l'époque Byzantine et Ottomane," Études byzantines d'histoire économique et sociale (Paris: Paul Genthner, 1938), pp. 168–77.

Constantinople; and Mehmed wanted the fish and grain of Pontic Europe to feed his new capital.[4]

The result of the new regime of the Straits, therefore, was sharply disadvantageous to the merchants, farmers, and fishers of the Black Sea coasts. Their loss was Constantinople's gain, for the measures taken by the sultan's government supplied enough foodstuffs to his capital to sustain a very rapid growth of population, from less than 100,000 in 1453 to between 500,000 and 800,000 in 1600.[5]

In 1474 matters took a new and decisive turn. The Crim Tartars in that year organized a large-scale raid against village populations of the Black Sea region and enslaved thousands of captives. This event inaugurated a long series of similar raids, with the result that during the 1480's slaves supplanted grain as the major export of Crimean ports.

There are several interesting aspects to this change in the commerce of Pontic Europe. Before 1474 the Crim Tartars, heirs though they were of the tradition of Genghis Khan, had struck a comparatively peaceable *modus vivendi* with the agricultural and urban populations of the Black Sea region. There were obvious attractions in such a relationship. In return for permitting peaceful passage down the rivers, Tartar horsemen received "protection money," whether in kind or in coin. This in turn allowed the rude Tartars of the

---

[4] Cf. Wilhelm Heyd, *Geschichte des Levanthandels im Mittlelalter*, II (Stuttgart: J. G. Cotta'schen Buchhandlung, 1879), pp. 393–400; J. Nistor, *Die auswärtigen Handelsbeziehungen der Moldau im XIV, XV und XVI Jahrhundert* (Gotha: Perthes, 1911), pp. 188 ff.

[5] Albert H. Lybyer, "Constantinople as Capital of the Ottoman Empire," *Annual Report of the American Historical Association* (1916), I, 377; Fernand Braudel, *La Méditerranée et le monde méditerranéen à l'époque de Philippe II* (Paris: Librairie Armand Colin, 1949), pp. 272, 283, 461–62; Nicholas Jorga, *Points de vue sur l'histoire du commerce de l'Orient à l'époque moderne* (Paris: Librairie universitaire J. Gamber, 1925), pp. 3–25; Walter Hahn, *Die Verpflegung Konstantinopels durch staatliche Zwangswirtschaft, nach türkischen Urkunden aus dem 16. Jahrhundert* (Beihefte zur Vierteljahrschrift für Sozial-und Wirtschaftsgeschichte, VIII [Stuttgart: W. Kohlhammer, 1926]), p. 11 and *passim*; Alfons Maria Schneider, "Die Bevölkerung Konstantinopels im XV. Jahrhundert," *Nachrichten der Akademie der Wissenschaften in Göttingen*, No. 1 (1949), pp. 233–44.

OTTOMAN ADVANCE

steppe to secure goods of urban manufacture from the merchants of the Crimea, some of which, e.g., metal knives and sabers, were of great value to their traditional warlike and nomadic existence. Some Tartars even began to settle down to agriculture, finding grain such a valuable supplement to the products of their herds as to justify the cultivator's ineluctable enslavement to the work-hungry land. Others served a vital role in the commerce of the region as caravan attendants.

But details of the relationship between the Crimean Tartars and Pontic farmers are most uncertain. All that is sure is that substantial grain exports from the Crimean ports occurred in the earlier part of the fifteenth century despite (or because of) the presence of the Tartar horde in the Crimea and the adjacent steppe land. After 1474, however, the grain trade speedily collapsed when Tartar raids began to harass and destroy the village settlements whence grain had come.[6] The outbreak and long continuance of these raids — whatever the circumstances that provoked and sustained them — seem clearly to have been a reversion on the part of the Tartars to ancestral patterns of predation upon an agricultural and comparatively helpless population.

From another point of view, however, the Crim Tartars were simply playing the age-old political game of balance of power; for in launching their raids against the farmers of Pontic Europe, the Tartar horsemen were attacking lands belonging to Polish-Lithuanian nobles whose military mode of life and lordly attitudes toward their peasants closely re-

[6] From the point of view of Constantinople, destruction of the grain supplies from the northern Black Sea coastal plains was tolerable because simultaneously a substantial increase in commercial grain production occurred in the lower Danubian region — in what is today northern Bulgaria and across the river in Wallachia. Cf. F. Braudel, *La Méditerranée*, p. 574, for travelers' reports of Bulgaria and the lower Danube as the granary of Turkey.

In effect, therefore, the Turks were exchanging an agricultural base nearer their capital for one more distant; an area firmly under their military dominance for one beyond their effective control; and by drawing grain from the closer region and human livestock from the further parts of Pontic Europe, they were in fact setting up a very rational division of labor between the two portions of their Pontic hinterland.

sembled the style familiar among the Magyar nobility of the same age. This collision was part of a larger diplomatic-military realignment of forces in eastern Europe, resulting from the rise of Muscovy and of Turkey and the parallel decay of the Golden Horde.

As a matter of fact, the Crim Tartar state itself was a fragment of the Golden Horde. During its first decades of separate political existence (from about 1430), the Crim Tartars' primary rival was the khan of the Kipchak horde, based at Astrakhan on the lower Volga. This enmity at first compelled the Crim Tartars to adopt a generally inoffensive policy toward both of the Christian powers that flanked them south and north — the Italian trading cities of the Crimea and the expanding aristocratic polity of Poland-Lithuania. The conquest of Constantinople, however, stimulated the Tartars in 1454 to attack the Genoese of the Crimea in alliance with the Ottoman Turks. When this effort failed, the Tartars lapsed again into a relatively demure diplomatic role vis à vis their Christian neighbors. In 1468, after a disputed succession, a new Tartar khan, Mingli-girai, came to power. Mingli-girai owed his victory in part to the help of Genoese mercenaries and used his office to repay the debt he had incurred.

Such an alignment failed to please the sultan in Constantinople. Matters came to a head in 1474–75, when the sultan's forces collided with the Polish-Lithuanian power in Moldavia. In January, 1475, the prince of Moldavia, Stephen the Great (d. 1504), with the help of Polish and Hungarian detachments, succeeded in inflicting a major defeat upon the Turkish field army. But though the sultan's land forces thus suffered disaster, the prestige of Turkish arms was in some measure rescued by the success that met the supporting maritime operation. For the Ottoman fleet, despatched against the Genoese in the Crimea, took Kaffa and other key ports of the northern Black Sea, making that body of water into an Ottoman lake for the first time.

This victory had definitive consequences for the Crim Tartars. Mingli-girai, as an ally of the Genoese, was taken captive and despatched to Constantinople, where he was condemned to death. On the eve of his execution, however, the sultan pardoned his defeated foe, formally invested him as khan once more, and sent him back to resume his reign over the Tartars.[7] A Turkish garrison was planted in Kaffa to keep the khan in line with Constantinople's policy; and the Turks also despatched a number of religious dignitaries, whose task was to tie the Tartar religious establishment firmly to Constantinople. The result, therefore, was that in 1475 the Crim Tartars, together with their Genoese trading partners, lost an independence they had only briefly enjoyed.

Five years later, in 1480, the new diplomatic-military line-up of Pontic Europe was confirmed by the conclusion of a treaty of alliance between Mingli-girai and Ivan III, the Grand Duke of Muscovy. This treaty was directed against Poland-Lithuania and the khanate of Astrakhan and suited the interests of both rulers very well. The alliance was not disturbed by the fact that a Tartar faction in Polish pay launched the first massive Tartar raid against Muscovy in 1512, thus making the Muscovite lands subject to the sort of slave hunting that had already been visited upon inhabitants of the more westerly Russian lands for a full generation.

This extension of Tartar enterprise eastward did not diminish operations further west. With Ottoman encouragement and support, the Tartars continued to ravage Polish-Lithuanian lands regularly, seizing livestock, burning villages, and enslaving the human population that fell within their grasp.

The Crim Tartars were, however, never tightly organized or effectively administered from any one center. Once the profits and excitement of raiding had been demonstrated, individual captains could and often did launch expeditions on their own initiative, sometimes even in defiance of the

[7] The slave raid of 1474 was organized by Mingli-girai's rivals for power; his restoration to office by the Ottoman Turks was the result of their failure to send a Tartar detachment to aid the Ottoman army in Moldavia. Even when restored to power, Mingli-girai was not able to control the actions of all the Tartars, who raided where they pleased and whom they pleased, with only prudential attention to the khan's wishes and instructions.

policy of the khan and his accredited agents. Constantinople's control was even more remote. Nevertheless, a shared Moslem tradition, in which military assault upon Christendom played a prominent role, and a pervasive coincidence of military-diplomatic interest between the sultans and the khans of the Crimea did establish a loose co-ordination between the disciplined imperial armies of Constantinople and the Tartar irregulars. In 1484, for example, the main Turkish field army resumed the campaign in Pontic Europe which had been broken off after the defeat of 1475. This time they completed the task of securing the Black Sea coast line by capturing Kilia and Akkerman, the forts that commanded the mouths of the Danube and Dniester Rivers. To support this operation the Tartars mounted a powerful diversionary raid against Kiev, which they took and sacked. Thereafter, Tartar raiding parties became a normal adjunct to Turkish armies operating in the field. Tartar horsemen served the sultan as scouts and couriers, and their bands ravaged the country through which Turkish troops passed. In short, instead of their earlier symbiosis with traders on the Russian rivers and in the Crimean ports, the Tartars struck a bargain after 1475 with their imperial coreligionaries to the south, establishing a new symbiosis with Constantinople in which resort to naked force played a far greater part than had been the case before.

The realignment of forces in Pontic Europe that occurred in the last decades of the fifteenth century may be described in yet a third fashion. The linkage between Tartar and Turkish military enterprise was only an aspect of a larger linkage that arose between the two communities. Culturally and economically, as well as militarily, Turkish Constantinople converted the entire Pontic coastland into a vast and valuable hinterland. Correspondingly, the slender but vigorous urban fringe in the Crimea and near the mouths of the principal rivers that flow into the Black Sea lost its earlier independent entrepreneurial function vis à vis the upcountry.

Constantinople's metropolitan role in Pontic Europe re-

OTTOMAN ADVANCE

quires further analysis, for the inhumanity of slave raiding, together with traditional Christian antipathy to the Turks, has obscured essential features of a relationship whose importance is attested by the fact that it endured for nearly two hundred years.

First of all, we must understand that Turkish slavery did not in the least resemble the slavery Europeans were simultaneously imposing upon plantation field workers in the New World, nor in most cases was it as onerous as the serfdom fastened upon the peasantries of eastern Europe in the same age. The comparatively mild character of Turkish slavery was due to the fact that slaves were not valued primarily for the economic usefulness of their labor. Slaves were used instead to satisfy the desire of upstart Ottoman notables (often slaves themselves) to accumulate a large household of attendants, thus attesting their own personal greatness. Competitive conspicuous display of enormous slave trains knew no intrinsic limit.[8] Moreover, since a numerous, well-equipped and loyal slave household helped to assure a great man's personal safety, precautionary considerations impelled every Turkish magnate to treat his slaves with at least a modicum of generosity and kindness.

Slaves in Ottoman society, therefore, were primarily personal servants and bodyguards.[9] Slave women also regularly played the role of concubine, and mothered the heirs of the Turkish ruling class. The sultan himself was the son of a slave mother. It followed that insofar as great dignitaries directed the affairs of Ottoman society — and in matters of statecraft and war they played the dominant role — they did so through their slave households. This meant, in turn, that slaves managed important facets of Ottoman life. In

[8] The sultan's household in the sixteenth century numbered between 20,000 and 25,000 men, women, and children; and when the Grand Vizier Rustem died in 1561, his household was recorded as embracing 1,700 slaves and 2,900 war horses! Cf. Franz Salamon, *Ungarn im Zeitalter der Türkenherrschaft* (Leipzig: Haessel, 1887), p. 199.

[9] Galley slaves were the only important exception. The emphasis upon their sufferings in Western travelers' accounts of Ottoman life is a backhanded testimony to the generally easy circumstances other slaves enjoyed.

particular, the imperial slave household administered the secular side of the sultan's government, and constituted the backbone of the sultan's field army. All this was far removed from our untutored assumptions as to what enslavement means. The brutalized Negro field hands of the New World, who constitute the Western archetype of an enslaved population, were different indeed from the slaves who strutted the streets and staffed the palaces of Constantinople.

Islam fully sanctioned slavery so long as the enslaved populations were not already Moslem and had not submitted to the sovereignty of a Moslem ruler by payment of the traditionally prescribed capitation tax. On every frontier against the Christian world, therefore, Ottoman fighting men gladly took prisoners and made their captives slaves. Indeed, since the supply of foreign slaves was not always adequate to meet the needs of the sultan's imperial household, the Turks adopted the policy of enslaving selected young men from inside the Ottoman borders. Thus, early in the fifteenth century in the wild and remote western Balkans, where money tributes would have been hard to collect, the sultan began to collect "child tribute" instead. Such regulated enslavement helped to keep the imperial household well staffed, but did nothing to supply lesser dignitaries' demands for recruits to their own households. Hence the slave market in Constantinople remained brisk, and the demand for captives from the frontiers could never be satiated.

Pirates in the Mediterranean as well as frontier fighters in Danubian Europe did something to meet this demand; but it was in the Pontic hinterland that the Ottoman slave market found its principal source of supply. The reasons are not difficult to understand. In Pontic Europe, a warlike population of slave raiders already existed in close juxtaposition to an experienced mercantile community. Moreover, merchants and Tartars were already accustomed to co-operating with one another. In Genoese times, Tartar caravan leaders had begun to collect goods from the countryside and deliver them to the merchants of Kaffa and other towns, who took over responsibility at the water's edge. No adjustment of this pattern was required when the goods in transit ceased to be bags of grain and became human captives. Tartar transport problems, indeed, were much simplified, for their captives could and did walk long distances to market.[10]

Nowhere else along the margins of the Ottoman empire did such a combination of circumstances prevail. Slave raiding in Hungary, for example, never attained more than sporadic importance because there was no marketing organization to deliver the captives to urban markets. Local Bosnian begs and Turkish pashas had only a limited use for slaves, since serfs attached to their estates already performed equivalent services, so far as the rude rural setting allowed. Consequently, the slave trade was never well organized or steadily pursued in Hungary.[11] In Pontic Europe, on the contrary, the insatiable urban markets of the Ottoman heartlands were easily accessible via Kaffa; and once this became evident to all parties, Tartar slave raiding became an annual enterprise that could be suspended only at substantial economic cost under very unusual political circumstances or in time of extraordinary pestilence.[12]

The social destructiveness of massive and repeated slave raiding needs no elaboration. There was, however, a second

[10] Tartar slave raiding thus constituted a special case of a general phenomenon familiar to economists, whereby in remote regions where transport is the principal limiting factor upon the exchange of goods, livestock — being both more mobile and more valuable per unit bulk — is more easily marketable than vegetable or mineral products.

[11] In Turkish Hungary, in fact, official policy appears to have allowed and perhaps deliberately encouraged Serbian settlement. Orthodox Serbs were obviously a more politically reliable population to plant near the Hapsburg frontier than local Magyars, who were tainted with Catholicism even after the Reformation and kept connections across the Turkish frontiers with their fellows in royal Hapsburg Hungary. On the progress of Serbian settlement, cf. Georg Stadtmüller, *Geschichte Südosteuropas* (Munich: R. Oldenbourg, 1950), pp. 278–81.

[12] Nikolaus Ernst, "Die ersten Einfälle der Krim Tartaren auf Süd-Russland," *Zeitschrift für Osteuropäische Geschichte*, III (1913), p. 49, tabulates Polish records of Tartar raids between 1474 and 1534. During this period of fifty years, no fewer than 37 separate expeditions were recorded, some of which lasted for several years at a stretch. Between 1482 and 1512, only five years passed without a recorded raid; and there is no reason to believe that such records are complete or notice any but unusually large-scale attacks.

aspect of the phenomenon. Individuals who survived capture and the hardships of transport to the urban slave markets entered a strange, rich, and wonderful new world. They migrated from remote, isolated, and often poverty-stricken villages to the metropolitan center of Ottoman civilization itself. The new style of life which opened to their eyes, with all its pomp and luxury, sophistication and scope, had wide appeal. This is not surprising, for a slave career among the Turks was sometimes extremely advantageous. As we have just seen, the most powerful and wealthy men of the empire were slaves of the imperial household. Slaves commanded the Ottoman armies, governed the provinces, and framed the policy of the Ottoman state. Rise to the pinnacle of the Ottoman power structure was always unusual, of course; yet in the households of the great, even the humblest slave enjoyed, if only as a spectator, a richly variegated experience of the great world. How fascinating it must have seemed, compared to the remembered monotony of village poverty and winter cold! Indignity and brutality sometimes existed between master and man — but this was no less true of the villages whence the slaves had come. The closed, familiar round of village life and custom certainly broke down in the megalopolitan milieu of Constantinople. But for most of the individuals who survived the transition from their native villages, we may take it for granted that the excitements and enlarged horizons of the new life more than made up for any loss of psychological security they may have felt. Broken family ties may, however, sometimes have countered the attractions of metropolitan living, as Ukrainian folk songs suggest.

The best evidence of the attractive power of Ottoman society for the slaves who were thrust into its midst was the regularity with which the newcomers accepted Islam. Physical force was not in question. Nor was there normally any systematic, organized proselytism. Rather, the force of social circumstance and expectation sufficed to persuade almost all of the slaves to conform, at least outwardly, to Moslem piety. This could be done without expressly repudiating the (sometimes only vaguely) Christian religious practices of their village past. Islam made an honorable place for Christianity by recognizing it as a forerunner of the Prophet's final revelation of the divine will for man. Christians, therefore, enjoyed a regulated, inferior, but perfectly legal and well-defined place in Ottoman society. In abandoning their Christian identity, slaves of Moslem great households were in effect only admitting that their new life had enhanced, indeed superseded, earlier, parochial religious experience. To become a Moslem must have seemed to most new recruits to the Ottoman system a natural part of the general process whereby they overcame and left behind earlier ignorances and foolish fears.

Heterodox Moslem tradition made such a view particularly plausible. Dervish orders like the Bektashi, with whom the sultan's slave household had close and special connections, taught that all organized religion — Christianity and Islam alike — was but an imperfect approximation to the truth, which lay in personal communion with God through mystic ecstasy. Hence, in accepting Moslem practices and insights, an ex-Christian slave could easily believe that he was repudiating nothing except the narrowness of his childhood training and the bigotry of ignorance.

In the fifteenth and sixteenth centuries, the energy and formidability of the Ottoman polity, the vigor of its officials, and the valor of its soldiers depended upon massive enslavement of peasant sons drawn from the fringes of the territories under Ottoman influence. Simple peasant boys, once drafted into the imperial household, were systematically trained for the tasks of defending, extending, and governing one of the world's greatest empires, all on behalf of a monarch, himself half slave. A career open to talent — wide open — regularly tended to project men of unusual abilities to the top of the official ladder; and as long as authority within the Ottoman state continued to be wielded by men who well remembered their peasant childhood in remote Balkan or Pontic villages, the bias of officials' actions and inactions, tended to show a modicum of sympathy for the peasantry whence they, as individuals, had sprung. This meant, in particular, that the high officials of the Ottoman Empire exhibited a general will to enforce legal limits upon the goods and services a Moslem landholder could require from the peasants living on the lands granted to him in return for military service with the sultan's army. A built-in tension between the sultan's slave officials and the Moslem cavalrymen and fief holders resulted: but it was from such a balance that both the sultan's personal power and the welfare of the Balkan peasantries under the sultan's administration proceeded. And as long as this balanced tension was maintained, the Ottoman polity remained formidable indeed. The entire fighting strength of the state could be mobilized for field operations with no fear or danger of revolt in the rear, while the field force itself was disciplined and obedient to a single imperial will to a degree no other great army of the age even approached. Every Turkish warrior knew that disobedience or defiance of orders from a duly constituted officer of the army would be visited with prompt and drastic punishment.

The operation of the Turkish administrative machine in the sixteenth century, therefore, had a curiously contradictory effect. The conservation of a comparatively lightly burdened peasantry at the center of the state and destructive raiding aimed against similar communities lying just beyond the limits of regular Turkish administration were complementary aspects of the same process. Indeed, the center could sustain organized military power on a large scale for an extended time *only* by preying upon peripheral communities, while keeping a secure home base where relatively easy economic circumstances and limited exploitation of the humbler ranks of society assured a modicum of stability in the rear.

Nor was this paradox unique to Turkey. On the contrary, in some form or other it is universal, for every civilized community must sustain itself by an unending process of recruitment from the borderlands. Indeed, conversion is the central task of civilization, for otherwise the civilized community will soon be overwhelmed by ever present barbarians without and within the gates. The contrived, radical, and to a Westerner, surprising institutional forms conversion took in the Ottoman world were therefore merely an unusually drastic and effective device for assuring the strength and prosperity of the metropolitan center.

Given the comparatively slender populations, crude techniques, and anarchic political traditions of eastern Europe in the fifteenth and sixteenth centuries, the only real alternative to the Janus-faced, centralized military regime exemplified by the Ottoman sultans was a much more local parasitism of a military class upon the rest of the population. Hungary's history in the fifteenth century shifted between these alternatives in paradigmatic fashion. The military-administrative centralization achieved by the crusading champion, John Hunyadi, and his son, Matthias Corvinus, depended directly upon a corps of military professionals who lived in substantial part on booty and preyed as ruthlessly as any Turk upon the populations that lay within the zones of their field operations.[13] Hence, one may argue that the transition from the fifteenth to the sixteenth century was simply a shift from one geographic locus of predation to another. In the earlier period, the Kingdom of Hungary extended its suzerainty over a wide band of plunderable borderlands; the collapse of Matthias' military machine after his death simply made room for Ottoman armies to penetrate what had been the heartland of the Hungarian state, in order to plunder it as thoroughly

---

[13] Matthias' clear preference for campaigns in central Europe becomes intelligible when one understands the problem he confronted in trying to maintain the mercenary troop upon which his power over his fellow Magyar magnates entirely depended. Earlier in the century, crusades against the Turks had begun to create a deserted zone south of the Danube, as comparable Ottoman operations were later to do in Danubian and Pontic Europe. Hence Matthias could not imitate his father's role as Christian champion against the Turk and also keep his troop of personal followers in good heart. Instead, he turned upon Bohemia, Moravia, Silesia, Austria, Carinthia, and Carniola, since plunder and taxes from these comparatively rich provinces made it easier to maintain his indispensable but costly "Black Troop." For details of Matthias' military establishment, which resembled the contemporary and later Ottoman arrangement very closely, cf. Wilhelm Fraknoi, *Matthias Corvinus, König von Ungarn 1458–1490* (Freiburg im Breisgau: Herder'sche Verlagshandlung, 1891), pp. 275–79.

as Hungarian crusaders had earlier plundered their neighbors.

The unpleasant alternative to such semi-predatory centralization was vividly demonstrated under the regime established by the Magyar nobility after King Matthias' death (1490) and before the Kingdom of Hungary fell within the zone of Ottoman military operations (1521–66). As we have already seen, the indignant and jealous nobles not only dismantled the instruments of royal centralization and declared their restoration forever illegal; they also fastened new and heavier burdens upon the peasantry, and in doing so provoked widespread rebellion and disastrous civil war on the very eve of the Turkish attacks. Decentralization of violence, in short, allowed intensification of local exploitation of the peasants by militarized aristocrats. In a sense, inequities inherent in any more centralized regime were dissolved in a common misery, for unrestrained aristocracy neither hurt the borderlands so much nor husbanded home resources so effectually as a centralized military autocracy could do. Yet equality in misery and the endemic insecurity of a countryside overrun by free and equal fighting men is not necessarily more admirable than the parasitic and imperial regimes Matthias Corvinus and the sultans established.

North of the Carpathians, the implications of unrestrained aristocracy found fuller expression; for in Poland-Lithuania, local military enterprise and aristocratic republicanism under the presidency of an elective king flourished longer and at first cost the country substantially less than in Hungary, owing to the initial absence of effectively centralized, militarily formidable, and territorially ambitious neighbors. Yet even in Poland-Lithuania, decentralized violence in the end led to loss of national independence; and even in the days of Poland's greatest military success and territorial extent, an unrestrained aristocratic dominance meant that the constriction of peasant life at the bottom of the social scale was matched by a comparable restriction upon court and urban cultural development. The range of cultural variety and achievement in Poland-Lithuania was therefore distinctly less than that attained under more centralized systems of predation, which sustained styles of courtly urbanity far more impressive than the aristocratic culture of even the greatest noble household or best endowed Jesuit college of Poland.

The real resemblance between the political-military structure created in Hungary by Matthias Corvinus and that erected by the Ottoman sultans does not, of course, imply identity between the two polities, or anything approaching it. The religious gulf between Islam and Christianity created a wide divergence between the high cultural traditions of the two states. To be sure, this gulf had not seemed unbridgeable in the fifteenth century, when Turkish appropriation of the Byzantine heritage was in full swing; and when echoes of the secularism of the Italian Renaissance, which resounded powerfully in Matthias Corvinus' Court, also attracted the favorable attention of Mehmed the Conqueror. But the sixteenth century saw a sharp revulsion from the doctrinal latitudinarianism which had been rife in courtly circles of Italy, Hungary, and Constantinople in the fifteenth. Each faith tended to encapsulate itself in a reinvigorated orthodoxy that made its champions increasingly impervious to intellectual or any other cultural challenge posed by the other. Moreover, the circumstances which provoked this reaction were similar on either side of the religious dividing line. The outburst of Shi'a rebellion in Azerbaijan and eastern Anatolia beginning in 1499 anticipated and in some respects paralleled the outburst of religious revolt in Germany and Northern Europe that was started by Martin Luther in 1517.

The sultans Selim the Grim (1512–20) and Suleiman the Lawgiver (1520–66) successfully repressed heresy and rebellion in their empire, as Charles V (1519–56) failed to do in his. As a result, the heterodox (often crypto-Shi'a) doctrines of dervish communities that had previously emphasized the resemblances between Islam and Christianity and constituted an effective bridge between the two faiths found less and less open expression in Turkish territory. The gap between the two religious communities within the empire tended, therefore, to widen. This was also true across Ottoman frontiers, for the hardening of Sunni orthodoxy among the Moslems coincided with the controversies kindled by the Reformation which fed the flames of Christian conviction among Protestant and Catholic alike. Under these circumstances, the learned men of Islam speedily came to be totally disinterested in Christian learning, and vice versa.

Suleiman's measures effectually froze the intellectual life of the Ottoman empire to fixed patterns. Instead of having to meet the challenges to the Sunni version of the Sacred Law on an intellectual plane, Turkish Moslems found it possible, with the energetic support of the Ottoman secular government, to resort to organization and persecution against Shi'a heresy. In the long run, this intellectual and moral abdication cost the Moslems dearly. Slowly but surely, the Turks' studied indifference to any but strictly traditional patternings of the life of the mind allowed Europe to outstrip the Ottoman world in one realm of thought and action after another, without provoking any Moslem response whatever.

In the short run, however, all the advantages lay on the Turkish side. Religious order and discipline on the Moslem side of the frontier confronted the riotous confusion of Reformation Europe, where the rival doctrines of Rome, Wittenberg, and Geneva clashed with one another and with still more radical sects of Baptists and Unitarians. Europe's failure to unite behind one emperor and under one church certainly facilitated Ottoman victories in Hungary and on the Mediterranean. In conquered regions, the Turks themselves did not usually intervene in Christian doctrinal disputes. Some Turkish (and Greek) authorities were perhaps more sympathetic to Calvinism than to other forms of Christianity, recognizing the Calvinist Reformed churches as the strongest domestic rival to the Roman Catholic and Hapsburg imperial power they opposed. Hence in the regions of Hungary that fell under Turkish control, Calvinism enjoyed a propitious political climate and took firm root by about the middle of the sixteenth century. In Transylvania, where Calvinism, Lutheranism, and Catholicism had all been declared official in 1557, Unitarian doctrine also won adherents, especially among communities of Szeklers. Accordingly, in 1571 Unitarianism was also accorded official toleration by the Transylvanian Diet. Religious variety had thus become the sign and palladium of Transylvania's ethnic diversity, a principle that fully accorded with the institutional structure of the Ottoman empire, where ethnic identity and religious affiliation were normally equated. Yet such accommodation to Ottoman forms did not change the fact that the intellectual font of the rival faiths of Hungary and Transylvania lay in western Europe; and their mutual strife kept alive a level of intellectual discourse and religious vituperation that had no analogue among the Moslems.

In addition to the religious and cultural watershed between Hungary and the Ottoman Empire, there were also important differences of social structure between them. Most important of all was the fact that the hereditary principle remained comparatively weak in Ottoman society. No magnate class remotely resembling that which so angrily dismantled King Matthias' power existed on Turkish soil. The magnates' stubborn self-assertion against a king who was, after all, no more than first among equals constituted the single most effective obstacle to the establishment of a centralized, absolutist Hungarian monarchy. The Ottoman sultan had no comparable check upon his personal authority; and the practical success of Turkish government, as contrasted to the utter failure of the Hungarian crown in the sixteenth century, was directly related to this fact.

Even among free-born Moslem fighting men, pride of descent and sense of family was lacking. Too many were social upstarts, come from nowhere, sons of slaves and concubines who so far outranked their ancestors as to be totally disinterested in them. Turkish domestic life and sexual manners were those of an army encamped. After the year's campaigning ended, Ottoman warriors were ready enough to take as wives and concubines whatever attractive women happened to be available. But when the command came to report for the new campaigning season, it was time to leave land, ladies, and offspring to fend for themselves — returning again in the fall, or perhaps not, depending on the chances of war, the availability of an alternative billet, or the will of some military superior.[14]

Projected upon society as a whole, the comparative weakness of family ties and of the hereditary principle among the military and ruling classes of the empire meant that resistance to centralized bureaucratic government was notably less in the Ottoman world than was the case in Hungary or anywhere else in Christendom. The urban element and Byzantine traditions worked powerfully in the same direction, strengthening the sultan against rural Moslem landholders, who were his servants in battle, but his potential rivals, too.

Until after about the middle of the sixteenth century, therefore, when Ottoman military operations reached their approximate geographic limits, the individual free-born fighting man who entered the sultan's service tended to detach himself from all past anchorages almost as completely as did the household slaves who commanded the Turkish cavalry in the field. Annual campaigning meant heavy losses, not only in battle, but from the diseases and accidents that distant campaigning along the far-flung frontiers of the empire inevitably involved. As a result, turnover of personnel and possessions remained very rapid. As long as the em-

---

[14] Most survivors of a campaign returned to the same billet from which they had departed; anything else would have produced administrative chaos. Suleiman in 1530 took official recognition of the right of fallen warriors' sons to an income sufficient for their maintenance. This shows, if proof be needed, that a sense of family solidarity was not absent among the Turks.

Moreover, donations to mosques and other religious enterprises, administered by suitably pious persons who might happen to be sons or other relatives of the donor, offered an avenue along which Moslems who wished to secure the economic interests of their offspring might legally pass. Many certainly availed themselves of this possibility. Yet these qualifications do not remove the real contrast between the territorially mobile military class of the Ottoman Empire and the locally rooted aristocracies of Christendom. Cf. F. Braudel, *La Méditerranée*, pp. 637–40; Richard Busch-Zantner, *Agrarverfassung, Gesellschaft und Siedlung in Südosteuropa* (Leipzig: Harrassowitz, 1938), pp. 67 ff.

pire was expanding, each new province provoked a further disturbance of the property system, since its lands, too, had to be parceled out among the victors. The result, therefore, must have been that most warriors shifted winter quarters frequently enough to prevent them from putting down roots and beginning to feel that a particular estate was their personal and permanent property, rather than merely a convenient source of income during a limited period of military inactivity.

Obviously, when the land was in the hands of such a class, local resistances to administrative centralization and rationality were vastly weaker than was characteristic of Christendom, where numerous and formidable aristocrats, attached to their family acres by strong sentiments and childhood memories, stubbornly resisted any innovation proposed by upstart clerks in the service of an overweening monarch.[15]

From the peasant viewpoint, the difference between Ottoman and Christian landholding was also important. The motility of Ottoman landholders gave a large scope for village autonomy, if only because the Turkish warrior was usually absent from the scene for several months each year, and could leave no real plenipotentiary behind when his own return to that particular spot was itself uncertain. By contrast, Christian noble landowners, attached to particular localities by long family tradition, had long since worked their way into the tissues of the village community itself, leaving much smaller scope for peasants to manage their own affairs. Sporadic brutality and sudden violent interruption of normal routines was the price villagers of the Ottoman Empire paid for their enlarged autonomy. Such violence came into play when-

[15] To be sure, in Bosnia and Albania, and in most of the empire's Asian provinces, local landowners survived Ottoman conquest. This happened when a pre-existing nobility was (or became) Moslem; for the Sacred Law of Islam did not allow wholesale expropriation of the lands of True Believers. Whenever a native aristocracy maintained itself on the ground, the sultan's power was, of course, circumscribed in almost the same fashion as prevailed universally in Christendom, although the institutional forms through which aristocratic power in local affairs found expression were quite different.

ever a Turkish overlord or predatory wayfarer intervened unexpectedly to demand some service or supply of goods beyond and above the comparatively light obligations legally imposed in accordance with the sultan's fiat.

Such sporadic violence did not, however, disrupt the normal autonomy of village life under the Turks. Moreover, this autonomy in the open country was supplemented even in towns by a comparably broad autonomy for the various religious communities of the Ottoman Empire. Each community was legally subordinated to a religious head, who with other clergy exercised judicial and other governmental powers vis à vis his coreligionaries, just as Moslem doctors of the Sacred Law exercised their jurisdiction within the Moslem community. Hence, in a sense, not one but several polities occupied Ottoman ground simultaneously, each ruled by its own law, following its own custom, judged by its own authorities, and entering into only a limited range of relationships with one another. The ruling Moslem polity and the subjected Christian and Jewish polities of course co-operated in important and traditional ways. Yet each remained a separate and distinct corporate entity.[16]

In the long run, Ottoman society and government developed serious weaknesses; but in the sixteenth century, all the advantages seemed to lie with the Turks. Weak hereditary feeling made the autocratic power of the sultan more effective; and the slave career created a body of men loyal to and absolutely dependent upon the sultan for the power and wealth of their offices. With such an administrative instrument, and with an obedient and well-equipped soldiery

[16] Traces of similar social-psychological fissures between conquerors and conquered may be detected in Hungary, where the peculiar harshness of noble-peasant relationships descended from a time when Magyar conquerors had first penetrated the Hungarian plain and subjugated its previous inhabitants and dwellers round about. Christianity, however, tended to knit the separate classes together, inasmuch as even the humblest peasant was admitted to have an immortal soul worthy of salvation; whereas in Ottoman lands the failure to convert conquered Christians to Islam — a process which ceased to predominate after the early decades of the fifteenth century — meant institutionalization and perpetuation of the initial social fissure between conqueror and conquered.

OTTOMAN ADVANCE

at his command, the sultan outmatched all rivals within marching range. Indeed, the only effective limit upon the expansion of Turkish power was the distance his army could travel from winter quarters in a single campaigning season and still return in time for the winter months. Armies that could fight all round the year and whose obedience was not conditional upon the personal presence of the monarch were not beyond Ottoman conception. Yet in practice, the main force of the sultan's household troops was seldom separated for long from the sultan's person. Without the imperial presence, the sultan could have no firm assurance of his effective control. At the same time, the sultan could not easily afford to immure himself for years on end in army camps on the periphery of his empire. To do so would have allowed the reins of administrative power to slip from his control.

In the sixteenth century, the sultans met this dilemma by usually spending part of the year on campaign with the troops and part of the year back in Constantinople. But this migratory pattern of life meant that the sultan's household troops, the central core of the field forces of the empire, had to sally forth each spring from Constantinople or its environs, and march to the scene of battle, which was usually to be found far from the capital on one or another of the frontiers of the empire. Imperial Turkish armies of Suleiman's time had elaborate camel trains and knew how to use Danube shipping for transporting supplies as well. Yet even with a well-organized commissariat, an army of several score thousand men, not all of whom were mounted and all of whom had to be fed, could not travel very fast across long distances, although in an emergency a march of twenty to thirty miles in a day was possible. Hence the effective range of the Turkish army's operation in a campaigning season was a 90 to 100-days' march, which amounted to between 700 and 800 air miles from Constantinople, but possibly twice as far on the ground. All of the year's good weather was required to march that far and back again. Operations at any longer range were entirely impractical.

It is true that small forces were despatched and maintained for indefinite periods at remote fortresses along the borders of the empire; and in special instances, as when Selim the Grim undertook the conquest of the Mameluke kingdom of Egypt and Syria, 1516–17, the sultan and his armies remained in the field for more than a single campaigning season. But these departures from the norm did not change the fact that in most years between the capture of Constantinople in 1453 and the death of Suleiman the Lawgiver in 1566, the slave troops of the imperial household, together with a large fraction of the landholding Turkish cavalrymen of the entire empire, took the field in the spring, marched toward the frontier appointed by the sultan for the year's campaigning, and then marched back again to winter quarters in or near the capital.

Even at the beginning of Suleiman's reign (1520–66), the Turkish land frontiers had been pushed so far from Constantinople that the imperial field army lost a good part of its effectiveness. Sieges that had to be broken off after only a few weeks, like the famous beleaguerment of Vienna in 1529 (started September 27, broken off October 15), were predestined to failure. Hence, after the superiority of the Ottoman imperial forces on the field of battle had been clearly demonstrated (Battle of Mohacz, 1526), the obvious strategy for Christian defenders of the Turkish frontier zone was to fortify as many strongholds as possible and retreat behind walls whenever the Turks appeared in force. Such tactics all but nullified the superiority of Suleiman's grand army, turning invasions of Hungary into a series of petty sieges, precariously won or lost not so much by direct military action as by calculations of weather and availability or scarcity of supplies.[17]

[17] In the last year of his life, Suleiman sallied forth from Constantinople on May 1 and traveled 97 days before his army met solid enemy resistance. For the next 34 days, the vast force Suleiman had brought with him was halted by a single stubbornly held fortified spot — Szigeth — and when the place fell to the Turks on September 8, the season was already so far spent that little more could have been done, even if, as actually happened, the sultan had not expired in his tent two days before the fall of Szigeth — an event which required the sultan's household troops

This stalemate did not really set in until after 1543, when the sultan took central Hungary under direct Turkish administration for the first time. As in other provinces, Suleiman assigned most of central Hungary to Moslem cavalrymen, who thenceforward acted as a local garrison and engaged in running struggles with their Magyar and Croat counterparts throughout the border regions. Cities and some open country he kept for the imperial fisc.

The consequences of this arrangement were painful indeed for the Hungarian peasants on the ground. For a few weeks in summer, if the sultan had elected to campaign in Hungary that year, his field forces could march whither they chose and besiege any fortified positions they decided to attack. Meanwhile, of course, the Turkish troops lived off the land or attempted to do so. For the rest of the year, however, no single military power enjoyed unambiguous supremacy. Local raiding parties freely traversed the landscape, to and fro, and like the imperial Ottoman troops, also sought to live off the land. Peace and security were far to seek under such a regime, where the balance of military power fluctuated so sharply with the season and with the unpredictable decision of Constantinople to invade or not to invade in any given year.

Despite all this, the plain of Hungary continued to be inhabited. Many villages were abandoned, as one would expect; and the population, when it was not killed out of hand, either fled to safe regions or, as slaves, migrated to the Turkish interior. Two alternative refuges attracted the harassed Hungarian peasants. On the one hand, there was hope of safety in numbers, so that a few larger settlements tended to attract refugees from smaller communities round about. Such migrants could hope, once acute local danger had subsided, to revisit their abandoned fields, even at a distance of a score of miles or more, and exploit the land in some marginal, part-time fashion; or, if vacant fields lay closer to the overgrown village-town, refugees could hope to survive by

to return to Constantinople and establish their relationship to the new ruler of the empire.

working unclaimed land lying closer to their new homes. Towns or villages assigned to the sultan's imperial fisc usually enjoyed distinctly better conditions than did those assigned to a Turkish warrior. Hence a stream of migration toward these locations set in.[18]

The other refuge zone lay in the mountain valleys of the Carpathians that ringed the Hungarian plain on the north. Here wooded slopes and narrow valleys made the sudden cavalry raid, which perpetually endangered villages of the open plain, unlikely, if only because limited routes of access gave wary villagers warning of the approach of hostile foraging parties and allowed them to flee into trackless mountain wastes. Hence there was a marked tendency to evacuate the plain, save for a few comparatively well-defended, large settlements, while mountain valleys to the north filled up with populations that sought survival through a combination of cultivation of any available arable patches with pasturage — mainly of sheep and goats, whose nimbleness in the mountains and voracity in the plain were conducive to escape and survival, even in the face of recurrent, chronic military raiding.[19]

Nevertheless, Turkish occupation of central Hungary after 1543 did not destroy the older political organization of the land. Magyar gentry remained and kept the former county assemblies in being. From the Turkish point of view, Christians were of course expected to manage their own affairs in any way they chose; and if the Christians of the part of Hungary under direct Ottoman administration preferred a Calvinist synodical organization of the church and a system of lay assemblies for dispensing justice, this in no way displeased or much affected the Turks, who had their own courts and

[18] Franz Salamon, *Ungarn im Zeitalter der Türkenherrschaft* (Leipzig: Haessel, 1887), pp. 212–18. The Turkish tax system, which exempted pasture lands from payments assessed upon cultivated acres, also sometimes seems to have encouraged landholders to clear peasants off portions of their estates in order to open the ground for herds of horses and other animals (*ibid.*, pp. 210–11).

[19] A. N. J. den Hollander, "The Great Hungarian Plain: A European Frontier Area," *Comparative Studies in Society and History*, III (1960–61), 74–88.

OTTOMAN ADVANCE

obeyed their own administrative superiors just as they expected the Magyars to obey theirs.

Both Turks and Magyars also agreed in maintaining a quite fictitious indivisibility of the Kingdom of Hungary. After 1543, from the Turkish point of view, the central portion of the kingdom was administered like any other province of the empire, flanked, however, by two vassal principalities: Transylvania, ruled first by John Zapolya (1526–40) and then by his son, John Sigismund (1540–71), and a northwestern strip where Ferdinand of Hapsburg (1526–64) and his successors held sway. Both the Zapolyas and the Hapsburgs paid tribute to the Turks for their parts of Hungary; and in Turkish eyes, each held his portion of the kingdom at the Turks' good pleasure, merely because it was more trouble to dislodge them by force of arms than the effort was worth.

The Hapsburgs and the Magyar nobility viewed the facts very differently. Ferdinand of Hapsburg claimed the crown of Hungary by inheritance. A family compact concluded in 1521, when Ferdinand married King Louis' sister, specified Hapsburg rights of succession to the crown of Hungary in the event of Louis' death without heirs, as in fact occurred at Mohacz. Immediately after that defeat, some of the Magyar nobility recognized the Hapsburgs as legitimate kings of all Hungary (a party led by the magnates); others (mostly the lesser gentry) preferred to support John Zapolya's claim to that dignity. But all the Magyar nobles agreed that succession to the throne of Hungary depended on election by the Diet and was not disposable by family compacts or through the private will of a reigning monarch.

The result, therefore, was extreme constitutional confusion. All parties boldly defended transparent legal fictions, while indulging in violence and rapacity that had little relation to any law. In some instances, at least, peasants found themselves required to support two distinct landlords and governments — a Turkish warrior, to whom lands had been assigned for his support by the sultan, and a Magyar gentleman, whose hereditary claim upon the village in question had not been canceled by the appearance of the Turk. Rents and taxes were sometimes transmitted from Turkish Hungary to imperial Hungary, where the great magnates who had survived Mohacz nearly all took up their residence. But the burden of such double exactions must have been all but intolerable for the peasantry. Efforts were indeed made to regulate the respective rights of Turks and Magyar landholders, but we cannot suppose that such moves had much practical effect. In 1548, for example, the sultan halved Hungarian taxes — good indication that the previous levies had been uncollectible in practice. Twenty years later, a treaty between the sultan and his Hapsburg vassal specified certain villages in Turkish Hungary that were liable to Hapsburg dues, and others in Hapsburg Hungary liable to Turkish claims.[20] In practice, in all probability, rival claims boiled down to what an armed and mounted man, now Turkish, now Christian, could extract from a cowering serf at any particular moment. Carefully husbanded legal claims upon the products and services of the agricultural population amounted in practice to little more than a convenient justification for whatever scale of violence a warrior-landlord felt like indulging at any particular moment and circumstance.

The situation in Transylvania and imperial Hungary was simpler in a sense, since only one prince and one landlord normally claimed a share of the peasants' produce. Yet the frequent raids of Turkish and Tartar troops must have had nearly the same effect upon the actual inhabitants and cultivators as did the multiple and conflicting claims that distressed the surviving cultivators of the central plain.

Further east, in Pontic Europe, fixed agricultural settlements in the open steppe had never been firmly established, and agricultural communities located on the grasslands soon disappeared when Tartar raiding became chronic. This was not the case in the oak and beech forests which covered the

[20] Franz Salamon, *Ungarn*, pp. 272, 284; cf. also Charles d'Eszlary, "L'administration et la vie dans la Hongrie occupée par les Turcs au cours des 16e et 17e siècles," *Ibla, Revue de l'Institut des Belles Lettres Arabes*, XX (1957), 351–68.

lower slopes of the Carpathians in Moldavia. Here a pastoral-farming population survived; for in such a landscape Tartar horsemen and their bows were severely handicapped. Threatened communities could disperse into the woods and hide until raiders had passed by; and in case of larger-scale attack, local clan groupings among the Moldavians could gather together the fighting manpower of the principality and with the help of forest stockades and similar primitive but effective fortification could sometimes withstand cavalry attack quite successfully.

To be sure, the prince of Moldavia usually found it convenient to recognize Turkish suzerainty; but control from Constantinople was very slight. Local political-military struggles threw up one victor after another, each of whom was, normally, recognized by the Turks as ruler of the principality and duly held office until some rival came along and unseated him. Foreign intervention was chronic. Both Hungary and Poland had claimed Moldavia as a dependency in late medieval times. Such claims gave standing ground for intervention, so that when propitious circumstances allowed, both Polish and Transylvanian rulers permitted filibustering expeditions to muster on their territory. These sometimes failed miserably, or sometimes succeeded in overthrowing the reigning prince and installing a new and presumably grateful ruler on the throne.

The most unusual such enterprise was the Polish-based venture that placed John II Basilikos on the Moldavian throne in 1561. John claimed descent from imperial rulers of Byzantium and had spent several years in Germany and other western Eurpoean countries attempting to stir up a crusade to restore him to the throne of his ancestors. In the course of this enterprise, he came into close association with Lutheran circles — Philip Melanchthon in particular. During his short tenure of power, John II therefore attempted to spread the Reformation in Moldavia. The movement was, in a sense, contagion from Poland, where Reformed doctrine was spreading like wildfire. Nevertheless, John's tampering with Orthodoxy provided effective ground for rousing revolt among the Moldavian chieftains, who in the absence of better equipped invading expeditions dominated the local military scene. John II's reign therefore came to an end after only two years. The only trace his zeal for the Reformation left behind was an increased religious distrust between the Orthodox religious community and their Polish-German-Magyar neighbors, whose religious instability had briefly seemed to threaten the eternal truths of Orthodoxy.[21]

By comparison with Moldavia, Wallachia was considerably more developed agriculturally, although the pastoralism which dominated Moldavian life was far from absent in the more southerly principality. The greater importance of agriculture implied sharper social differentiation between ploughing peasant and landowners. The rough and ready military self-defense characteristic of the Moldavian clans and local groups was less rough and a good deal less ready in Wallachia, since leaders and followers no longer had an implicit mutual confidence or unanimity of outlook. This comparative military weakness meant that local resistance to Turkish jurisdiction over Wallachian political struggles was less formidable. Characteristically, the rivalries and quarrels among ambitious candidates for the princely dignity were resolved more effectually in Constantinople by intrigue and administrative process than with arms in hand, as happened regularly in Moldavia. In other words, the grand vizier was often in a position to choose between rival candidates in Wallachia, whereas in Moldavia he was usually confronted by a *fait accompli*, which he could refuse to ratify only at the cost of a distant and difficult campaign. Geographical propinquity and the fact that the Danube offered an easy route for armies as well as goods moving between Constantinople and Wallachia reinforced the comparatively firm bonds uniting Wallachia to the Ottoman capital in the sixteenth century.

It is not clear to what extent the food supply of Constantinople depended on Wallachian export of agricultural surpluses. One reason the Turks and Tartars could sacrifice the

[21] For details of this extraordinary episode, cf. Ernst Benz, *Wittenberg und Byzanz* (Marburg: Elwert Gräfe und Unzer Verlag, 1949), pp. 34–58.

produce of Ukranian fields so wantonly was that adequate supplies for the capital could be found nearer at hand. Both banks of the lower Danube, as well as the Thracian and Bulgarian hinterland of Constantinople, played their part here. Nevertheless, insofar as commercial agriculture established or maintained itself in Wallachia as a result of the urban market Constantinople offered, an economic circulation began to support the political-military subordination of Wallachia to the Turks. This became much more strongly developed in the seventeenth century, when boyar landowners began to extract heavy labor dues from their ex-followers and fellow clansmen in order to raise wheat for sale in Constantinople. By so doing they lost the basis for any sort of effective independent political-military power vis-à-vis Constantinople, while sharing, at least in a provincial and marginal way, in the intellectual culture and material luxuries enjoyed by urban Christians of the upper classes under the Ottoman system of society.

As in the Moldavian forests, so also far to the north, village communities survived the Tartar ravages, even though raids repeatedly penetrated to the lands around such distant towns as Vilna and Moscow, not to mention closer targets like Lvov and Kiev. Nor did the desert zone that came to separate Tartar headquarters in the Crimea from the inhabited lands of Poland-Lithuania and Muscovy entirely lack population, even when settled village life on the steppe became impossible. River fishermen and hunters, together with individuals whose only available means of support was some fortunate windfall that could only be secured through violence, never disappeared; and from this kernel the Cossack hordes developed by about 1550. Their mode of life closely resembled that of their Tartar counterparts, with the difference that by preference they raided Moslem communities on the Black Sea coast and sought to intercept booty-laden Tartars returning from successful enterprises in the north.[22]

The development of militarily formidable Cossack com-

[22] Günter Stökl, *Die Entstehung des Kossakentums (Veröffentlichungen des Osteuropa-Instituts München*, III [Munich: Isar Verlag, 1953]).

munities, together with the retreat of agricultural settlement beyond easy operating range of the Black Sea ports, combined to make the Tartar slave raids less and less financially rewarding. During the second half of the sixteenth century, the balance gradually shifted. The attrition which agricultural populations continued to suffer from Tartar raiding was met and then surpassed by natural increase, so that behind the Cossack screen, agricultural settlement presently began once more to advance southward despite the continuance of Tartar harassment.

By approximately the same date and for comparable reasons, the main thrust of Turkish expansion into Danubian Europe also came to an end. For when the extreme radius of effective field operations from a base in Constantinople had been reached, so that the concerted effort of the sultan's armies could no longer do more than reduce a handful of trifling fortresses in a season's campaigning — as was repeatedly demonstrated in the years 1551–62 when Turks and Austrians fought a long drawn-out and desultory war in Hungary — the practical possibility of any dramatic further expansion of Ottoman power had disappeared. Stalemate, characterized by sharply fluctuating local balances of military forces throughout a frontier zone of a couple of hundred miles depth, came to prevail; and the fact that the Kingdom of Hungary lay athwart this precarious frontier zone, claimed by both Turk and Hapsburg and harassed impartially by Moslem and Christian men-at-arms, soon made that land into unfavorable campaigning ground, where a large army could not sustain itself for any length of time. Thus the very operation of the Turkish field armies tended, like the operations of the Tartar raiding parties, to create conditions at the extreme range of their effective radius of action that prevented them from going further.

Irregular Christian forces matched irregular Turkish forces on the disputed frontier itself, as the rising Cossack communities matched and mirrored the Tartars further east. But an organized professional field force comparable to that commanded by Suleiman the Lawgiver had not yet challenged

Turkish supremacy in the open field. The appearance of such a force under Hapsburg command eventually changed the balance of forces in Danubian Europe in a fundamental fashion. But before this happened, a troubled time of counterpoise intervened. Its closer examination will be the subject of the next chapter.

TIME OF TROUBLES

1570–1650

THE FRUITLESS campaign into Hungary in the course of which Suleiman the Lawgiver died (1566) demonstrated that even the full imperial muster of the Ottoman Empire no longer sufficed to win more than trifling successes along that sector of the empire's frontier. The march to the middle Danube took too long; too many fortified places had sprung up; and when a brave and determined captain happened to be in charge, the resistance of a mere handful of men behind skillfully constructed fortifications could last an embarrassingly long time. Since supply lines could not be left unprotected, such a check was capable of halting the entire imperial army in its tracks for days or weeks on end.

To the east, the frontier still lay open, for in Pontic Europe the thick-strewn fortresses that blocked advance into Hungary scarcely existed. Wide and potentially fertile lands lay open to the first power that could establish a regime favorable to settlement. But Turkish power in that region rested on symbiosis with the Crim Tartars, whose slave raids, far from encouraging settlement, had actually created a desert in much of the region. Some Ottoman statesmen and strategists were not content to leave the area north of the Black Sea in this undeveloped state. Accordingly, in 1569–70 an Ottoman expeditionary force penetrated as far as Astrakhan (recently captured by the Russians from the Kipchak khans) and started to construct a canal between the Don and the Volga, so as to link the Black and Caspian Seas into a single waterway. But Russian resistance at Astrakhan, the unwillingness of the Crim Tartars to co-operate with Turkish regulars in an enterprise which, if successful, would have hemmed the Tartars in as never before, and the deserted countryside itself, which made living off the land impractical, combined to inflict resounding failure on the Turks. Of the more than 30,000 men who sailed from Constantinople in 1569, only 7,000 returned the next year, with nothing whatever to show for their efforts.[1] After such a debacle, the enterprise was never resumed.

The year 1570, therefore, besides being a conveniently round number, aptly signifies the exhaustion of Ottoman expansive capacity, both in Danubian and in Pontic Europe. Military stalemate succeeded the earlier Ottoman superiority; and the other frontiers of the empire failed to offer any adequate substitute for victories in Europe, by which the Ottoman military machine and ruling elite had previously been both tested and sustained. Expansion on other frontiers did not cease. Naval and military expeditions to the Red Sea asserted Ottoman control over Hejaz in southern Arabia in 1571; and war with Venice and other Christian naval powers in 1571–81 secured the useful way station of Cyprus for the Turks.[2] Even more impressive, at least on a map, were Turkish territorial acquisitions in Georgia, Azerbaijan, and Shirwan, which resulted from a long war with Persia, 1577–90. But the reality of Ottoman administrative control of

---

[1] Cf. Joseph von Hammer, *Geschichte des osmanischen Reiches*, III, 531 ff. The plan of linking the two seas was calculated to take the Shi'a heretics of Persia in the rear by connecting Ottoman with Uzbek orthodoxy via the Caspian. The grandiose enterprise was itself part of a still larger scheme, for the grand vizier, Mehmed Sökölli, also planned a canal through the Isthmus of Suez to allow Turkish fleets and merchant vessels to pass freely between the Mediterranean Sea and the Indian Ocean. Not until the twentieth century have both his enginering plans been realized; and then under divided political regimes, so that the physical possibility of navigating from Kazan or Ghilan to Constantinople, and from Constantinople to the Indian Ocean, has not yet had much importance. Under the umbrella of a single Ottoman administration, such a far-flung network of inland waterways might have changed the whole military-political balance between Islam and Christendom.

[2] The famous Battle of Lepanto, which occurred off the western coast of Greece in 1571, was an incident in this war. Christian Europe hailed it as a great victory, which in fact it was; yet it had remarkably little effect, since the Turks were able to launch a new fleet the following year almost as formidable as that which had been destroyed at Lepanto, and ended the war with the acquisition of Cyprus. Lepanto, therefore, merely reconfirmed a naval stalemate, according to which naval supremacy in the eastern Mediterranean remained in Moslem hands while the western Mediterranean remained predominantly under Christian control. For details, cf. R. C. Anderson, *Naval Wars in the Levant, 1559–1853*, (Princeton, N.J.: Princeton University Press, 1952) pp. 8–54.

these regions was always questionable. Azerbaijan and Shir-wan were already Moslem; and the local landowners and tribal leaders were therefore not superseded; Georgia remained under its own Christian rulers, in a status analogous to the principality of Transylvania. Hence, with the exception of Cyprus, these new provinces did not actually offer the Ottoman warriors new fief lands to be divided among the victors.

Without important new territories to move in to, particular warriors tended to settle down as tenants of particular estates. The mutability and flexibility of earlier Turkish society and of the Ottoman armed establishment thereby underwent drastic and quite rapid alteration. Venturesome and rootless warriors who lived in the saddle as part of an ever victorious army and cared not overmuch about their children, if any, gave way to lazy landholders, located in some provincial town where the peasants assigned to their maintenance could bring them the dues upon which they lived. Venturesome warrior and lazy landlord had always been appropriate roles for Turkish cavalrymen, each having its proper season of the year. At first, therefore, the change amounted to no more than an increasing self-identification on the part of the Moslem military class with winter-quarters routine in a particular billet.

But growing attachment to a particular spot carried with it additional complications. A natural desire to pass on property and position to one's own sons put a severe strain upon the legal principle whereby properties were granted only to fighting men as a recompense for services rendered. Sons might not be of age when their father died. Even in Suleiman's time this had led to difficulties, and in 1530 the great sultan had promulgated elaborate regulations prescribing just what proportion of a deceased warrior's income should go to his sons not yet of age, with higher percentages assigned to those whose fathers had died in battle than to those whose fathers had died of natural causes. In subsequent decades and generations, the drive toward hereditary succession among the military elite of the empire gathered strength, incessantly nibbling away at the bureaucratic rationality of the regime Suleiman had inherited and perfected. As a result, during the first half of the seventeenth century, the sultan's power itself came to be seriously undermined. Financial stringency accentuated the disorder that hereditary pressures brought to bear upon the Ottoman administrative and military machine, while the personal insignificance of most of the sultans who succeeded Suleiman made reform from the top difficult.

Thus we see how the whetted blade, wielded so long and with such effect by a conquering clique of Ottoman warriors, naturally and inevitably blunted itself with use. But the fabric of Ottoman society and government remained, grand and imposing; and Ottoman culture retained its power of attracting strangers from without the gates until long after 1570. The Ottoman Empire did not decay; it merely descended toward the normal level of fiscal and administrative confusion and cross purposes to which the states of western Europe and of Moslem India and north Africa had long been accustomed.

It is, nevertheless, traditional to call these changes "decay." In a sense all change is decay; and the change in ethos among the ruling military class of the Ottoman Empire did reduce individual recklessness in battle and administrative flexibility in the rear. The effective power at the sultan's personal disposal was thereby decreased. But what occurred could equally well be described as a process of acculturation whereby arbitrary power was limited by countervailing forces within Ottoman society, while a rude and violent group of warriors acquired at least an outward acquaintance with the amenities of civil life — including religion and poetry as well as dancing girls and tobacco.

Whichever way one chooses to describe the transformations of Ottoman society, it is well to remember that the Ottoman Empire remained a great world power until the very close of the seventeenth century. Retreat before expanding European empires did not become definite until 1699. Between the period of Ottoman advance and the beginning of the empire's territorial retreat, Ottoman government settled down for more than a century within the far-flung frontiers set for it by the technical limits of Turkish campaigning. Simultaneously Ottoman political institutions, after some initial oscillation between bureaucratic and hereditary principles, also settled down toward a confused compromise between the two.

As normal confusion and variety thus set in, Moslem and Christian rulers began to operate within comparable limitations. The conflict between bureaucratic rationality and hereditary privilege, which manifested itself in Turkish ruling circles, had parallels in Christendom, where the struggle was inextricably entangled with Reformation and Counter Reformation in the West, and with Orthodox resistance to Latin schismatics in Russia. It would be false to suggest that the causes for which men fought, the words they used, and the ideals they professed did not affect their behavior and the outcome of the various conflicts into which they plunged. Yet this side of historical reality should not blind us to the fact that the political struggles in Western, Orthodox, and Ottoman communities everywhere pitted an hereditary, landed elite against monarchical and bureaucratic absolutisms served by appointed officials who had no hereditary claim to power.

This struggle took particularly drastic and dramatic forms in Russia, where the period has traditionally been called "The Time of Troubles." Use of the same term to describe the internal political difficulties confronted by the Hapsburg, Polish, and Ottoman monarchies between 1570 and 1650 seems a useful device to emphasize the common element in the institutional evolution of each society during these decades. The term is also applicable to the region of Danubian and Pontic Europe which centrally concerns us here; for the efforts of local rulers and polities to assert effective independence — whether in Transylvania, Wallachia and Moldavia, Crim Tartary, or among the Zaporozhian Cossacks — shared some of the same traits. Partial paralysis of the adjacent empires through prolonged internal crises was what allowed the local captains and princes of Danubian and Pontic Europe to make headway against imperial claims to their lands; and the process of political consolidation within each of the separate polities which seriously strove, however briefly or uncertainly, for real sovereignty and independence recapitulated *in parvo* the struggles between aristocracy and monarchy simultaneously going on in the greater states lying on the region's flanks.

In trying to reduce such complexity to comprehensibility, it seems best to summarize the manifestations of the Time of Troubles within each of the limitrophic empires before trying to put the pattern of their interaction with the states and peoples of Danubian and Pontic Europe, 1570–1650, into focus.

The Ottoman Time of Troubles. The Turks remained almost continually at war, as aforetime, but campaigns were no longer decisive; and the scale of effort put into distant enterprises in the Mediterranean against Spanish and Italian naval powers, in eastern Anatolia against the Persians, or in Hungary against the Hapsburgs tended to lessen as the prospect of any important gain from such enterprises evaporated. The willingness of individual fief holders to report for military service that promised nothing but hardship and danger decreased, while various devices outside or barely within the law allowed heirs, even if militarily incompetent, to succeed to their fathers' lands without accepting the obligation of effective military service. At the same time, the sultan's slave household, which had been the agency through which the sultan exercised personal control over Ottoman military and civil affairs, also threatened to get out of hand. The imperial finances, like those of individual Turkish warriors, had formerly depended on substantial booty income. Rents and taxes were all very well; but what conferred the decisive superiority upon Ottoman arms in the first half of the sixteenth century was the sultan's ability to maintain a larger, better equipped, and better disciplined military force than any rival succeeded in doing. He did so by preying upon the borderlands where the imperial field army operated each summer. This ceased to be possible when summer operations, instead of enriching, were more likely to impoverish the warriors who took part in lengthy march and countermarch, only to besiege a few desolate frontier posts which, even when captured, yielded no booty worth the name.

On the other hand, what could no longer be picked up along the frontiers of the empire could, in part at least, be made good by exacting more from subject populations at home. Landholders could and did demand extra payments from the peasants on their estates. Officials of the sultan's slave household could and did demand extra payments, either for the performance of the duties of their office, or for nonperformance of such duties, i.e., for granting exceptions to the rule. Such devices allowed the Turkish cavalrymen and the officials of the sultan's slave family to live more luxuriously than their predecessors had done in the days of rapid territorial expansion and abundant booty income.

The humbler ranks of the armed establishment, however, had few such opportunities. Quite the contrary: with a general inflation of prices, resulting at least in part from the influx of American silver into Mediterranean economies, their pay became quite inadequate. The solution here was to allow the imperial footsoldiers, the famous slave corps of Janissaries, to work as artisans during their idle time in garrison, so that income from sale of the goods they had made might supplement the imperial pay. But just as hard-bitten Turkish cavalrymen of an earlier generation tended to transform themselves into parasitic landlords who shrank from the costs and exertions of a campaign, so also the humbler soldiery, when its maintenance came to depend on sale of artisan products, tended to dissolve into the Moslem artisan population of Constantinople and other garrison towns of the empire and lost much of the old-time discipline and eagerness for battle.

Nor could the hereditary principle be checked when individual Janissaries took up artisan trades and began to mix freely with the civil population. Sons of Janissaries were at first admitted to the corps only by virtue of a legal fiction — for no born Moslem could lawfully be enslaved. Later, under

Selim II (1566–74) a quota was established for admission of Janissaries' sons to the muster rolls; and then in 1638, Sultan Murad IV formally abolished the old style of recruitment to the imperial slave household through child tribute from the villages of the western Balkans. The legal enactment merely legitimated an accomplished fact. Place holders' sons had long been eager to gain admission to the privileged ranks of the sultan's household; all available jobs were filled and over-filled without recourse to forcible recruitment from remote villages.

This evolution of Ottoman institutions conspicuously fa-vored towns and town populations at the expense of the peas-antry of the heartlands of the empire. When the rulers of the Ottoman state had been enslaved village boys, a vestigial sympathy for the peasant populations from whence they had themselves come held townsmen and the landholding class in check. No such sentiments affected the conduct of men who had grown up in towns and entered the sultan's slave family thanks to paternal "pull" or through direct purchase of office. Such men tended to make their careers on the strength of fiscal ruthlessness, which, if cleverly enough pur-sued, allowed purchase of ever higher office.

Skill in personal intrigue also helped a man to advance rapidly upward. The old military virtues still mattered from time to time; but even competent commanders frequently lost their reputations on some distant frontier, since easy victory, though still expected, could no longer often be at-tained. By contrast, a clever man who stayed close to the seat of power in Constantinople might profit as much from mili-tary failure as from success — if he joined the winning clique soon enough or paid the right superior enough money to buy a new and more lucrative office. Cynical cleverness flourished in this environment; but the men who rose to the top sur-vived extremely rigorous as well as ruthless competition. As a result, they were normally endowed with unsual energy and intelligence, even though trained in a very narrow, backward-looking, and morally unscrupulous tradition.

The growing weight of towns in the body social sustained

and was itself sustained by an increase in the luxury of life, level of cultivation, and mere number of the upper classes. Rude warriors, sons or grandsons of humble villagers or poor tribesmen, had accepted a spartan life while on campaign as part of the natural order of things and, in winter quarters, lacked time and opportunity to develop much acquaintance with the seductions of urbanity. Not so their successors, leisured landlords, who took seldom and reluctantly to the saddle. Such individuals, brought up to the life of a gentleman, Turkish style, living in towns from childhood and exposed both to Moslem learning and to age-old vices and luxuries, provided an enlarged market for artisans and merchants, on the one hand, and demanded more from the peasantry who sustained them, on the other.

The gap between town and country widened enormously. Villagers were systematically alienated from the Ottoman establishment, as had not been the case in earlier generations. The rise of brigandage and local guerrilla is a good index of this shift; for young men, who in an earlier time might have been drafted into the sultan's household and emerged as rulers of the empire, now tended to become local bandits, whose occasional Robin Hood assaults upon Turkish landlords or townsmen did not prevent them from living most of the time as parasites upon the Christian peasantry.

What happened may be described in another way by saying that the armed establishment and administrative bureaucracy which had initially sustained itself in a good part by plundering the borderlands of the Ottoman state shifted the locus of its predation toward the center of the empire as the borderlands became exhausted. Pressure upon the borderlands relaxed somewhat and increased very considerably in the heartlands of the empire, thus tending to equalize the burden geographically. The extraordinary and contrived social system of the fifteenth-sixteenth centuries, having reached the socio-technical limits of expansion, had painfully to readjust to a style of life from which booty windfalls of any significant scale had been abstracted. In doing so, Turkish administrators and warriors inevitably weakened their military striking power and divided their own society against itself far more acutely than had before been necessary, when an adequate supply of appropriate victims lay waiting just across the frontier.

The most conspicuous manifestation of the strains introduced into Ottoman institutions by the cessation of territorial expansion and booty income was a long series of riots in Constantinople, led, characteristically, by Janissaries, by the cavalry garrison force (spahis of the Porte), or even on several occasions, by the students and officers of the religious establishments of the city. In 1589 the Janissaries mutinied when their pay was delivered in debased coinage; and before order was restored to the city, the grand vizier and other high officials of the state had to be replaced according to the Janissaries' demand.[3] This was the first time that common soldiers had intervened successfully in Ottoman high politics; but once the possibility became apparent, similar and more prolonged and violent uprisings became frequent. In 1622 a new landmark was reached when the reigning sultan, Osman II, was deposed and executed, and a helpless incompetent put on the throne in his place — again at the demand of mutinous Janissaries who broke into the palace itself to wreak their will upon the cowering imperial inmates.[4]

Yet despite these and many less drastic riots, the Ottoman system of government and military organization was still capable of sporadic recovery. In 1596, for example, after severe setbacks in war with Austria, special prayers and other religious observances in Constantinople prefaced an all-out mobilization of the empire's resources. The sultan, Mehmed III, took the field in person, and his troops won a hard-fought battle at Keresztes. This success had the happy side effect of bringing in plunder on something like the old scale. A more dramatic revival came under the eye of Sultan Murad IV (1623–40), a man of extraordinary muscular strength and personal prowess who strove mightily, and not without success,

[3] For details, see Joseph von Hammer, *Geschichte des osmanischen Reiches*, IV, 193–95.
[4] *Ibid.*, IV, 541–53.

to restore and reform ancient institutions which had fallen out of order. Murad's victorious wars against Persia were matched by wholesale executions at home. Whoever the sultan thought inimical to his regime or merely inefficient or disobedient was destroyed out of hand. Such violence, like that of Peter the Great half a century later, was not merely wanton. Murad planned wholesale military reform, aimed at producing a smaller, fully professional force that could be paid a money wage from the resources available to the Ottoman government. But an early death, brought on in part by his intemperate personal habits, made all his reforms stillborn, save those, like the suspension of child tribute levies, which happened to coincide with the self-interest of the ruling cliques of the empire.

Under normal conditions, however, when the central authority was not exercised by a ruthless, energetic sultan or grand vizier, the hardening of vested interests proceeded apace. Any effort to galvanize the machine of government to effective military action required progressively greater effort, i.e., demanded the bloodletting of malingerers and opponents on a larger and larger scale. Such extreme measures, threatening everyone's routine enjoyment of his position in life, whatever it might be, could win general support only in face of immediate foreign danger.

Ottoman rulers were, in fact, caught in a difficult dilemma. Military or any other effective reform implied innovation. Vested interests regularly opposed such moves by explaining that what was needed to keep the empire great was not innovation but a faithful adherence to old precedent; in particular, Janissary customs and privileges should not be infringed and the traditional equipment and deployment of Turkish armies should not be altered. Military technological development in Europe or elsewhere was irrelevant. The will of Allah, having indorsed ancient custom by granting the Turks their enormous success, could not change. Woe, therefore, to the impious man who tried deliberately to change what had been handed down from the past!

No effective riposte was possible. Had Turkish successes

not been so great, had the past not been so persuasive as a model of successful behavior, self-transformation of the sort Ivan the Terrible and then Peter the Great carried through in Russia would have been far easier. The Russians, being without a great imperial past, could afford to model themselves on foreigners; the Turks could never really do so as long as they remained loyal to the Ottoman ideal and self-conception.

A corollary of this profoundly conservative outlook was that the erosion of autocratic power in the Ottoman Empire could never go as far as it did in states where no such compelling past inhibited the narrow localisms of town and nobility. The instruments of absolutism were always latent in the Turkish body social, even when weaklings and children occupied the throne. Ruthless, competent men continued to staff the Ottoman bureaucracy, although they ceased to aim primarily at matters of public concern, concentrating instead on the narrower, but no less engrossing, game of self-aggrandizement, enrichment, and defense against rivals. The appearance of a strong-willed and violent man at the top of such a hierarchy could, within relatively short time, polarize the ranks of officialdom like the molecules of a magnet, making them into an obedient instrument of a single sovereign will once more. Sultan Murad IV won his successes in just this fashion: the grand vizier Mehmed Köprülu (1656–61) did so a little later. But the traditionalism of Turkish society which permitted such revivals also limited the effective action of the restored bureaucratic instrument to traditional means and goals.

The same conservative frame of mind greatly weakened hereditary privilege. Even when hereditary privilege became widespread in fact, dominating landholding and affecting entry into many branches of government, it was still felt to be fundamentally wrong, a usurpation which could rightfully be overridden by a strong ruler and his chosen agents. Hence, however dramatic sporadic manifestations in Constantinople may have been, the Ottoman "Time of Troubles" was comparatively superficial, leading to no lasting alteration in the balance of forces within that society and requiring no fundamental departure from established ideas and ideals of life and government.

The Time of Troubles in Austria. Upper and Lower Austria, with the adjacent kingdoms, duchies, counties, and lands of less exalted degree that clustered in Hapsburg hands by the middle of the sixteenth century, stood at an opposite extreme from the contrived rationality and radical centralization of power which characterized the Ottoman government when it was in working order. Multiplicities, autonomies, immunities, privileges pullulated everywhere; and the imperial prerogative, pretending to all Germany and Italy together with such client kingdoms as Bohemia and Hungary, was spread so thin as to be but little effective. Even after Charles V abdicated (1556), assigning Spain and its dependencies to his son Philip II and the imperial title to his brother, Ferdinand, the distractions of a position which required negotiation and cajolery rather than command vis à vis the princely rulers of Germany were still enormous. Religious controversy between Lutherans, Calvinists, and Catholics threatened irremediable civil war in Germany, partly because the locus of sovereignty — whether imperial, local, or princely — was as profoundly in doubt as were the truths of religion.

Ferdinand and his heir, the emperor Maximilian II (1564–76), played a cautious role amid such confusions. In his youth Maximilian was personally inclined to Lutheranism, but as emperor and prince of the Austrian hereditary lands, with an eye also to the possibility of some future reunion of the Hapsburg possesions if the Spanish line should die out, Maximilian could not let his personal inclinations interfere with considerations of state. And these required, or seemed to require, the emperor to uphold Catholicism in Germany against usurping Protestant princes. Within the hereditary lands, Protestantism speedily became the banner behind which burghers and nobles who aspired toward greater independence or larger immunities rallied. Such a program, if successful, would have whittled down the tax income and reduced the effective administrative power of the Hapsburgs, just as the Protestant

TIME OF TROUBLES

confiscation of church properties and the abrogation of ecclesiastical jurisdiction had whittled away the income and administrative authority of the prelates of the Roman church. To
embrace such a program seemed out of the question, but to
oppose it with anything more than a passive tenacity of imperial and hereditary prerogatives was not in Maximilian's
nature. When pressed, he made concessions to Protestants,
as, for example, his recognition (1574) of the right of nobles
to keep Protestant ministers in their town houses, even when,
as was the case in most of the towns of Austria, Protestantism
remained illegal.

Such countervailing concessions simply intensified the confrontation between Catholic and Protestant in the Hapsburg
hereditary lands without doing anything to tip the balance
decisively one way or the other. The fact that Maximilian
sent his eldest son, Rudolf, to be educated in Spain had far
more important consequences.[5] In Spain Rudolf absorbed the
militant spirit of Spanish Catholicism from his Jesuit teachers;
and when in 1576 he inherited all of his father's titles and
functions, Rudolf set out to establish in the Austrian lands
as near a replica of the Spanish power as he could. Intimate
alliance with Catholicism and energetic repression of religious and political rivals were Rudolf's policies. Weaknesses
in his own personality — Rudolf remained a bachelor all his
life, and in old age grew increasingly suspicious and eccen-
tric — together with the lively dissatisfactions of his brothers
who, contrary to earlier family custom, had been excluded
by Maximilian II's will from any share in regalian rights to
the hereditary lands, prevented Rudolf from achieving any
dramatic success. Nevertheless, during his reign formidable
champions of the Catholic cause like Cardinal Khlesl (d. 1630)
of Vienna and Cardinal Pazmany (d. 1637) of Hungary, both
of whom were converts from Protestantism and of humble
social origin, rose to leadership of a revitalized church and
carried forward a very successful propaganda on behalf of the

---

[5] Rudolf's Spanish education was initially calculated to make him
acceptable in Spain as a potential heir to Philip II, whose succession long
remained in doubt owing to the precarious health of his sons.

old faith. Thus, by 1589 the governments of eleven of the principal towns of Austria had been reconverted to Catholicism, largely through the missionary energies of Jesuits and other clergy. But the princely power was never far behind. In 1585, for example, Rudolf decreed that only Catholics could enjoy burgher rights in the towns of Austria. By such measures, the secular arm effectively reinforced the theological arguments of Catholic preachers.

In Upper and Lower Austria and in Bohemia, where towns were comparatively numerous and well developed, the balance of power between Hapsburg monarchical bureaucracy and the nobility rested in large degree with the burghers. If townsmen's taxes flowed smoothly into Hapsburg coffers, then the administrative skeleton wherewith to match and in case of necessity to overpower the nobility could easily come into existence; but if the towns allied themselves with the nobility in defiance of Hapsburg agents, then the power of the central government could not be sustained. Much the same balance of forces existed in Germany as a whole; but after the Reformation had come to most of the important cities of the empire, the Hapsburgs had small chance of making an effective alliance with Protestant burghers against local princes and nobles. Only a radical policy of championing a national German church, cutting all ties with the Spanish and Catholic worlds in which the Hapsburgs were deeply rooted, might have made such an alliance possible.

Within the hereditary lands, however, matters were much more in doubt. In Maximilian II's time, town and noble had generally found it possible to co-operate under the banner of Protestantism.[6] Under Rudolf, however, as the towns were recaptured for Catholicism and the prince, Protestantism became more nearly identified with aristocratic resistance to centralization. In Hungary towns were comparatively unim-

[6] Herein lay the importance of Maximilian's concession which legalized Protestant services in a noble's town house. Burghers who had to visit such houses to hear Lutheran worship were driven into the arms of the nobility, who in maintaining such places of worship also asserted their solidarity with the burghers.

68

portant, and religious affiliation among the only class that mattered, the nobility, became a sign, more than anything else, of loyalty toward — or distrust of — the Hapsburg king. Generally speaking, after the initial force of the Reformation had spent itself in Hungary, the magnates readily returned to Catholicism. The stronghold of Protestantism came to be the small gentry, particularly in Transylvania and Turkish Hungary. Religious division among the Magyars, therefore, carried into the seventeenth century the sociopolitical fissure which had become critical immediately after the death of Matthias Corvinus in 1490. Sectarian differences lost much of their doctrinal vigor, and religion became little more than a quarry providing suitable rallying cries for each side in the ongoing struggle between the magnates and the rank and file of the nobility.

Matters came to acute crisis in the last years of Rudolf's reign. War with the Turks, begun in 1593 in alliance with the prince of Transylvania and aimed at the liberation of all Hungary, bogged down into squalid intrigue and violent coup and countercoup until Stephen Bocskay, appointed prince of Transylvania by the Turks, rallied enough support among the Protestant Magyar gentry to endanger the Austrian forces. Thereupon, Rudolf reluctantly agreed to a peace with the Turks (1606), in which he recognized Bocskay as prince of Transylvania. The emperor also secured exemption from further tribute payments for the part of Hungary he controlled by agreeing to pay the sultan a lump sum in redemption of annual payments.

This setback was accompanied by and entangled with a bitter intrigue within the Hapsburg family. Matthias, the emperor's youngest brother and prospective heir, was unwilling to acquiesce longer in Rudolf's rule, which became more and more erratic. Rudolf, on the other hand, was not in the least inclined to yield office or authority to Matthias. Each therefore began to bid against the other for support, with the ironical result that Matthias gave away regalian rights in Hungary (1606) and Austria (1607) to the predominantly Protestant nobility in order to win their support against the emperor, while Rudolf was doing the same thing in Bohemia in order to thwart Matthias' ambitions.

The effect of this struggle between the two brothers was to reverse (Majestätsbrief, 1609) the whole policy of Rudolf's reign. When Matthias found himself successful at last, and inherited all his brother's titles and powers (1612), he therefore found it difficult or impossible to discard his alliances and repudiate his promises to the nobility. As a result, he failed to re-establish the regalian rights he had so recklessly squandered during his quarrels with Rudolf. Efforts to recover lost ground in Bohemia led to disturbances in Prague, from which, in due course, the Thirty Years' War (1618–48) developed.

Matthias died in 1619 and was succeeded by his cousin, Ferdinand of Styria (1619–37). At the time of his accession, Ferdinand confronted rebellious nobles in Bohemia and Austria who feared the energy and determination he had shown as duke of Styria. Nevertheless, within two years Ferdinand won relatively easy success in the Hapsburg hereditary lands. This merely transferred the scene of struggle to Germany as a whole, where the contest between centralized bureaucracy and local sovereignty played itself out to a contrary conclusion. For a while, Ferdinand seemed on the verge of making the imperial power a reality in Germany. The instrument of his success was a large imperial army that was able, like the earlier armies of Matthias Corvinus and of the sultans in eastern Europe, to sustain itself in large part by plundering the country where it operated. The result was very costly to many parts of Germany and offended Ferdinand's moral sense. He also had reason to fear the overweening ambition of the commander, Albert of Wallenstein, under whom the imperial army won its early successes. Wallenstein's assassination in 1634 actually relieved the emperor of a major political embarrassment. Hence even after massive foreign intervention by Sweden and then by France brought new forces to oppose the Hapsburg imperial cause, neither Ferdinand II nor his son, Ferdinand III (1637–57), opted for an all-out policy of victory at any cost.

Radical Caesarism à la Wallenstein, disregarding all traditional limitations and institutional niceties, might conceivably have united Germany but could have done so only at the cost of creating a zone of devastation in the borderlands between the German and the French (as well as Swedish) power centers, i.e., in the very heartland of European civilization. The Catholic conscience of the emperors prevented them from personally pursuing such a policy, and to intrust an army of plundering mercenaries to anyone else was to run the risk of usurpation. Hence in the end the Hapsburgs settled for half measures: the evisceration of imperial powers over Germany, published to the world by the treaties of Westphalia (1648), was counterbalanced by the war-born consolidation of monarchical-bureaucratic power in the hereditary lands of Austria and Bohemia.

Despite failure in Germany, Hapsburg power emerged enormously strengthened from the Thirty Years' War. The reduction of Bohemia at the beginning of that war gave the king-emperor a secure and relatively wealthy base for his power, where neither rebellious noble nor purse-proud burgher any longer dared to challenge the twin pillars of the new regime: a reinvigorated Catholic clergy and an appointed officialdom. Styria had been organized in the same mold before Ferdinand became emperor; Upper and Lower Austria soon followed.

The achievement was not merely a matter of military force, though violence was assuredly an essential ingredient of Hapsburg success against both nobles and towns. But the use made of military victory depended largely upon schools and universities, which were founded or reorganized in the course of the Hapsburg "Time of Troubles," and which began to provide Hapsburg officialdom, both lay and ecclesiastical, with a quite new level of education. A body of men arose who were able to use subtler and more impressive techniques, both of administration and of argument, against insubordinate elements in society than had been available before. The educational establishment also inculcated new moral attitudes by emphasizing the Hapsburg-Catholic mission of bringing peace, order, justice, and civilization to the frontier zone of east-central Europe. This mission was directed in the first instance to the salvation of unruly Protestant heretics in the Austrian and Bohemian lands. Success there foreshadowed transfer of the mission field to the Hungarian lands, where, however, military victory against the Turks was a necessary preface to the work of civilization as conceived by the Hapsburgs and their disciplined, educated, and (moderately) dedicated servants.

For the time being, the Hapsburg state had no military energies to spare for Hungary and the Turks. Until 1648, the struggle in Germany overrode every other consideration; and that effort was so great that a considerable period of recuperation intervened after the Peace of Westphalia before the Hapsburgs directed any major effort eastward. In the interim, however, the Catholic Counter Reformation made great progress in Hungary. Most of the Magyar nobility ceased to be Protestant; but this success was won, in part at least, because the Hapsburgs refrained from pursuing political and administrative consolidation in the portion of Hungary under their nominal control. With the privileges and powers of the Diet unchallenged, there was no need to rally to the defense of a threatened constitution; and Protestantism therefore lost much of its meaning to the Magyar nobility. Under these circumstances, the superiority of Catholic educational institutions and propaganda had a relatively clear field. Only a minority among the Magyar gentry, who remained unaffected by higher education and cherished deep suspicion of the magnates' "foreign" ways, clung to Calvinism as a mark of their distrust of the new currents sweeping into Hungary with the Catholic Counter Reformation.

Three points deserve emphasis in connection with the institutional and social balance that emerged from the Hapsburg "Time of Troubles."

a) There was no clear, sharp resolution of the triangular relationship between monarch, nobles, and burghers. Many of the former ambiguities survived, even in Bohemia, which saw a radical replacement of old noble families by newcomers, loyal, presumably, to the Hapsburgs. There was plenty of room for nobles and burghers to advance to high office in the Hapsburg service; and many ambitious and energetic young men made their careers in this way. The church, likewise, opened its ranks to men of high and low degree, allowing even peasants' and artisans' sons to rise to high office, at least occasionally. Jesuit schools and the universities played the critical role here in making possible an effective rapprochement within the ranks of the Hapsburg bureaucracy between these diverse social groups. For it was expanded and improved institutions of formal education that provided a common set of values and ideas, as well as more technical and specifically professional training in theology and public administration for the recruits to governmental and ecclesiastical office.

Such an institutional system built great flexibility into Hapsburg (and still more into European) society. New social groups and new ideas could rise to power by grasping the educational ladder. At a time when social mobility in Ottoman society was decreasing, and when the path from peasant village to imperial slave family was being blocked by entrenched urban privilege, in the Hapsburg lands an institutional arrangement allowing less dramatic but nonetheless effective social climbing by individuals of unusual ability achieved a much enlarged scope. The contrasting fates of the two empires in the following two centuries may in large part be attributed to this difference.

b) Even within the hereditary lands, no clear, rational, and radical administrative centralization developed from the Hapsburg "Time of Troubles." Compromises with traditional local immunities and privileges was the stuff and substance of the equipoise that emerged from the convulsion of the Thirty Years' War. Each land within the cluster of the hereditary lands remained administratively separate; and local political bodies — diets, town councils, manorial courts, and the like — continued to function. The difference lay in the fact that new officials, or rather officials with newly effective powers, divided actual authority with all the tangle of local and traditional bodies. Under such a regime, the total energies and manpower of society could not be mobilized for any given end. Indeed, it was his refusal to attempt any such ruthless radicalism that lay behind Ferdinand II's quarrel with Wallenstein. This meant restriction of the effectiveness of the Hapsburg power — at least in the short run; but, again, making room in the political system for divergent interests and privileged groups may also have had the longer-range effect of maintaining flexibility, and therefore durability, within the body politic.

c) Despite these limits upon Hapsburg power, the long travail of the Thirty Years' War did lead to the establishment of a small, technically well-equipped standing army. After the close of hostilities in Germany, the emperor kept in being nine regiments of foot and ten of horse.[7] The tax income now available to the emperor from the hereditary lands sufficed to sustain such a force. It was not large, by the standards of Wallenstein's army, nor, indeed, by the standards long familiar to the Turks. Yet it was always available to the emperor, ready at short notice to bring a very considerable force to bear at any point within or adjacent to the hereditary lands. The local insubordination on the part of groups of restless nobles or towns that had plagued the Hapsburgs at the beginning of the seventeenth century thereby became utterly and permanently impractical. This in turn cleared the way for officials to collect more taxes which might be used to maintain a larger army capable of meeting other European armies on even terms and, by the end of the century, able also to defeat the Turks, not by matching Turkish numbers, but by surpassing Turkish troops in maneuverability, armament, discipline, and strategic skill.

In summary, therefore, we may say that the Hapsburg "Time of Troubles" wrought far more significant changes in the texture of Hapsburg society than was the case within the

[7] Hans Meier-Welcker, *Deutsches Heerwesen im Wandel der Zeit* (Frankfort on the Main: Bernard & Greife, 1956), p. 18.

Ottoman empire. By the middle of the seventeenth century, new ideas, new techniques, new men acquired far greater scope in Hapsburg lands than was the case in Turkey. The convulsive capacity of Ottoman institutions to recover their original formidability confronted Hapsburg capacity for slower but sustained institutional self-transformation. In such a confrontation, the long-range advantage clearly now lay with the Hapsburgs; but before we examine the consequences of this change for Danubian Europe, it will be best to consider the parallel evolution of the Polish and Russian lands, where the Time of Troubles had its classic manifestation.

The Time of Troubles in Poland and Russia. In 1570 as in 1650, extreme contrast prevailed between the political institutions of the aristocratic republic of Poland-Lithuania and the autocratic tsardom of Muscovy. Yet events of the intervening decades demonstrated how nearly akin the contrasting polities in fact were. Abortive plans for establishing Polish monarchical absolutism were matched by active, but in the end unsuccessful efforts to dismantle the Russian tsar's autocracy in favor of some largely undefined, but clearly aristocratic alternative. Moreover, in both Russia and Poland the anarchic, politically inchoate will of the peasantry confronted tsar and noble with a sporadically dangerous and angry challenge to their exercise of power.

The "Time of Troubles" that afflicted Poland and Russia in the late sixteenth and early seventeenth centuries found particularly dramatic expression, because the extremes among possible alternative forms of constitutional organization achieved unusual visibility within societies whose resources and manpower were chronically and severely strained by the effort needed to attain or to maintain the status of a great power. In more anciently civilized areas, like those ruled by the Hapsburgs and Osmanlis, resources were not stretched so thin as they were in Poland and Russia. Larger means existed wherewith to maintain systems of political power, so that choices between alternative modes of social organization and patterns of wealth distribution did not have to be made so ruthlessly. Only the Hungarian and Swedish kingdoms exhibited a comparable sociopolitical extremism, and for the same reason, since these states too erected a transiently great state power on the basis of comparatively slender home resources.

Between 1570 and 1650, Poland was passing through the last decades of what her patriotic historians have reverenced as a period of national greatness. It would be more accurate to describe it as a period of the greatness of the Polish and Lithuanian landowners, whose liberation from royal and ecclesiastical jurisdiction had been sealed by events of the immediately preceding period. Two circumstances, one economic and one political, coincided to allow the Polish landowners to dominate society. First, as Polish grain became a staple of west European urban markets, local landowners organized peasant labor for export production and secured for themselves most of the money income that accrued from the entire enterprise. Under these circumstances, taste for the amenities of life as known to men of wealth in western Europe easily rooted itself among the Polish landowners, who thus began to share more fully than before in the refinements of European civilization. The peasants, on the other hand, were enserfed to stabilize the labor supply needed to assure tillage of the grain fields. They remained culturally in a different world from their westernized, noble masters.

In the second place, after 1410, when the medieval Polish kingdom decisively repulsed the Teutonic knights, no important outside military threat compelled the Polish landowners to share their power and wealth with public functionaries. A divided Germany on one side, and a divided and subjugated Russia, on the other, offered no real danger to the Polish kingdom; and the pricks from the steppe which became apparent after 1484, when the Crim Tartars started their slave raids, were not really felt in the northerly centers of the Polish-Lithuanian state. Hence, after 1410 the medieval kingship that had arisen to withstand the attack of German knights could be dismantled with impunity, and was. An aristocratic republic developed in the course of the fifteenth and sixteenth centuries in which representatives of the great landowners of the country exercised effective control over the initiatives of the central authorities.

Yet this potentially anarchic polity worked fairly well, as long as no very severe military threats had to be met. It had remarkable success along the Polish eastern borderlands in persuading first Lithuanian clan chieftains and then a variety of Russian (and even Moldavian) magnates to take out membership in the Polish noble republic. Rapid territorial growth was one result, so that the vision, never quite attained, of a state extending right across Europe from the Baltic to the Black Sea seemed on the verge of practical realization. The spread of Polish culture and style of life among the landowning classes of most of this vast territory was another and somewhat more lasting consequence.

By 1570, the days of Polish aristocracy liberty and prosperity were coming to a close. To the east, the rise of a sternly centralized autocracy, centered in Moscow, put a formidable rival into the field along Poland's eastern frontier. On the south, the local military initiative of Polish landlords failed to hold Turkish and Tartar harassments very successfully in check; and the rise of a powerful military brotherhood among mere commoners — the Cossack Sech — put a potentially dangerous military rival in the field. Meanwhile, to the north, a precariously centralized Swedish monarchy, whose military strength depended directly upon a royal army recruited from a peasantry that was still, for the most part, free from landlord oppression,[8] offered a new and immediate threat along the Baltic coast, where Polish and Swedish imperial ambitions clashed.

The new international constellation of forces became apparent during the Livonian War (1557–82). This began when Polish success in concluding an alliance with the grand master of the Knights of the Sword (who then controlled most of Livonia) persuaded Tsar Ivan IV the Terrible (1533–84) to invade that Baltic land. The Swedes and Danes entered the fray

[8] Ingmar Andersson, *A History of Sweden* (New York: Prager, 1956) pp. 142–52.

soon afterward. As the long struggle proceeded, the need to mount ever increasing military force against these Scandinavian rivals and against each other provoked sharp domestic crises in both Poland and Muscovy.

In Poland's case, the initial response seemed to strengthen the state. In 1569, union between Lithuania and Poland was concluded. The grand duchy of Lithuania thereby acquired Polish institutions, so that the Lithuanian petty nobility, previously largely overbalanced in political questions by a handful of great magnates, acquired the same pre-eminence that their Polish counterparts had enjoyed for several decades. This constituted a solid victory for the Polish gentry, who had previously feared an alliance between king, Catholic clergy, and Lithuanian magnates to deprive them of sovereignty in domestic affairs. The king, in effect, reversed himself. By accepting gentry predominance at home in return for enlarged support of the war abroad, King Sigismund II Augustus (1548–72) prepared the way for his elected successor, the former prince of Transylvania, Stephen Bathory (1575–86), to lead Polish armies to a series of military victories over the Muscovites and thus end the Livonian War victoriously, with Poland in possession of all of Livonia, together with the provinces of Polotsk and Velich, which had formerly belonged to the tsar.

But Stephen Bathory's military successes had been won only with the help of an infantry army, recruited from among the peasants of the royal estates and paid by tax moneys voted by the nobles' Sejm, or Diet. Bathory also elected to use state money to "enrol" a limited number of Cossacks as paid border guards against Tartar raids from the south. These military policies cost the Polish-Lithuanian landlords more than they were willing to pay. The taxes the king collected from peasants diminished the sums collectible as rents, and thus directly reduced (or threatened to reduce) noble income. This was bad enough; but the fact that the king used such money to create a military force that might countervail the supremacy of noble cavalry levies was far worse. With such an instrument, an ambitious king might break through all the constitutional limitations the gentry had woven around his power and try to introduce absolutism. The fact that such a policy could be pursued under the guise of a crusade against either Orthodox or Moslem error — depending on whether Muscovy or Turkey were attacked first — did not make the Polish gentry any less suspicious.[9] It was, in fact, the refusal of the Sejm to vote further taxes that compelled Stephen Bathory to come to terms with Ivan IV in 1582 when he felt himself on the eve of decisive success against Muscovy.

For Muscovy, on the other hand, the struggle over Livonia was an unlimited disaster. Not only did the Russians lose important territories, but the violent revolution from above which Ivan the Terrible loosed against the boyars, beginning in 1565 and sustained with varying degrees of intensity until the end of his life in 1584, instead of succeeding in mobilizing sufficient forces to defeat the Poles and Swedes had the result of fragmenting the Russian ruling and land-holding class into mutually distrustful, frightened, and at least in some cases, also angry individuals, who were quite incapable of acting together effectively without a tyrannous master's compulsion. In many cases, Ivan's policy broke traditional ties between particular boyar families and particular regions or estates. This probably inhibited the effective mobilization of aristocratic military power when unrestrained political chaos paralyzed Muscovy twenty some years after Ivan's death.

Yet the breaking up of traditional boyar power was at most a negative accomplishment. In the long and painful Livonian War, Poles and Swedes had succeeded where Russians had failed, and this despite the fact that the tsar's government had mobilized a far larger proportion of Russia's available resources and manpower than either the Polish or the Swedish government had done.

In an ironic sense, this demonstration of Russia's continu-

[9] Stephen Bathory talked freely with agents of the pope and others of his intention of using the resources of a conquered Muscovy together with those of Poland-Lithuania and all other Christian states that would cooperate for a grand crusade against the Turk — with whom he meanwhile was at considerable pains to keep good relations.

ing backwardness as against her western neighbors nonetheless implied eventual victory. Russians could not escape the conclusion that still greater efforts were necessary to cope with Western military pressures, whereas their successes in the Livonian War convinced the Polish nobles that Poland could survive as a great power without a standing army and without any form of taxation that would give the king independent power against the gentry landowners. The decision to repudiate the innovations Bathory had made meant that the existing imbalance between Russian and Polish strength did not in fact prove fatal to Moscow's political independence, as Bathory had intended and expected.

Instead, violent dissension broke out within Poland during the last year of Bathory's life. This was followed by a brief but pregnant interregnum before the Sejm intrusted the royal office to the heir to the Swedish throne, Sigismund III Vasa.

Sigismund was ill-content with the web of restraints the Polish nobles imposed upon him. He therefore encouraged a party of magnates, Catholic prelates, and malcontents who sought to strengthen the monarchy against the gentry of the Sejm. When Sigismund inherited the Swedish crown (1592), his position was further complicated by the fact that he needed, if possible, to use Polish resources against Swedish insurgents who resisted his rule. This the Poles refused, and by 1600 he had, indeed, lost all semblance of authority in Sweden. With this upshot, the hope of Swedish-Polish collaboration against Muscovy, which had been one of the arguments for Sigismund's election as king of Poland, glimmered toward extinction. Instead, the two kingdoms launched a desultory war against each other that lasted more than half a century.

Matters came to a head in 1606, when a faction of the Polish Sejm revolted against Sigismund's demand for the establishment of a standing army wherewith to pursue the war against Sweden. Peace was patched up three years later, when the king agreed to abandon all his projects for constitutional reform. A major factor facilitating this pacification was the sudden opening of glittering possibilities in the east, where the Muscovite state was in the throes of an even more drastic internal crisis. When Ivan the Terrible's son Fëdor died without heirs in 1598, hereditary tsardom lapsed, and no successor, unhallowed by ancestral legitimation, could control the explosive tensions tearing Muscovite society apart. Hence, despite Tsar Boris Gudunov's personal abilities, the grievances, personal and collective, of every rank of society came out into the open during his tumultuous and precarious reign. Boyars and Ivan's "service nobility," merchants, peasants, Cossacks, and adventurers of every sort began to aspire to influence or control the state. Rival ambitions and intrigues boiled toward open and wholesale violence; and after Tsar Boris' death in 1605, the Time of Troubles (in its traditional and strict definition), distracted Russia for the next eight years.

Such confusion offered Polish adventurers irresistible opportunities for taking up Stephen Bathory's crusade once more. Thus, in 1608 most of the fighting men who had entered the field against King Sigismund in 1606–7 rallied to the banners of the second "False Dimitri," who was consequently able to invade Russia with some 18,000 Poles at his back. A year later, King Sigismund transferred Polish broils to Russian ground by besieging Smolensk with a royal army of his own. But the prospect of opening all Muscovy to aristocratic enterprise and Catholic culture seemed to offer such advantages to all the Polish factions that Sigismund was willing and able to negotiate a reconciliation with his political rivals who controlled the Polish army that had preceded him into Russia. Both parties agreed to transfer their support to Sigismund's son, Ladislas, as candidate for tsar. This agreement was shortlived, for the assassination of the False Dimitri in 1610 encouraged Sigismund to advance his own candidacy for the tsardom.[10]

[10] This act cost him the sympathy of a faction of Russian nobles, among whom Filaret Romanov, father of Michael, the first Romanov tsar, was numbered. Indeed, the subsequent arrest of Filaret by the Poles was a factor in making his son acceptable as a "patriot" candidate for the va-

For a while, the dubious tide of battle — psychological as well as military — left it unclear whether a Polish-aristocratic-Catholic party would prevail, or whether Muscovite traditions of autocracy and Orthodoxy would command enough support to be able to restore the fabric of Russian state power. From the Polish point of view, the capture of Smolensk (1611) scarcely compensated for their expulsion from Moscow (1612). Meanwhile, Polish soldiers, back from the Muscovite wars with pay claims unsatisfied, made the countryside unsafe. Thus the anarchic, popular will, exemplified in Russia by the Cossack hordes with which some of the Poles had been closely associated, threatened to find a Polish expression through the operations of plundering bands of veterans. Such a danger persuaded the Sejm to approve the collection of taxes sufficient to pay off the returned soldiery (1613); but the necessity for doing so also had the effect of convincing the gentry that it was dangerous to support further foreign wars and dynastic adventures.[11] Indeed, soon afterward, when the defense of Polish territories became critical, both against the Turks in the south and against the Swedes in Livonia (1617–29), the Sejm acted only reluctantly and usually in-

cant tsardom when Russian reactions against Polish domination gathered way (1613).

[11] In Sweden, the nobles came to the exactly opposite conclusion at almost precisely the same time. For by the constitutional charter of 1611, the Swedish aristocracy in effect made peace with the monarchy by electing to serve as officials and officers of the newly strengthened royal government and army. Cf. Michael Roberts, *Gustavus Adolphus: A History of Sweden 1611–1632* (London: Longmans, Green & Co., 1953) I, 255–315.

The army, recruited from the peasantry, officered by local nobles, and sustained by port dues from the Baltic lands it conquered, together with plunder, subsidy from western powers (Netherlands, France), and modest direct taxation, created the instrument of Sweden's imperial aggrandisement at the exact time when the Polish nobility shrank from the cost and danger of arming the peasantry of Poland. Clearly, in Sweden the survival of a free peasantry and of patriarchal relations between local nobles and farmers aided the construction of a modern army; whereas the prior development of commercial farming in Poland, with the fissure between social classes that resulted, made it difficult if not impossible to arm peasants without simultaneously provoking civil war against aristocratic privilege.

TIME OF TROUBLES

effectually to authorize the recruitment of a Polish army that could defend the frontiers.

This was not at first an impracticable policy. Muscovy was sufficiently exhausted by the devastations of 1604–18 (when a Polish-Russian truce sanctioned Polish possession of Smolensk) that no immediate danger threatened from that quarter. The Thirty Years' War in Germany likewise diverted Swedish power from endangering the Polish state. And in the south, carefully calculated concessions to the Cossacks, allowing a larger number of them to enrol as paid border guards against the Turks and Tartars, seemed sufficient to ward off any embarrassment their unruliness might threaten. Indeed, the internal evolution of Cossack society, whereby a class of landowning gentry began to develop within Cossack ranks, meant the emergence of a social group with whom Polish nobles could deal on easy and equal terms. The self-interest of such Cossack "nobles" could also be counted on to favor the Polish connection and to check peasant egalitarian radicalism, which found recurrent expression through peasant collaboration in the destructive plunderings of Cossack war bands.

Thus by about 1629 the Polish gentry could take satisfaction from the fact that everything seemed safely back under control, after a rough and dangerous passage indeed. Peace with Moscow in 1634 on the basis of the earlier truce sealed and symbolized the new calm. The loss of the Baltic coast to Sweden was no doubt deplorable; the failure to add Muscovy to the Polish-Lithuanian polity was unfortunate; but the acquisition of Smolensk counterbalanced the loss of Livonia, and the specter of peasant revolt, which had briefly haunted the land, seemed effectively laid to rest. The liberties of the noble class remained unrestricted, both as against the peasants beneath and the king above; and this seemed more important to the Polish landlords than any other consideration.

For their part, the Russians under Michael Romanov (1613–45) licked their wounds and withdrew, so far as possible, within a protective shell. Despite — nay, because of —

tsardom's practical weakness and initial insecurity, the principle of autocracy, rooted deep in the Muscovite past, was emphatically reasserted; and with autocracy an Orthodoxy profoundly suspicious of all religious inquiry and innovation was also restored.

In a real, though scarcely demonstrable sense, this upshot of Russia's Time of Troubles was far more popular than was the aristocratic Polish regime. The peasants, although compelled to accept a burdensome serfdom, saw a rude sort of justice in the service state, which required landowners to serve the tsar just as the peasants were compelled to serve their masters, the landowners. Moreover, the holy figure of a distant tsar, chosen by God for his high office, and himself God's servant, fitted peasant expectations better than an elective monarchy, hampered at every turn by a landowners' assembly where peasants had neither voice nor sympathy, could ever do. If government were inescapable and an evil — as Russian, along with all other peasants, no doubt felt — at least the autocratic, Orthodox tsar, as mirrored forth once more by Michael Romanov, was an intellegible power-wielder. His oppressions were the more tolerable because he oppressed everyone, rich and poor, landholder and cultivator, merchant and soldier.

Against this sort of psychological appeal to the peasant majority of the land, the Polish aristocratic polity could only offer the theatrical, but real grandeur of the baroque Catholic Counter Reformation. For anyone with the opportunity to acquire an education, and endowed with the curiosity to explore the ramifications of Catholic baroque culture, it was indeed impressive and intellectually as well as artistically far more attractive than anything then known to Russian Orthodoxy. Hence the higher clergy and educated officials of Russia faced a constant struggle to maintain their own convictions and cultural heritage against Catholic learning and propaganda, and this despite the fact that Polish Catholicism was so thoroughly tainted by detestable heresy and hateful foreignness. The best evidence of the power of the Catholic baroque was the success with which Polish culture spread among the nobles of Lithuania, White Russia, and the Ukraine, and the enduring character of that cultural orientation even in later times, when political advantage pulled in the Russian direction. The not inconsiderable success of the Uniate church (established 1596) likewise attested the power of Catholic education and propaganda among Orthodox prelates and lesser ecclesiastics of the western Russian lands.

But a serious vulnerability was a function of these successes. To understand and share in the cultural tradition brought into Poland by the Jesuits (from 1565) and other devoted agents of the Counter Reformation required years of schooling. Only a small segment of the population could attain such sophistication; in particular, the vast bulk of the peasantry was excluded, save insofar as the ornate grandeur of ecclesiastical art conveyed a meaning to untutored observers. Hence even the conversion of the hierarchy to the Uniate creed did not much affect the Orthodoxy of the peasantry, who clearly continued to cherish the old prejudices against Rome, and whenever free to do so, opted for Orthodoxy. The cultural achievement of the Polish Counter Reformation as a whole thus remained something of a tour de force, the creation of a comparatively small body of specially privileged persons.

The brevity of Poland's cultural efflorescence was perhaps related to this sociological fact. After about 1650, the levels of learning and artistic creativity attained prior to that time began perceptibly to decrease. Schooling addressed almost entirely to privileged landholders is unlikely to remain rigorous in the absence of intense and serious intellectual controversy, such as that brought to Poland in the second half of the sixteenth century by the Reformation. It is ironical to reflect upon the fact that the extraordinary success with which the Jesuits and their allies in Poland were able to overpower Protestantism with education and propaganda deprived their successors of an environment capable of stimulating really vigorous intellectual (or any other form of high cultural) activity.

Poland's cultural circumstance was further complicated by the importance of German and Jewish communities in the Polish towns. Jewish cultural life was largely autonomous and therefore interposed itself as a more or less impenetrable barrier between the peasant and noble worlds. In more western lands, there was an almost imperceptible gradation between the untutored rustic and the most recondite cultural innovators, for men were able to move from country to town and to ascend occupational and educational ladders as chance and ability might dictate. Upward mobility was sharply checked at the very bottom in Poland, for humble urban occupations — the first lodgment of a peasant coming from the countryside in other countries — were nearly all pre-empted by Jews, while privileged occupations were almost entirely in German hands. The church, therefore, constituted the only important avenue of escape from peasant status; and much of the vitality of the Catholic church in Poland resulted from its near monopoly of upward social movement. On the other hand, for those Orthodox peasantries which did not accept Catholicism, the church remained, like the landowners with whom it was so closely associated, persistently alien.

The comparative cultural crudity of Orthodox Russia under the first Romanovs meant that the gap between upper and lower classes was more easily bridged than was the case in Poland. An inchoate popular acquiescence certainly constituted a great reserve strength for the restored tsardom. In addition, the autocratic principle permitted the maintenance and even improvement of the country's armed establishment. Dutch cannon founders, a standing army as large as tax income could support, and the levy of landholders whose estates were granted in return for military (or other) service constituted, at least potentially, a more balanced and disciplined force than did the unsupported cavalry levy of the Polish nobility. Russia's future victories over Poland were guaranteed by these psychological and technological superiorities.

Russia's enhanced potential became apparent after 1648,

when a massive Cossack rising in the Ukraine invited Moscow's intervention against the Polish overlords of that portion of Pontic Europe. But before we examine this phase of our theme, it will be well to survey the uses and abuses of their greater neighbors' Times of Trouble made by the peoples and princes of the border zones.[12]

Danubian and Pontic Europe, 1570–1650. The interstitial principalities and armed freebooting communities occupying most of Danubian and Pontic Europe in 1570 eagerly took advantage of their various suzerains' preoccupations with domestic broils to increase the scope of their independence. One of them, in fact, emerged by the mid-seventeenth century as a full-fledged sovereign state; for the principality of Transylvania was among the signers of the treaties of Westphalia (1648). But Europe's recognition of Transylvanian sovereignty did not commit the Turks, who still regarded the principality as their own somewhat unruly vassal — a point of view they made good, arms in hand, a mere thirteen years after the signature of the treaties of Westphalia.

Transylvania's independence was therefore a fragile thing, the transitory product of times of trouble in Turkey, Austria, and Russia. The same was a true *a fortiori* of the less developed and more loosely articulated states that lay eastward along the European steppe lands. Piratical enterprise in the

[12] In connection with these remarks on Polish and Russian history, I consulted the following books: W. F. Reddaway *et al.* (eds.), *The Cambridge History of Poland* (Cambridge: Cambridge University Press, 1950), I, 250–502; Oscar Halecki, *A History of Poland* (New York: Roy Publishers, 1943), pp. 106–53; Jan Rutowski, *Histoire économique de la Pologne avant les Partages* (Paris: Librairie Ancienne Honore Champion, 1927), pp. 89–119 and *passim*; George Vernadsky, *Russia at the Dawn of the Modern Age* (New Haven, Conn.: Yale University Press, 1959), pp. 171–292; B. H. Sumner, *Survey of Russian History* (rev. ed.; London: Gerald Duckworth & Co., 1947), *passim*; Michael T. Florinsky, *Russia: A History and an Interpretation* (New York: Macmillan, 1947), I, 182–306; V. O. Kluchevsky, *A History of Russia* (New York: Russell & Russell, 1960), II, III; S. F. Platonov, *History of Russia* (New York: Macmillan, 1929), pp. 125–75; M. N. Pokrovsky, *History of Russia from the Earliest Times to the Rise of Commercial Capitalism* (New York: International Publishers, 1931), pp. 109–257.

Black Sea and freebooting on land certainly made the Cossack hosts a factor in the international politics of eastern Europe. The challenge their rough and ready war-band spirit offered to the lords of enserfed peasants gave the Cossack polity an even greater force in the domestic affairs of Poland-Lithuania and Russia. Yet a basic instability was built into the Cossack war-band organization, for without betraying the freedom they cherished, the Cossacks could not attain the status of a fully organized state. In addition, Cossack war bands required supplies of powder and shot, if nothing else, and this necessity placed them permanently at the mercy of their suppliers. Hence despite striking ventures and extraordinary daring, and despite the undertone of peasant *jacquerie* that accompanied Cossack enterprises in the early seventeenth century, the Cossack hordes failed to achieve real sovereignty.

Similar economic weaknesses, together with the seductions of Ottoman urbanity, prevented the Tartar khanate of Crimea and the two Rumanian principalities of Moldavia and Wallachia from persevering in any of the bids for political independence that were initiated by particularly ambitious or unusually rash or unfortunate rulers of these states. Michael the Brave of Wallachia (1593–1601), who looked to the Hapsburg emperor for the means to make good his independence from the Turks, and Khan Mehmed Girai III (1622–27), who probably expected assistance from Persia in the same enterprise, both met the melancholy fate of being assassinated by angry or disappointed allies: Michael by the orders of the imperial general, George Basta, and Mehmed Girai by a band of Cossacks whom he had hired to help him recover his lost throne. Their careers, however briefly brilliant, scarcely encouraged others to try for real sovereignty; and in fact, Constantinople's mercantile and cultural penetration of the Black Sea littoral advanced so rapidly in the latter sixteenth and early seventeenth centuries as to persuade the politically and economically dominant classes of Crim Tartary and of the Rumanian principalities that it was sweeter as well as more prudent to submit gracefully to Turkish suzerainty than to struggle against it.

Details of political and military events are extremely complex and turn upon such matters as the personalities of rulers, the presence or absence of dynastic heirs, successful and unsuccessful assassinations, poisonings, bribes, marriages, and the tortuosities of an unusually unscrupulous diplomacy. Nevertheless, it seems possible to detect longer-range changes behind the façade of rulership which help to explain the distressing confusion and amorality of the region's politics, and give intelligible form and pattern to what transpired.

The basic change was the slackening of Ottoman military expansion. This meant that throughout the frontier zone the lands laid waste in the sixteenth century became once more capable of sustaining settled agricultural populations. But the reflux of farming communities into Danubian and Pontic Europe posed in an unusually acute form basic questions of social structure and control.

In the Ukraine, the egalitarian and anarchic liberty of the Cossack hordes confronted the hauteur of Polish nobles, whose liberties were based upon the labor of an enserfed peasantry. This polarity between aristocracy and equality, which roughly coincided with the religious dividing line between Catholic and Orthodox, went very deep. Yet, with what is only an apparent paradox, Cossacks and Poles had important traits in common. Both polities successfully institutionalized sporadic fluctuation between anarchy and absolutism. Polish nobles and Cossack commoners could at any time suspend anarchy by instituting a war band, whose members voluntarily accepted absolute obedience to a commander chosen for the occasion, who was unquestioningly obeyed, but only for a limited period of time. This institution reconciled the conflicting requirements of military effectiveness and domestic liberty in reasonably effective fashion, but allowed no continuity to state power and recognized no permanent hierarchy among free men. Professional administration and professional soldiers could not exist in such polities; and in proportion as professionalism in government and war outdistanced what even gifted amateurs could do, Polish and Cossack institutions became archaic and incapable of effective self-defense. This, however, became evident only after 1650, with the arrival on the Polish scene of well-drilled Swedish infantry, trained in the hard school of the Thirty Years' War.

In the Rumanian provinces, and also among the Tartars, traditional social leadership of kinship groupings, whose cohesion rested upon the daily requirements of pastoral and warlike enterprise, gave way to more civilized societies in which commercial agriculture, based upon enserfed or enslaved cultivators, played an increasingly prominent role. Under these circumstances, old lines of kinship solidarity were broken, and the rapidity of the development was such that no new moral linkage between serf and master arose. Instead, the masters became provincial participants in the cultural and political world of Constantinople, while the serfs nursed their grievances in ignorance and isolation.

In Transylvania, matters were more complicated, and the polarities were correspondingly less sharp. Transylvanian social patterns underwent no such abrupt changes as occurred further east. Magnates, gentry, townsmen, and a numerically important free (and therefore "noble") peasantry maintained an uneasy internal balance which had been inherited from medieval times. The prince with his officials and small standing army at one extreme, and peasant serfs at the other, completed the social spectrum. None of this was new; and whatever progress agriculture may have made in Transylvania had ample precedent. What to do with a Vlach wanderer turned cultivator had been decided in 1438 when, after suppressing a peasant revolt, the victorious gentry gave legal definition to serfdom in Transylvania.

Nevertheless, one result of the long and destructive war between Ottoman and Hapsburg armies, 1593–1606, was to produce a new class of footloose adventurers and runaway serfs in Transylvania. The rapid rise of the princely power in the period 1606–1648 was certainly assisted by the fact that the princes were able to enlist these men in their armies by offering them freehold land tenures along the frontiers of Turkish Hungary. This sort of alliance between prince and plebs corresponded to the special linkage between tsar and Cossacks which achieved systematic definition in 1571,[13] and matched the relation between Hapsburg emperor and the Slavic "Grenzers" of Slavonia and Croatia, which had achieved its first legal definition in 1535.[14] Anarchy and absolutism often meet and the history of eastern Europe in the early seventeenth century nicely illustrates this fact.

Remarks about each of the local polities of Danubian and Pontic Europe will perhaps bring somewhat greater precision to these observations about the region as a whole.

Transylvania, 1570–1650. The history of the principality of Transylvania divides into three fairly distinct periods: from 1571–1593, Stephen Bathory (prince, 1571–75) and his relatives, Christopher Bathory (vice-regent and then prince, 1575–81) and Sigismund Bathory (prince, 1581–1601) sought to make Transylvania serve as a base upon which to construct an east European empire embracing Poland-Lithuania, Muscovy, and, potentially, Hungary and who knows what else besides. After the death of Stephen Bathory in 1586, this dream faded, to be replaced by an attempt to repel the Turk from Hungary with Hapsburg aid and, if need be, under Hapsburg rule. The war which ensued between Turkish and Hapsburg forces, 1593–1606, involved extensive devastation in Transylvania, Wallachia, and Moldavia, and many abrupt, dramatic shifts of power between the protagonists, who were operating near the extreme limit of their effective military range, so that small changes could work drastic shifts in the local balance of forces. In the years 1601–4, the Emperor Rudolf's general, George Basta, seemed on the verge of fastening Hapsburg power upon Transylvania by dint of an army that lived off the country through a combination of outright plunder with legalized extortion from Protestants and other opponents. This effort failed when the local gentry

[13] Günter Stökl, *Die Enstehung des Kossakentums (Veröffentlichungen des Osteusropas-Instituts München*, III [Munich: Isar Verlag, 1953]), p. 150.

[14] Gunther Rothenberg, *The Austrian Military Border in Croatia, 1522–1747* (Urbana: University of Illinois Press, 1960), p. 24.

rallied to the standards of Stephen Bocskay and drove the imperialists from the country. Bocskay's revolt (1604–6) inaugurated a new phase in Transylvania's history, characterized by a pro-Turkish, anti-Hapsburg governmental policy, aiming above all else at repairing the damages of the long war and strengthening the princely power.

During the first of our three periods, Transylvania was for the first time effectually separated from the Kingdom of Hungary. In the time of John Zapolya (1526–40) and his son, John Sigismund (1540–71), the voivodship of Transylvania had been only incidental to their claim to the crown of Hungary. John Zapolya had, indeed, secured support far beyond the borders of Transylvania; his son less so; and after John Sigismund's death (1571), the newly elected voivod or prince, Stephen Bathory, made no claim whatever to the Hungarian crown. He soon, however, made good this defect by winning election to the Polish throne. This was a victory over the Hapsburg emperor Maximilian, his principal rival for the Polish crown. Even when King Stephen's enterprises took him deep into Muscovy and Livonia, Transylvania continued to play a role far greater than its modest territorial extent or limited resources might suggest. For it was his home ground, where he could and did raise soldiers who would obey him regardless of what the Polish Sejm might do or fail to do. Transylvania thus provided King Stephen with a small but stout military bastion which he held in his own right and which therefore lay quite beyond the reach of the Polish nobility. This was one of the reasons why the Poles quarreled with him so violently in his last years.

At home in Transylvania, however, the Bathorys faced no such cantankerous opposition. The Diet, with its separate representation of the three "political" nations — Saxons, Magyars, and Szeklers — did not seek to imitate the Polish Sejm, but granted the taxes demanded of it without very much resistance. As Catholics, the Bathorys patronized Jesuits and the Counter Reformation, but did so with such moderation as to give the Protestants of the principality no very strong ground for complaint.

The fact that Stephen Bathory came to power in Transylvania in 1571 at a time when a singular surge of popular religious excitement had just passed its crest greatly facilitated the success of his moderate Catholic policy. The central figure of this episode was a Calvinist bishop of Transylvania named Franz David, who embraced Unitarian doctrines and presently convinced himself and numerous followers (including Prince John Sigismund Zapolya) that the world was coming to an end in the year 1570. For a short period, this expectation gripped great multitudes; but when the year 1570 came and went without the expected opening of the skies, only a fringe of fanatics remained faithful to David's further prophecies. The hard core of his following concentrated among the Szeklers, whose difficulties in resisting landlords who sought to reduce them to serfdom encouraged them to embrace an extreme, millennial view of the wicked world. Stephen Bathory put David in prison and deprived the Szeklers of many of their traditional immunities, thus convincing the stubborn remnant that the reign of Antichrist had indeed begun. In doing so, however, Bathory had the support of the conservative and organized Protestant churches. Unexpected exposure to the perfervid heat of millenarian prophecy with its implicit social revolution undoubtedly frightened many Lutherans and Calvinists; and to avoid official proscription, the more conservative fraction of the Unitarian community that boggled at Franz David's later visions was also constrained to follow a particularly circumspect line with respect to the new prince's official Catholicism. Hence, in reaction to the religious broils of the immediately preceding years, Stephen Bathory and his successors were able to follow a cautiously Catholic policy without exciting serious resistance from the Protestant majority of the principality.[15]

[15] A small sect of David's followers survived official persecution and eventually became Jews in the eighteenth century.

The war of 1593–1606 entirely upset Transylvania's internal balance. The effort to unite all Hungary under the Hapsburgs with which the struggle began proved far more costly than either the Hapsburgs or the Magyars had expected. Turkish field armies, though defeated in 1595 by Michael the Brave of Wallachia (with the help of Cossack and Transylvanian detachments) at the battle of Calugareni, were victorious the next year over Hapsburg and Hungarian forces at Keresztes. A prolonged military stalemate ensued. Hapsburg finances were not yet equal to the task of paying an army regularly over a period of years. Unpaid soldiers were permitted to pillage; and the ravages of the imperialists were rivaled by those of the emperor's client, Michael the Brave, whose troops briefly occupied Transylvania in 1599–1600 and again in 1601. Turkish forces, reinforced by Tartar detachments, also harried the countryside of Transylvania and central Hungary with their wonted thoroughness. Polish troops, supported by Cossack and even on one occasion by Tartar raiders, added a fourth dimension to the principality's distresses.

A decisive change in this unhappy situation came in 1604, when the Magyar magnate, Stephen Bocskay, rose in rebellion against the Hapsburg occupying armies and quickly succeeded in compelling them to withdraw from Transylvania and most of "royal" Hungary as well. The core of Bocskay's forces, around which other classes and nations eventually coalesced, was composed of "haiduks," i.e., of broken, landless men who inhabited the no-man's land of central Hungary and lived by hunting, fishing, herding, and plundering quite in the manner of the more numerous Cossack communities of the Ukraine. By promising these haiduks land to be awarded at end of the hostilities, Bocskay gathered a formidable fighting force in short order. He was also able to attract the support of many Magyar nobles by appealing to their dislike of German domination and to their Protestantism. Defense of the Hungarian constitution and of the rights of the landowning class enshrined in Verböczi's *Tripartitum* was also at issue, since Rudolf's agents had set out both to crush Protestantism and to erect a modern, efficient, and bureaucratic government on the debris of Hungarian constitutional privilege.

With Turkish and Magyar support, therefore, Bocskay's armies rapidly snowballed into a really formidable force; and the Hapsburgs — already paralyzed by bitter quarrels between Emperor Rudolf and his brother Matthias — were constrained to yield. The Treaty of Vienna (1606) redefined the relationship between the Hapsburg crown and the Hungarian Diet in a sense entirely favorable to Magyar constitutional claims. A palatine was to be appointed and endowed with full royal powers whenever the king was absent from Hungary. Save for two fortresses, garrisons in Hungary were to be commanded only by Hungarians. The nobles were to enjoy full religious liberty, and the emperor recognized Bocskay as prince of Transylvania and wielder of sovereign rights in two adjacent counties of Hungary that had been formerly part of the Hapsburg domains. He was also intrusted with the task of arranging a peace with the Turks, whose own difficulties at home predisposed them to agree to terms.

The Treaty of Zitva-Torok (1606) which emerged from Bocskay's diplomatic mediation distinctly favored the Turks. As we have seen, the emperor no longer paid tribute for his part of Hungary, but instead redeemed annual tributes with a lump sum. Frontier delineation, however, favored the Turks in most cases where possession of a particular fortress was in question; and the aspiration toward a united and obedient Hungary with which the Hapsburg forces had begun the war was definitively — and as far as obedience was concerned, also permanently — surrendered. The deeds of Hapsburg soldiers and administrators during the war had instead created or enormously reinforced a pro-Turkish, anti-imperialist party among the Magyar gentry. Stephen Bocskay and the enlarged and self-consciously Protestant principality of Transylvania were the tangible political embodiment of this realignment of sentiment.

Bocskay died in 1606, almost immediately after his victory had been assured. Sharp upheavals ensued, and a stable regime in Transylvania did not emerge until a Turkish army once more intervened and dictated the election of Gabriel Bethlen as prince (1613). Like the Bathorys before him, Bethlen sought to build up the princely power in all circumspect ways. A cowed and obedient Diet generally voted according to his instructions, and the princely income from taxes and rents was enough to sustain a small but quite efficient standing army. In addition, the traditional noble levy brought a significant cavalry force into the field. The geographical location of this force, combined with Bethlen's ambitious temperament and his ingrained hostility to the Hapsburgs, sufficed to make Transylvania a minor but ever present factor in the diplomacy of the European great powers throughout the troubled period of the Thirty Years' War.

Yet in fact, Bethlen and Transylvania suffered a setback at the beginning of that war from which the principality never recovered. Its own resources were too slender to support independence. But by becoming the kernel around which the entire Kingdom of Hungary might coalesce, the prince of Transylvania might expect to make his throne and power really secure. Only under such circumstances, indeed, could he hope to escape the galling alternatives of dependency either on Turkish or on Hapsburg good will. With this object in view, Bethlen boldly plunged into the Hapsburgs' tangled affairs in 1619, acting in concert with the rebellious estates of Bohemia and Austria. At first the Hungarian nobility rallied to his side in substantial number, and a meeting of the Diet in Pressburg, the traditional capital of Hapsburg Hungary, elected Bethlen king.

But almost at once a fundamental discrepancy of aim crippled Bethlen's enterprise. In raising the Magyar nobility against Ferdinand II, Bethlen had appealed to constitutional rights and immunities; but as king-designate — he postponed coronation and therefore never became king in legal fact — the prince of Transylvania let it be known that he expected to use the larger resources of royal Hungary to support an army like the one he already commanded on the basis of

Transylvania's resources. The prospect of allowing royal power to assume such tangible form on their home ground did not appeal to the Magyar nobles. From their point of view, the precious liberties enshrined in the *Tripartitum* seemed as much endangered by Bethlen's restless ambition as they were by a distant Hapsburg monarch who, happily, was fully engaged against rebellious German princes. Moreover, Ferdinand's victory at the Battle of White Mountain (1620) and the subsequent fate of the Bohemian noble opposition did not encourage reckless defiance of what were undoubtedly the legitimate claims of the duly crowned king of Hungary. Hence, the Magyar gentry decided to play safe by deserting Bethlen while there was still time, even though his Transylvanian troops remained in occupation of much of royal Hungary.

Their fickleness persuaded Bethlen to abandon his ambitions — at least for the moment. A truce, then a treaty of peace (Nicholsburg, 1621) ended his first war against Ferdinand. The terms, indeed, were favorable to Bethlen, for he acquired regalian rights in seven counties of royal Hungary, thus nearly doubling the territory under his command, in return for which he withdrew his forces from the rest of the country and relinquished all pretension to the Hungarian crown.

In the portion of royal Hungary he had thus acquired, Bethlen proceeded to institute the same sort of centralizing regime he had inherited in Transylvania. In Ferdinand's part of the kingdom, however, a very different evolution set in. The Hapsburg emperor had his hands full elsewhere, and after his narrow escape of 1619–20 carefully refrained from any infringement of the Hungarian constitution. Ferdinand's restraint opened wide the doors for a most effective Roman Catholic religious propaganda. The Jesuit Peter Pazmany, archbishop of Esztergom (1616–37), and cardinal (1629–37), was the key figure. Pazmany's initial tactic was to insist upon the complete restoration of all the legal prerogatives of the Roman church which had fallen into desuetude during the sixteenth century, when the incumbents of many Hungarian sees and parishes had become Protestant, along with nearly the entire noble class. In most cases, the various offices, rights, and jurisdictions that were surrendered by clergymen who left the Roman communion were not legally abolished, so when Archbishop Pazmany and his agents began to demand the restoration of Catholic rights, they stood on firm legal ground. This put even theologically opinionated Magyar Protestants in a difficult position — and many nobles had become Protestants more for secular reasons and as a gesture of defiance against a distant, distrusted, and distinctly Catholic king than by reason of theological conviction of any sort. Being such stout defenders of legality and of their own privilege as defined by the Hungarian constitution, the Magyar nobility could scarcely disagree with Pazmany's demands, which, however, put most of the high offices of the kingdom into the hands of Catholic prelates.

With the church's political power thus assured, Pazmany and his fellows found it relatively easy to convert a majority of the Magyar nobles to Catholicism. Schools and two universities assisted the process. In addition, vigorous pamphleteering (in Magyar as well as in Latin) against Protestant theological error, skilful appeals to patriotic piety based on a view of medieval history that made Hungary the special protégé of the papacy and the bulwark of Catholicism in southeastern Europe, together with an effective exploitation of the dislike Magyar nobles felt for the German, Lutheran townsmen in their midst, all contributed to Pazmany's success. Catholicism in Hungary thus was able to wed itself to Magyar noble privilege and to the ancient constitution of the land. The marriage was a lasting one: the survival of Hungary's archaic political and social order into the nineteenth century was the direct result of Pazmany's policy and Ferdinand's necessity. This stood in diametric opposition to the course of events in Bohemia, where Catholicism and monarchical absolutism marched hand in hand over the prostrate corpse of noble privilege.

Three subsequent military interventions from Transylvania (1623–24, 1626, and 1644–45) probably accelerated the

TIME OF TROUBLES

progress of the Counter Reformation in royal Hungary. Certainly Bethlen and his piously Calvinistic successor, George I Rakoczi (1629–48) failed to rouse any lasting support among the Magyar nobles in Hapsburg Hungary. Perhaps the Magyar nobility saw in the peasant foot soldiery, who constituted an important part of the Transylvanian army, an implicit challenge to their prerogatives; for such a force demonstrated all too clearly that in an age of firearms, peasant foot soldiers could be effective in battle even against noble cavalry. Hapsburg infantry at least had the virtue of being foreign, unable to communicate freely with the Magyar peasantry, and hated by all for their plundering. Such a force threatened noble privilege only from the outside; and the Treaty of Vienna (1606) prescribed that such troops should come under Hungarian command if stationed on Hungarian soil. Bethlen's infantry, by contrast, offered an internal and far more dangerous challenge to aristocratic predominance. It is therefore perhaps not surprising that the Magyar nobles opted decisively for the Hapsburg and Catholic connection in those parts of Hungary where the prince of Transylvania did not rule.

Within the boundaries of the principality, however, Bethlen and George I Rakoczi followed absolutist policies that closely resembled those pursued by their royal and princely contemporaries in central and western Europe. Like other princes elsewhere, they sought to build up an efficient army and a centralized, professional administration. Within the modest limits set by the principality's resources, they succeeded. Patronage of learning went hand in hand with repression of overmighty subjects. Town autonomies were restricted, though not abolished; and almost all magnates saw their Transylvanian lands confiscated by the prince in retaliation for real or suspected political intrigue against his power. Transylvania thus became a gentry-dominated land, fringed by an unusual proportion of free peasants of military habit, and studded with small, not particularly flourishing, towns.

All this much resembled the state of affairs prevailing in

any small German principality after the storms of the Thirty Years' War subsided. Transylvania's distinction from most other European states lay in the field of religion. Special favors to Protestants, particularly to Calvinists, to which communion both Bethlen and Rakoczi themselves belonged,[16] did not prevent the prince from following an official policy of religious toleration toward each of the four "received" religions of the land—Catholicism, Lutheranism, Calvinism, and Unitarianism.

Turkish precedents undoubtedly made a policy of such broad religious toleration seem practicable to the rulers and inhabitants of Transylvania; the comparative weakness of aristocracy in the Transylvanian polity and the effectiveness of princely absolutism likewise may have owed something to Turkish example and modes of thought. These linkages with the Ottoman world were nevertheless of smaller importance than the links with western Europe. In this connection, the central feature that distinguished Transylvania from its Polish, Hungarian, and Moldavian-Wallachian neighbors was the presence of fairly numerous towns in the principality. These towns, naturally, constituted a local market for agricultural products, accessible to peasants without need for any mediation more elaborate than a donkey cart. Town artisans were also in a position to offer goods of value to the peasants in return for their agricultural surplus, although in all probability most of what ordinary, i.e., unfree, peasants received for their goods was transferred in rents and taxes to their social superiors—thus sustaining the fabric of prince-

---

[16] Bethlen ennobled all Calvinist ministers and their children, according to Ladislas Makkai, *Histoire de Transylvanie* (Paris: Presses universitaires de France, 1936) , p. 231. Grants of nobility to whole classes of individuals had begun in Transylvania with Stephen Bathory, who ennobled his discharged soldiers, thereby creating a "service class" attached directly to the prince. As a result, a large proportion of the Szekler community as well as ex-haiduks were legally ennobled under Bocskay and Bethlen. Such "nobles" were in fact peasant cultivators, often poverty-stricken, but legally free of all servile dues and obligations.

Transylvanian Calvinism and this poor but proud group of noble cultivators came to be closely identified. They remain a feature of Hungarian society to the present.

ly power almost as directly as did the privileged, rent-free peasants who served as soldiers in the prince's armies.

By contrast, in Poland, central Hungary, and other regions of eastern Europe where local town life was weak, commercial agriculture required elaborate entrepreneurial operations to carry grain and other goods to market. These remained beyond peasant ken and had the effect of concentrating wealth and political power in the hands of noble landowners and wholesale grain merchants.[17]

Transylvania, in short, continued to be an islanded community, surrounded by societies that differed significantly in internal structure as well as in their political regimes and cultural achievements from what prevailed within the sheltering crook of the Carpathians.[18]

Wallachia and Moldavia, 1570–1650. Anyone who tries to come to grips with the history of Wallachia and Moldavia in the sixteenth and early seventeenth centuries will, at least

[17] The rise of megalopolitan centers in western Europe and at Constantinople, requiring massive food imports from long distances, had the side effect of helping to fasten serfdom and aristocracy on broad stretches of eastern Europe, whence came the needed grain and other foods. This appears paradoxically contrary to the effect of the rise of western European towns in medieval times; but peasant participation in medieval town markets and the practical exclusion of peasant entrepreneurs from long-distance trading sufficiently accounts for the contrary social consequences of the two phases of urban growth.

The phenomenon is to be compared with the contrasting consequences of military enterprise when monopolized by central authority and when dispersed among an armed nobility. See above, pp. 32–35.

[18] In connection with these remarks on Transylvania and Hungary, the following books were consulted: Heinrich Marczali, *Ungarische Verfassungsgeschichte* (Tübingen: J. C. B. Mohr, 1910), pp. 73–85; Albert Lefaivre, *Les Magyars pendant la domination ottomane en Hongrie, 1526–1722* (Paris: Perrin et Cie., 1902), I, 174–423; Maja Depner, *Das Fürstentum Siebenbürgen im Kampf gegen Hapsburg* (Stuttgart: W. Kohlhammer, 1938); Ladislas Makkai, *Histoire de Transylvanie* (Paris: Presses universitaires de France, 1946), pp. 176–237; Mihaly Bucsay, *Geschichte des Protestantismus in Ungarn.* (Stuttgart: Evangelische Verlagswerk, 1959), pp. 40–87; Nikolaus Mester, "Siebenbürgen als selbstständiger Fürstentum," in Emerich Tukinich (ed.), *Die siebenbürgische Frage* (Budapest: Verlag des Osteuropa Instituts, 1940), pp. 61–83; Franz Salamon, *Ungarn im Zeitalter der Türkenherrschaft* (Leipzig: Haessel, 1887).

initially, be oppressed by a sense of utter confusion. Both principalities exhibited an unending political instability. According to one tabulation, Wallachia suffered under twenty-three, Moldavia under twenty-six princes between 1570 and 1650; and if separate reigns were counted, the numbers would rise still higher.[19] Individual princes frequently ruled first in one and then in the other principality; or changes in the wheel of fortune might bring an individual back to the same throne he had occupied one or more times before. Some princes were isolated adventurers who appeared from nowhere and then disappeared from the historical record at the end of their term of office. Others founded amorphous dynasties like the series of five Movila princes who governed Moldavia on and off between 1595 and 1634. No rules of succession existed. Individual princes secured office either (a) by military coup d'état sanctioned after the event (normally at a price) by the sultan in Constantinople, or (b) by purchase of office in the Ottoman capital itself, which might then have to be made good on the ground by appropriate military coups. In the sixteenth century, particularly in Moldavia, succession by coup d'état was more common than it became in the seventeenth century, when intrigue and bribery at Constantinople became more effective and large-scale resort to violence as the mode for determining succession usually ceased to be necessary.

This distressingly complex political jungle reflected the breakdown of older kinship groups which had allowed Stephen the Great of Moldavia (1457–1504) to hold the Turks precariously at bay for half a century by mustering the fighting manpower of his people for almost annual campaigns. A century later, in the time of Michael the Brave of Wallachia (1593–1601), the basis of military power had shifted. Not a general levy of the male population of the entire principality, in the style of Stephen the Great, but a body of noble horse supplemented by a hard core of foreign mercenaries — Cossacks, South Slavs, Transylvanians — consti-

[19] Cf. chronological table of ruling princes in Nicholas Iorga, *A History of Rumania* (London: T. Fisher Unwin, Ltd., 1925), pp. 267–68.

tuted the strength of Michael's army; and its effectiveness depended in no small part on subsidy from the distant Hapsburg emperor. Clearly, something drastic had happened between Stephen's death and Michael's accession to disrupt the old local solidarities between boyar leader and his clan followers.

The nature of this change is not particularly difficult to discern, although precise data seem to be unattainable. Yet even without statistics, there is no doubt that agriculture made great strides in the two Rumanian provinces during the sixteenth and early seventeenth centuries. Grain and cattle were exported to Constantinople in growing quantity, and the capital city paid for the food it thus secured not so much by exporting artisan goods as by disbursing the ever growing sums of tribute [20] and bribes that were remitted to Constantinople by the ruling cliques of the two provinces as the price of their tenure of office.

Serfdom was imposed by law in Wallachia in 1595, in Moldavia in 1621. The essence of such legislation was to forbid peasant cultivators from leaving the land they worked, while authorizing their masters to search for and bring runaways back by main force if need be. Shortage of labor to sustain an expanding commercial cultivation lay behind this legislation. But the imposition of serfdom also signified profound psychological alienation between landlord and cultivator. As long as pasturage had produced the only important commercial product of the principalities, old kindred organization with traditional boyar leadership continued to be a living reality; and agriculture was conducted primarily as a

[20] Tribute in Wallachia rose from 8,000 "galbeni" in 1503 to 155,000 galbeni in 1593, after which date no further increase in the direct tribute occurred. In Moldavia the tribute in 1503 was 4,000 galbeni and in 1593 the figure had become (and subsequently remained) 65,000 galbeni. Cf. Academia Republicii Populare Romine, *Istoria Rominiei* (Bucharest, n.d.), II, 779–80. Direct tribute, however, was only a small part of the levy Constantinople made on the two provinces. Bribes took vast additional sums, and controlled prices for Rumanian wheat and livestock made the money Constantinople thus secured far more valuable than would otherwise have been the case.

subsistence activity, each family consuming more or less what it had raised. This relationship crumbled as grain sales became more lucrative than the traditional export of cattle and sheep. Vastly greater labor was of course required to till the fields; and cultivators were no longer free to dispose of their product as they themselves pleased. The grain went instead to agricultural entrepreneurs turned landlords, who by the legislation of 1595 and 1621 could legally compel the newly enserfed peasants to work for them.

It seems clear that this socioeconomic transformation proceeded mainly from the top. That is to say, it was the demand for taxes and other moneys required to recoup the costs of acquiring office from the Turks that set the process in motion and pricked it on. Vast sums of cash spent in Constantinople as the price of office had somehow to be recovered by exactions from the provinces; one obvious way was to sell subordinate offices in the government and, indeed, to invent new and more dignified positions (preferably with high-sounding Byzantine titles and no duties) that could be auctioned off to ambitious boyars on the spot. To recoup their costs, such officeholders had to act as fiscal agents of the prince in the only practicable way available to them: that is by compelling their ex-followers and future serfs to cultivate more grain for sale.[21]

Simultaneously, Jews, Greeks, and other foreigners penetrated the country to purchase grain and arrange for its transport to market. These intermediaries, who had the advantage of being already alien, were obviouly in a better position to make new demands upon the commoners than their former (and perhaps somewhat shamefaced) local leaders and kinsmen could be. Hence not infrequently, prince and boyars intrusted the collection of public taxes and all the "private" administrative procedures required to organize and maintain the grain trade to these strangers.

[21] Cf. G. I. Bratianu, "Servage de la glèbe et régime fiscale; essai d'histoire comparée roumaine, slave et byzantine," *Études byzantines d'histoire économique et sociale* (Paris: Paul Genthner, 1938), pp. 245–51.

TIME OF TROUBLES

The role of such social outsiders was definitely greater in Moldavia than it became in Wallachia, presumably because the native boyar class of the former province remained closer to ancestral solidarities with the rank and file and therefore stood more in need of the services of strangers as intermediaries than was the case in Wallachia, where large-scale and at least semi-commercial agriculture was older and social distance between boyars and commoners had already become greater in the fifteenth century than in the more backward, remote, and pastoral Moldavia. As a result, Moldavia's sixteenth-century backwardness gave way in the seventeenth century to an agricultural and commercial boom, accompanied by rapid and unrestrained Hellenization. The slower, more uninterrupted development of commercial agriculture in Wallachia allowed local boyar leadership to adjust itself to changed circumstances instead of crumbling, as happened in Moldavia, before the clever and ruthless fiscality of alien agents of the Ottoman and princely government. The result was to give Wallachia a more Rumanian and a somewhat archaic aspect in the seventeenth century by comparison to Moldavia: an exact reversal of the relationship between the two provinces in the preceding century.

It will be readily understood how this rapid and drastic transformation from a traditional ordering of society put severe strains upon pre-existing moral codes. Boyars who began by betraying their dependents and followers obviously sloughed off most traditional restraints upon their behavior. The utter amorality and unmitigated self-aggrandizement which found flamboyant expression in the politics of the two principalities during the sixteenth century was a natural consequence.[22]

[22] In the nineteenth and early twentieth centuries, analogous behavior among ex-peasant politicians who had left the restraints of the village community behind them in order to plunge into the fascinating world of westernizing urbanism gave a bad name to all the Balkan peoples. Rumanians remain unique in having undergone the moral dislocations of two successive acculturations in modern times: one to the Ottoman-Hellenic style of civilization in the sixteenth to eighteenth centuries, and

By the seventeenth century the peak of the crisis was past. The boyars began to construct for themselves new moral codes of an urban, courtly character. Its elements were part Turk, part Greek; part consciously created on the basis of scholarly investigation of Byzantine court manuals and part spontaneously developed by use and wont in the princely entourages. The development of a new pattern of manners for the upper classes sustained a stabilization of the political regime that became apparent soon after the beginning of the seventeenth century and lasted until the nineteenth.

This upshot could scarcely have been foreseen in the sixteenth century. The first effect of the expansion of commercial agriculture upon the boyar-landlords of Moldavia and Wallachia was to expand both their incomes and their intellectual horizons, with the result that a number of alternative cultural models began to exert competing influence. In Moldavia, for example, several boyar families assimilated themselves completely into the Polish nobility; and a Polish party became a persistent fact in Moldavian domestic politics. Similarly in Wallachia, a party among the boyars supported Michael the Brave's policy of aspiring toward a Transylvanian (or Hapsburg) alliance, with the aim of throwing off Ottoman suzerainty with Western assistance. Westernizing architectural styles and a vernacular Rumanian written literature also penetrated the two provinces during the sixteenth century; and most disturbing of all were the Protestant echoes which resounded in the Rumanian church and to some degree among the laity. This openness to variant foreign influences was an important factor sustaining the political instability of the sixteenth century. Disappointed factions could and regularly did look for support abroad, and such exiles could count on ready-made resonances within the ruling group at home. Even small gestures of outside intervention were therefore often able to set political revolt in train.

a second to Western patterns of life in the eighteenth to twentieth centuries.

This double exposure to a widespread dissolution of moral codes accounts for the sting of the familiar slander, to the effect that "Rumanian" is not a nationality but a profession.

But the gravitational pull of Constantinople in the end prevailed. Flirtations with Poland or with Transylvania, with reformed Christianity, Gothic architecture, and German *Landsknechten* (who constituted the backbone of Michael the Brave's army in 1601 when he reconquered Transylvania for the second time) were all predestined to failure as long as steady intensification of economic dependence on Constantinople reinforced traditional lines of political dependency.

This elementary fact became evident in the seventeenth century. Michael the Brave's failure (1601) did not encourage reliance on help from the West. It is true, however, that a party of boyars continued to look towards Transylvania; and one of his successors, Radu Serban (1602–11), dallied with the idea of renewing Michael's bold defiance of the Turks. Not until 1632, when Matthew Basarab ascended the throne of Wallachia, where he remained for the unprecedentedly long time of twenty-two years, did the flirtation with the West come definitely to an end. Almost simultaneously, Basil the Wolf, a man of Albanian origin, became prince of Moldavia (1634) and held office until 1653. Under his alien hand, Moldavia definitely outstripped Wallachia in developing the new, archaistic Byzantinophile court culture that was destined to supply the boyar class of the two principalities with a cultural identity and code of conduct until the first decades of the nineteenth century.

The inherent attractions of the new cultural style should not be discounted in any effort to explain its success against competing Western (and Moslem) models.[23] Splendid and

[23] Westerners are often inclined to such warm self-appraisal as to suppose that any population, when exposed to Western culture, will normally wish to accept it. The Rumanians of the sixteenth-seventeenth centuries clearly had the chance and refused; but this rejection was as nothing compared to the rebuff Rumanian behavior administered to the Moslem Turks, whose ranks always remained open to converts to Islam and whose geographical propinquity multiplied opportunities for contact and conversion.

Rumanians in search of a civilized style of life — as the boyars of the sixteenth century were — had little in their own immediate cultural inheritance upon which to draw. Instead, they found in Byzantinism a glorious substitute for their own unsatisfactory and undistinguished local

stately court robes, precise hierarchy of rank determined anew by each prince upon arrival at his capital, whether Bucharest or Jassy, combined with comfortable wealth deriving from the labor of an oppressed peasantry raising grain for export: all these had their charms. Yet it is hard, at least for a Westerner, to escape the feeling that the Rumanian boyars and princes nevertheless were in some sense retreating into an artificially fashioned and deliberately insulated cultural world. Ideals of political independence and military prowess they abandoned utterly. Instead, the Rumanians settled for local autonomy at the cost of heavy payments and subservience in all matters of political or military importance. The harsh realities of their position were disguised, no doubt, by a gorgeous court ceremonial, quite consciously resurrected from the Byzantine past. But such archaism, however intricate and admirable in its detail and finish, nevertheless smacks of retreat from reality. Yet by confusing life with play-acting and play-acting with life, one may perhaps construct a tolerable moral world from shattered fragments of the past; and insofar as this is what the courtiers of Jassy or Bucharest achieved, the historian should rather admire the skill with which they glossed over realities of their position than criticize them for not altering what they could in fact not change except by becoming Turks themselves: i.e., their economic and political dependence on culturally alien masters.

In a second and perhaps more important, because more popular, sense, Rumanian culture in the first half of the seventeenth century rejected the West and encapsulated itself in a past that seems to an outsider deliberately artificial. I have in mind the repudiation of theological speculation and argument, which had been brought to Orthodox attention by the propaganda first of Protestants and then more urgently by

past. Above all, Byzantinism had the advantage of being neither Turkish nor Western, and therefore offered to the Rumanian boyars a cultural identity which could become peculiarly their own. Other peoples emerging from barbarism on the margins of great civilizations have often sought to safeguard their cultural autonomy by behaving similarly, e.g., the Khazars of the Volga, who became Jews in the eighth century, or the Uighurs of Turkestan, who became Manichaeans a little earlier.

champions of the Catholic Counter Reformation. The major crisis came not in Rumania, but in Poland and Constantinople, and centered upon the career of Cyril Loukaris, born in Crete, educated at Padua, Orthodox agent in Poland when the negotiations culminating in the Union of Brest (1595–96) were in course, and finally ecumenical patriarch of Constantinople (with two periods of exile) from 1621 to 1638, when he was executed by the sultan's orders. Loukaris attempted to meet the Catholic challenge on its own ground, with educational improvement, theological argument, and historical scholarship. His ideas were affected by Protestantism, though it would be misleading to call him a Protestant; and this gave his opponents a chance to attack and eventually to overthrow him. Thereafter, no successor proved interested in confronting Catholicism intellectually. Instead, emphatic assertion of every jot and tittle of traditional formulae, and piety that rested upon ritual rather than reasoned conviction, dominated all the provinces of Orthodoxy that fell within the jurisdiction of the ecumenical patriarch of Constantinople.

By the mid-seventeenth century, the Rumanian provinces came to share this ecclesiastical rigidity. Earlier, this had not been the case, for in the sixteenth century Rumanian ecclesiastical affairs exhibited some of the confusion that dominated secular politics. In administrative matters, rivalry between the patriarchates of Constantinople and Peć for control of the Orthodox churches in the Rumanian provinces opened a way for sporadic assertions of autocephaly. Three languages competed for liturgical use: Church Slavonic (the oldest and most popular), Greek, and Rumanian. In the second half of the sixteenth century, Protestants of Transylvania made concerted efforts to proselytize Rumanians in Transylvania. Translations of the Bible and of catechetical materials into Rumanian aided their missionary effort. This provoked counter activity among the Orthodox on both sides of the Carpathians. Between the two theological camps, the Rumanian language achieved its modern literary definition. Some scholarly distinction, as well as a good deal of theological venom, developed in the course of controversy; and individuals were not lacking who tried to steer a middle course by somehow combining aspects of Calvinism and Orthodoxy.

Such enterprises came speedily to a halt when the ecclesiastical supremacy of Constantinople became unambiguous by the mid-seventeenth century. Constantinople itself was then in full cry against the Westernizing and innovating spirit of Cyril Loukaris; and Rumanian prelates, with their own experience of militant Calvinism in Transylvania and of militant Catholicism in Poland, found it easier to follow the mode of Constantinople and retreat behind old rites and formulae than to continue the effort and sustain the risks of debate and intellectual controversy with Calvinist and Catholic rivals. In the second half of the seventeenth century, therefore, intellectual vigor drained away from the Rumanian church, leaving only a shell of ritual piety behind.[24]

The imperial city on the Bosphorus, with is mixed population of Turks, Greeks, Jews, Armenians, and smaller numbers of all the other peoples of the Mediterranean lands, had indeed taken the two Rumanian provinces in tow by 1650, making them fully a part of its economic and cultural hinterland. The extraordinary fiscality whereby the city supplied itself with food, while exporting nothing more tangible than political legitimacy in return, is indeed remarkable. A more direct and efficient way of concentrating goods into the hands of the ruling cliques of Constantinople and of the two provinces could scarcely be imagined.

Political-military power has been used for similar economic purposes both before and since in eastern Europe. Indeed, it may be illuminating to compare the exaction of economically unrequited goods from the Rumanian peasantry by boyars or their intermediary agents in the seventeenth century with the manner in which Stalin's agents in machine-tractor stations collected unrequited grain from the Russian peasantry in

[24] This judgment seems fair, despite the fact that the greatest achievement of Rumanian ecclesiastical scholarship, the translation of "Serban's Bible," was not completed until 1688. The philological learning that lay behind this collaborative achievement turned out to be only the first stage in a general retreat from rational or at least rationalistic theology.

the 1930's, when collectivization was new and manufactured consumers goods could not conveniently be supplied from towns whose work force was otherwise engaged. Turkish townsmen, too, were otherwise engaged — primarily in the manifold tasks of sustaining and elaborating the apparatus of military-political domination. This involved not merely soldiers and administrators, but a systematic conspicuous display, taking such forms as luxury handicrafts and the maintenance of enormous slave trains by the Turkish magnates. Compared to such vital pursuits, the tasks of supplying Rumanian or any other sort of peasants with something they might find useful in return for their grain lacked all charm. Unlike Stalin's Russia, the very idea was absent, for the grain and cattle the city needed came in regularly and almost automatically in an ever increasing flow, despite the fact that it was economically unrequited. The only apparent limits were those set by geography and by the fiscal ingenuity of the swarm of agents who collected and delivered the agricultural surplus of the two provinces. Neither of these ultimate limits upon Constantinople's economic parasitism had even begun to be felt before 1650.[25]

Tartars and Cossacks. In the year 1571 the Tartars made a great raid upon Moscow, sacked the city, and ravaged its en-

[25] This section derives from Nicholas Iorga, *Geschichte des rumänischen Volkes im Rahmen seiner Staatsbildungen* (Gotha: F. A. Perthes, 1905) II, 1–121; Nicholas Iorga, *A History of Roumania: Land, People, Civilization* (London: T. Fisher Unwin Ltd., 1925) pp. 108–78; R. W. Seton-Watson, *A History of the Roumanians from Roman Times to the Completion of Unity* (Cambridge: Cambridge University Press, 1934), pp. 50–126; George A. Hadjiantoniou, *Protestant Patriarch: The Life of Cyril Lucaris, Patriarch of Constantinople* (Richmond, Va.: John Knox Press, 1961); J. Nistor, *Die auswärtigen Handelsbeziehungen der Moldau im XIV, XV und XVI Jahrhundert* (Gotha: F. A. Perthes, 1911), pp. 206–21; Nicholas Iorga, *Histoire des Roumains de Transylvanie et de Hongrie* (Bucharest: Imprimerie "Gutenberg," 1918) I, 197–335; Ladislas Galdi and Ladislas Makkai, *Geschichte der Rumänen* (Budapest: Sarkany Buchdruckerie, 1942), pp. 120–85; I. Lupas, *Zur Geschichte der Rumänen, Aufsätze, und Vorträge* (Sibiu: Druck Krafft und Drotleff, 1943), pp. 226–43, 267–337. The flavor of the age can be sampled through Grégoire Urechi, *Chronique de Moldavie jusqu'à l'an 1594*, Emile Picot (trans.) (Paris: Ernest Leroux, 1878).

virons with unprecedented thoroughness. In the same year, both Muscovy and Poland took steps to organize an effective frontier defense system.[26] In both states, a series of modest fortifications was supplemented by a system of sentinel posts backed up by "registered" Cossacks, i.e., frontiersmen who accepted military subordination to an agent of the distant monarch in return for a small annual payment in cash.

Such a system of frontier guard was expensive, and salaries were often unpaid. Nor was the obedience of the registered Cossacks always assured; for while they were willing enough to fight against the Tartars, they were by no means so ready to turn their arms against their fellows, the unregistered Cossacks, whose depredations and feats of arms were not infrequently directed against Christian noble landowners when raids against the Tartars palled.

Despite these difficulties and defects, which kept the Ukraine in an heroic turmoil for more than a century, the border guard thus instituted by the two great Slavic monarchies of eastern Europe did suffice[27] to check Tartar raiding. As a result, the drain of peasant population into Ottoman slavery was much reduced; life on the steppe became more nearly safe — at least for a man who slept light and kept a horse and a gun at his side; and the population began to increase very rapidly, being fed by adventurers and rebels from the north who sought to escape the trammels of serfdom by taking up the frontiersman's free life in the south. Hunting, fishing, beekeeping, and fighting had been the main occupations of the "Cossacks" who first adjusted themselves to the dangerous life of the southern steppe; newcomers crowded into these occupations, especially the latter; but many of them preferred (or were compelled by scant hauls of booty) to follow the life of a cultivator, while claiming the full liberties of a Cossack and recognizing no master.

[26] Poland had accepted responsibility for frontier guard against the Tartars as part of the terms of the Union of Lublin, negotiated between the Kingdom of Poland and the Grand Duchy of Lithuania in 1569.

[27] In conjunction perhaps with sociological changes within the Tartar community, about which there seems to be no adequate information. See below, p. 120, 176–77.

The growth of such a rough and ready frontier community constituted a sharp challenge to the aristocratic polity prevailing in Poland. Yet the Cossacks were always divided among themselves and never attained stable political institutions of their own that could stand against the apparatus of a civilized state. Despite the extraordinary and far-ranging military prowess of the Cossack hosts, and despite the effectiveness with which individual heroes were able to control and command large armies of Cossacks, a profound, mercurial instability was never overcome; for to overcome it the anarchic individual freedom upon which the Cossack communities were founded would have had first to be crippled. And this the Cossack fighting men were never prepared to do of their own free will.

Cossack political organization existed at three distinct levels. In the wild steppe, small groups of five to ten habitually lived and worked co-operatively, as fishers, hunters, bee-keepers, and casual brigands. Such groups often sallied forth from some village home in the north in the spring and returned in the fall with the products of their summer's adventures. Among such groups, leadership depended on personality; and common dangers, gains and losses created, at least in the early days of pioneering, a strong sentiment of solidarity.

The villages from which such men ventured forth were often free communities, owning no master and dealing with the outside world through an elder — "starosta" — chosen by some informal process of consensus. This sort of rudely egalitarian polity attracted runaways from villages to the north, where noble landowners were imposing serfdom and steadily extending its geographical limits throughout the latter sixteenth and early seventeenth centuries. From the peasant point of view (both those already subjected to serfdom and those who feared they soon might fall into some landowner's clutches), the compulsory labor required for large-scale commercial grain farming was the result of an outright and unwarranted usurpation by the nobles. Their hatred of such oppressors imparted a recurrently revolutionary tinge to Cossack politics.

The third form of Cossack political organization was the

war band, formed around a particular captain for a particular enterprise. Initially, perhaps, such war bands had gathered in the steppe by consolidation of separate small groups for quite local and temporary enterprises: e.g., an attack upon a caravan or harassment of the flank of a Tartar raiding party that was returning home with booty and captives. In some instances, war-band leaders also held the office of *starosta* of a village.

War-band organization achieved a new importance and stability after 1557, when Dimitri Vishnevetsky, the *starosta* of Cherkassy (a large village or small town on the Dnieper) established a fortified refuge on an island in the lower Dnieper River below the rapids which interrupted navigation of that river some hundred miles from its mouth. In succeeding decades, this "sech" became the center from which raids were launched in every direction. A rather highly developed set of rules governed the conduct of the men who set foot within its bounds. No women were admitted under any pretext; and a communal life, organized on military principles by regiments, hundreds, and tens, prevailed. Each regiment chose delegates to a council; and the council chose a "hetman" who held office indefinitely, though his power always depended on the readiness of the rank and file to follow where he chose to lead. Membership in the sech was open to anyone who presented himself before the hetman and submitted to a simple ritual, of which the central feature was making the sign of the cross. This excluded Moslems and Jews; anyone else was welcome, with no questions asked about the individual's previous existence. By the same token, individuals could leave the sech freely; and between campaigns, when no enterprise was afoot, only a few men remained to guard the camp.[28]

The institutionalized war band of the Zaporozhian Sech preserved for a few decades the egalitarian camaraderie that had distinguished the life of the first Cossack fishers and

[28] Knightly crusading orders, Moslem religious-military brotherhoods, and mercenary companies of German *Landesknechten* all probably contributed something to the customs, spirit, and organization of the Cossack sech. To distinguish them from the wider Cossack community, members of the sech were often called Zaporozhian Cossacks, from "za parogi," meaning "below the rapids."

hunters who had once scattered over the steppe and along the rivers in their small, dispersed groups. But as population grew and as cultivation increased, the old liberties and equality of circumstance inevitably underwent decay. Indeed, the successes of Cossack raiding parties contributed to the change, since a successful pirate could hope to use his new-found wealth to set himself up as a landowner on the model of the Polish-Lithuanian nobility; and many did so. The heirs of Vishnevetsky, for example (Polonized as Wiśniowiecki) distinguished themselves by the energy with which they asserted their own and others' noble rights against Cossack contumacy. From the beginning, therefore, the Cossack community leaked at the top and was fed from below by runaways and adventurers of all sorts, drawn mostly from the western Russian lands, but including representatives of practically every nationality of Europe in its ranks.[29] Such an engine of depredation and social escalation both resembled and in a sense reversed the Tartar-Turkish mode of enslavement and acculturation which had operated so effectively in the same regions during the immediately preceding decades. Obviously, the cultural model was changed. Not the Ottoman Moslem, but Polish-Lithuanian Catholic, and later Russian Orthodox styles of civilization were the models toward which unusually successful Cossack veterans aspired. In addition, Cossack depredation was directed mainly toward goods rather than the human cattle which Tartar raiders had found so attractive. This meant that cities and other seats of civilization, e.g., a Polish noble's house, offered by far the best targets for a raid, whereas fellow-feeling with enserfed villagers and the poverty of the peasants discouraged Cossack depredation in the countryside.

The contrast may therefore be expressed as follows: In the time of Turkish-Tartar ascendancy, city folk preyed upon villagers, whereas in the time of Cossack apogee, villagers

[29] The Barbary pirates constituted the Moslem equivalent to the Cossacks; and the lesser pirate communities of the Caribbean and of the Indian Ocean which also flourished in the interstices of civilized political power during the sixteenth-seventeenth centuries constituted remoter instances of the same phenomenon.

attacked cities and city folk. In the former case, the process of acculturation was unambiguous: the movement of persons and of styles of life was toward a center whose superiority all participants in the process recognized. In the second case, however, this was no longer so. Cossack heroes valued their rude comradeship in arms; and any veteran who left the community and joined the noble camp became in some degree a traitor to his earlier loyalties and self-image. The acerbity with which Polish and newly Polonized nobles asserted their rights as landlords against the peasantry of the Ukraine, particularly in the period between 1619 and 1648, must in part have been due to the presence among the nobles of a significant number of renegades from the ethos of Cossackdom. Such men, having broken, perhaps reluctantly, with the Cossack brotherhood, were liable to press for extreme measures against their erstwhile fellows; for only so could their new identity be proven to themselves and to nobles of older standing.

The first heroic period of Cossack history extended from 1582 until 1638. During this time, the Cossack war bands spread the terror of their name from the very walls of Constantinople and the shores of all parts of the Black Sea to Moscow and the Baltic. The Polish government found itself in an ambiguous relation to these bands. Insofar as they threatened noble predominance in society, they were the objects of radical distrust by the Sejm. But insofar as the Cossacks stood ready to put a hardy and very effective force of fighting men into the field in hope of booty and for the mere promise of pay, the Cossack hosts constituted a precious resource for the Polish kingdom which could not be safely squandered. Sharp fluctations in the policy of the Polish government toward the Cossacks resulted from this situation. When armies were needed, concessions were offered to the Cossack hetman; when peace threatened to break out — which was seldom — efforts to restrict, regulate, and control Cossack power regularly led to conflict between agents of the Polish crown and Cossack bands.

Two weaknesses plagued the Cossacks in their conflicts with the Polish authorities. For one thing, booty seldom or never came in quite the right assortment to permit continuation of raiding operations. Supplies of powder and shot, of clothes, and perhaps of food had to be found; and if such supplies could be interdicted, the military effectiveness of even the bravest men rapidly declined. Some Polish victories over pillaging Cossack bands were probably due as much to pre-emption of available supplies of powder and shot by Polish noble forces as to any overt military action by the Polish nobility.

The second Cossack weakness was the fact that "registered" Cossacks and others in the Ukraine whose social and economic status had begun to solidify tended to hesitate between supporting an insurrectionary band and obeying the Polish authorities. Much depended on circumstances and on the charisma of particular leaders; but the balance of forces was always precarious from the time when the sech was founded until 1638, when the combination of Turkish fortification of the Black Sea coasts and Polish repression of unlicensed raiding gave the forces of order and social hierarchy the upper hand for a decade.

Before depredations were thus brought under more or less effective control, the range and energy of their action amazed all Europe. The first great coups against Turkish fortresses and towns guarding the Black Sea were really a sequel to the disbanding of King Stephen Bathory's armies after their long but victorious wars against Russia (1582). Cossack contingents that had served with him provided the spearheads for vastly expanded and more professionally expert operations against the Turks. By 1590, raids against the Turkish towns that ringed and guarded the shores of the Black Sea were supplemented by the operations of almost equally unwelcome foraging parties demanding supplies from Polish nobles and towns. This first ebullience was checked in 1596 when the Polish army defeated and almost annihilated a Cossack force that had been ravaging as far north as White Russia. But the Cossack forces soon recovered numbers and morale. Cossack troops served with the Poles in Moldavia against Michael the Brave (1600) and in Livonia against the Swedes (1601); but this was merely the preface to their great enterprise into

Russia in support of the False Dimitri in conjunction with Polish aristocratic adventurers (1604).

Nor were Cossack operations confined to land. River boats sufficed to carry bands of freebooters into the Black Sea, where they launched a series of daring and dramatic raids against the cities that lined its shores. Varna was plundered in 1606; Sinope and Trebizond and the outskirts of Constantinople itself were pillaged between 1613 and 1615. Simultaneously, other Cossack bands were ravaging the Russian countryside, when the Muscovite Time of Troubles temporarily paralyzed Moscow's power.

This was the Cossacks' apogee. Like the Varangians of old, from a headquarters on the Dnieper interrelated bands operated all the way from the Baltic coast to the walls of Constantinople and from the Volga to the Carpathians; and everywhere booty-raiding and trading went hand in hand. Such military prowess inevitably implied involvement in politics; and in Peter Sahaidachny the Cossacks found a leader who for half-a-dozen years seemed on the verge of constructing a semi-independent Cossack-Ukrainian state. Sahaidachny first achieved prominence by leading a remarkably successful raid against Sinope (1614), on the south shore of the Black Sea. He subsequently became both hetman of the Zaporozhian Sech and the commander of the "registered" Cossacks. Sahaidachny used his extraordinary position to re-establish an Orthodox hierarchy in the Ukraine, thus putting a serious obstacle in the way of the success of the Polish Uniate church. But he also used Cossack fighting manpower in behalf of — or in alliance with — the Polish crown. Thus in 1616 he sent a Cossack contingent to the aid of King Ladislas IV, who was still fighting in Russia; and in 1621 he himself came to the rescue of a Polish army which was surrounded by a numerically much superior Turkish army near Khotim. Sahaidachny was himself wounded on this occasion and died soon afterward. But in using a Cossack army to determine the upshot of a struggle between the full imperial muster of the Ottoman Empire (Sultan Osman II was personally present at the siege of Khotim) and the Polish kingdom, he had brought Cossack power to a peak from which it rapidly declined in the succeeding decades.

What happened was simple in essence, though confused in detail. The Poles and Turks began to co-operate to check Cossack and Tartar raids. In response, there were some tentative gestures of co-operation between particular Cossack hordes and factions among the Tartars; but this alignment was never stable, since the whole tradition of both partners repudiated co-operation with the hereditary foe.

After their check at Khotim (1621), the Turks made peace with the Poles, each side undertaking to restrain irregular raids by their respective subjects. Not trusting to Polish ability or will to control the Cossacks, the Turks also established a new border regime, strengthened old fortifications, and built some new ones. A Nogai Tartar chieftain named Kantemir was put in charge of the forts and cities of what was thenceforward called "Budjuk," i.e., the region between the Dniester and the Danube mouths. The next year, the Turks took steps to fasten their control more securely upon Crim Tartary itself. This, however, backfired at first, when the khan whose removal had been decreed in Constantinople refused meekly to submit, and instead besieged the Turkish admiral who had come to depose him. Threatened with disaster, the Turks yielded and invested the rebellious khan once more with the symbols of authority; and since the Ottoman government was then engaged in a large-scale campaign against Persia, the home authorities for the time being agreed to recognize what they could not alter. In 1628, however, a fresh naval detachment was despatched from Constantinople against the Crimea. Being supported on land by Khan Kantemir, this expedition succeeded in deposing the rebel Tartar khan and installing an Ottoman nominee, despite Cossack contingents which had come to serve the rebel khan's cause. Trouble flared afresh in 1636, when the khan of the Crim Tartars quarreled with Khan Kantemir and demanded his dismissal and the withdrawal of Ottoman forces from the Crimea. But this second rebellion was nipped in the bud. In 1638 peace with Persia freed the main Ottoman forces; and detachments of Janissaries were despatched to stiffen defenses all along the Black Sea coastline. In particular, the city of Azov, which had been captured by Cossacks in 1637,[30] was recovered and strongly garrisoned by Turkish regulars (1642).

The internal evolution of Tartar society in the Crimea does not seem to be recoverable. Perhaps the changes were not very sharp, for the Crim Tartars were heirs of an ancient polity adjusted to a strictly and traditionally defined social stratification between the ruling family, nobles, commoners, slaves, and foreigners. Nevertheless, the checks to slave- and booty-raiding which set in after the great and successful raid of 1571 must have hampered the free enterprise of fresh-sprung war captains and correspondingly strengthened the relative weight of more pacific (and aristocratic?) elements in Tartar society. Something analogous to the recurrent tension between free warriors and aristocratic lords that manifested itself on the Christian side of the frontier may therefore have existed also among the Moslems; but the bare chronicles of personal and dynastic quarrels upon which Western scholarly literature is based do not seem enough even to sustain plausible guesswork.

[30] En route, incidentally, to serve in the armies of the Persian shah against the Turks. The Cossacks' decision to attack Azov destroyed all chance of real collaboration between themselves and the Tartars at a time when both were under mounting pressure from the more civilized governments on the flank of Danubian Europe. It had the further effect of providing the occasion for Patriarch Cyril Loukaris' execution; for his enemies enraged the sultan against him by asserting (quite falsely) that the patriarch had connived at the Cossacks' *coup de main*. Repercussions within the Orthodox church were decisive for the evolution of that institution over the ensuing two hundred years; the failure of Cossacks and Tartars to make an effective common front against their civilized rivals was decisive forever. An undertaking so casually determined upon and so surprisingly successful has seldom had such remote and important consequences.

It was also the first occasion upon which the ambitions of restored tsardom found carefully disguised expression, for the Cossack success depended on the skill of a German military engineer, who was shipped down the Don from Muscovy with supplies of powder sufficient to blow up Azov's fortifications by means of underground mines that were constructed by the Cossacks under the engineer's supervision.

TIME OF TROUBLES

Turkish precautionary measures against Tartar and Cossack disorder were matched by equally energetic repression from the north. The Polish nobility, having glimpsed in Russia and in their own lands the incendiary possibilities of peasant revolt provoked by Cossack war bands, were fully determined to bring the danger under control. The king, however, was not always so enthusiastic, seeing in the Cossacks a useful military resource and a potential counterweight to the Polish nobility.

This ambiguous internal situation made Polish actions against the Cossacks sporadic. Involvements in foreign war, where Cossack aid against Russians and Swedes was once more needed, also delayed the process. Nevertheless, in 1634 a threatened war between Turkey and Poland failed to come off and the two powers made a treaty instead, whereby each once more promised to discipline its subjects and stop border raids. As a result, circumstances became most unfavorable for upholders of old-style Cossack independence. Resort to open revolt merely hardened Polish hearts against the unruly revolutionaries; and many Cossacks refrained from joining the extremists who attempted to defy the Polish nobles and government. By 1638 the Polish armies, together with detachments of "registered" Cossacks, had seemingly won a decisive victory. All unruly war bands had been dispersed. The Sejm therefore felt free to pass a new set of Cossack regulations, reducing the number of registered Cossacks and putting them under the command of noble appointees of the Polish crown. The sech lay abandoned and desolate; the peculiar Cossack political institutions were all suppressed.

For the next ten years, peace prevailed; and it looked as though the administrative and military measures taken by the two civilized states adjacent to Pontic Europe would suffice to contain and subdue the frontier populations of the Ukrainian steppe. But in fact this possibility was ruled out by the presence of a third force, the Russian tsardom, whose caution in declining to accept the suzerainty of Azov from the Cossacks in 1642 was no measure of its strength or ambitions. The outbreak of another revolt among the Cossacks in 1648, directed against Polish landlords who had been trying highhandedly to fasten serfdom upon all non-registered Cossacks, provided an opportunity for Russian intervention, and postponed for another half century or so the decisive taming of the Pontic steppe to agricultural, aristocratic civilization.

Nevertheless, the temporary success which Polish arms and laws enjoyed between 1638 and 1648, no less than the stability of Ottoman control of the shore line, showed unmistakably the direction of social evolution in the region. Within the Cossack community itself, social differentiation created allies for the Poles in their effort to reduce the rank and file to servile status. The old camaraderie of the war band could, indeed, even be harnessed to safeguard the privileges of "registered" Cossacks against the interests of the non-registered majority. The spirit of the war band was, after all, an extremely exclusive one. Members were brothers in arms indeed; everyone else legitimate targets of opportunity. Moreover, each band, formed for a particular enterprise under a particular leader, dissolved automatically at the end of the campaign, when its members divided up their booty and betook themselves homeward. Such political institutions carried the fragility (as well as the occasional military effectiveness) of the Polish republic of nobles to its logical extreme. Every Cossack constituted a Polish noble *in posse*, lacking only lands and serfs to become as haughty, harsh, and overweening toward all who lay outside the brotherhood of nobles as the Polish *szlachta* had long since become.

Only the association between Orthodoxy and Cossackdom gave a modicum of reality to the polarity between Polish aristocracy and Cossack commonalty which has seemed so deep a gulf to Ukrainian nationalists ever since. Polish institutions, too, had emerged from medieval war bands not unlike those of the Cossack communities of the sixteenth-seventeenth centuries; and the internal momentum of Cossack development was clearly carrying them closer and closer to the Polish aristocratic pattern. Consideration of how Moscow's counter-

attraction disturbed this evolution must await the next
chapter.[31]

[31] Books consulted in connection with these remarks about Pontic development are: W. E. D. Allen, *The Ukraine: A History* (Cambridge: Cambridge University Press, 1940), pp. 64–132; Michael Hrushevsky, *A History of Ukraine* (New Haven, Conn.: Yale University Press, 1941), pp. 144–276; D. Doroshenko, *History of the Ukraine* (Edmonton, Alberta: Institute Press, 1939), pp. 123–224; Elie Borschak, *La Legende historique de l'Ukraine* (Paris: Institut d'Études Slaves, 1949), pp. 52–114; Dorothy M. Vaughn, *Europe and the Turk: A Pattern of Alliances, 1350–1700* (Liverpool: Liverpool University Press, 1954), pp. 175–204; *Cambridge History of Poland* (Cambridge: Cambridge University Press, 1950), I., 369–501; Günter Stökl, *Die Entstehung des Kossakentums (Veröffentlichungen des Osteuropa-Instituts München*, III; [Munich: Isar Verlag, 1953]); Henry H. Howorth, *History of the Mongols from the Ninth to the Nineteenth Century* (London: Longmans, Green & Co., 1880), Part 2, division i, pp. 512–52; Josef Hammer-Purgstall, *Geschichte der Chane der Krim unter osmanischer Herrschaft* (Wien: K und K Hof– Staatsdruckerei, 1856), pp. 58–126; Berthold Spuler, *Les Mongols dans l'histoire* (Paris: Payot, 1961), pp. 172–80.

CHAPTER FOUR

THE VICTORY OF
BUREAUCRATIC EMPIRE

1650–1740

IN the first half of the seventeenth century, two principles of social organization were everywhere at loggerheads in the anciently civilized agricultural lands adjacent to Danubian and Pontic Europe. Local leadership, lodged in the hands of a hereditary landowning class, opposed the bureaucratic principle that gave power to the appointees of a distant monarch, regardless of the individual official's origin. Convulsions provoked in large part by the clash of these rival principles allowed the rise of a series of interstitial polities in the no-man's land of the westernmost Eurasian steppe. Their degree of effective sovereignty and level of institutional elaboration varied markedly; and the amorphous quality of the interstitial political entities, as well as the complexity introduced by the mere number of competing power centers, is what gives the political history of this part of the world such a distressingly confused character in the late sixteenth and early seventeenth centuries.

After about 1650, the political history of Danubian and Pontic Europe takes on a new form. South, west, and north, the Ottoman, Hapsburg, and Russian empires consolidated bureaucratic monarchies, though each of these empires simultaneously gave some scope for the local exercise of power by aristocratic landlords. Stabilization of power at home meant a great increase in the effectiveness with which bureaucratic power could be brought to bear along the frontiers of each empire; and by 1711, when the peace of Szatmar ended Francis Rakoczi's rebellion against the Hapsburgs, and when Peter the Great secured his own control over most of the Ukraine by retroceding Azov to the Turks, it became clear that the enhanced power of the limitrophic empires far outmatched the strength of any interstitial polity. Thereafter, the full incorporation of Danubian and Pontic Europe into the body politic of one or other of the three neighboring agricultural societies was merely a question of time. What remained was

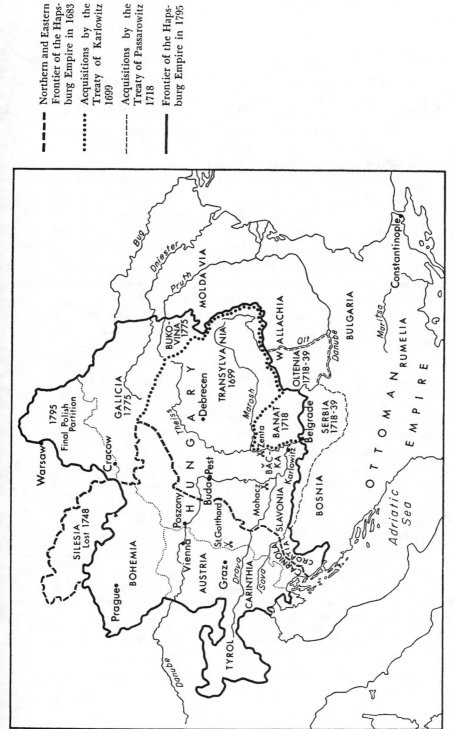

AUSTRIAN ADVANCE 1683–1739

Northern and Eastern Frontier of the Haps-burg Empire in 1683

Acquisitions by the Treaty of Karlowitz 1699

Acquisitions by the Treaty of Passarowitz 1718

Frontier of the Haps-burg Empire in 1795

exact demarcation of boundaries between the three competing empires, and little else.

The victory of monarchical bureaucratism rested ultimately on the energy and assertiveness of individual officials, clustered in the capitals or scattered out over the provinces of eastern Europe, pressed both from above and from below, yet everywhere sustained by an ideal of obedience and by a vision of collective as well as personal power — if not, in every case, also of law. But what gave scope for the individual energy of appointed officials was a change in military organization and tactics that rewarded bureaucratized armies with victory and condemned older forms of military endeavor to defeat. Professional infantry, trained like automata to deploy, maneuver, and fire on word of command even in the face of a troublesome enemy, proved able to withstand the most furious cavalry charge — at least if the battleground had been chosen with reasonable skill and there was time enough to deploy. Such professional infantry forces, when supported by artillery, not merely withstood cavalry charges; they could massacre their attackers. The more vigorous the charge and the braver the assault, the more disastrous the outcome for old-fashioned cavalry troops of the type which had formerly dominated the battlefields of eastern Europe.[1]

To be sure, it was no easy thing to create and maintain an army combining infantry, artillery, and cavalry in the most effective proportions, much less a navy, whose technical com-

---

[1] Cavalry continued, of course, to have a conspicuous and highly honorific part in the professionalized art of war. Cavalry were needed for reconnaisance of enemy positions and pursuit of a broken foe; and when the balance of discipline and fire power between opposing infantry-artillery forces hung by a hair, then a dashing cavalry charge might still decide the battle, breaking an already shaken infantry line into fleeing remnants.

But these roles had nothing to do with the traditional tactics of Polish, Magyar, Tartar, and Cossack cavalry. Nor could the aristocratic social order traditional in Hungary, Poland, and the Crimea (and which rapidly developed among the Cossacks) raise professional troops of infantry without either endangering the landowners' local power (if command lay in bureaucratic hands) or else precipitating intensified and painfully expensive local violence between rival landowners (if command of infantry detachments rested with local aristocrats).

plexities and costs were always substantially greater than those of land forces. Peter the Great discovered this to his and Russia's cost; but so did every other ruler of the time. Moreover, docked warships and unused armies tended rapidly to lose efficiency in war, so that even an expensively maintained armed establishment might prove distressingly defective when first put to the test of action. Older and less organized military establishments, by contrast, fluctuated less; for a Magyar hussar was — statistically speaking — just as good as his warrior father or grandfather had been — and just as pridefully undisciplined.

Yet these deficiencies and drawbacks to the more elaborate professionalized military establishments of the seventeenth century did not change the fact that when they were in good working order they could sweep all opponents from the field who were not organized, equipped, and trained in substantially the same fashion. Secure and stable sovereignties therefore depended on the ability to create and maintain such forces. Only fairly large states, whose rulers commanded a substantial tax income, could hope to do so. These facts not merely favored bureaucratic and imperial monarchy in Danubian and Pontic Europe: they imposed it.

The military-political transformation that became apparent in the second half of the seventeenth century may be described in a slightly different way, as follows. Standing armies, comprising infantry, artillery, and cavalry, had been known in eastern Europe as early as the fifteenth century. But in the days of John Hunyadi, Matthias Corvinus, and Mehmed the Conqueror, such forces could be sustained only by an unending process of plundering hostile border lands. This system had the serious drawback of being unstable, for no war captain could be sure of an unending supply of plunderable borderlands. We have already seen that even the Turks, who raised their plunder-based military system to logical perfection, could not sustain the indefinite geographical expansion such a system required.

What was new in eastern Europe in the seventeenth century, therefore, was neither the idea nor the reality of a professional standing army, but the mode whereby such forces were sustained. Taxes replaced plunder as the main source of supply. Taxes came through bureaucratic operation against townsmen, peasants, and (sometimes) landlords, backed by armed force, while armed forces willing to back bureaucrats were sustained by taxes the bureaucrats collected. This circularity could become vigorous only when it rested upon the availability of money (to be taxed) and of goods (to be bought) for the army — guns, powder, and thousands of other items, including the proverbial last gaiter button.

The first of these *conditio sine qua non* arose in eastern Europe without much deliberate official action. The penetration of a money economy into the region was rather the result of a collaboration between foreign merchants (Germans, Dutch, English, Jews, Greeks, Serbs, Armenians) and enterprising landlords and dated back to the Middle Ages in geographically favored and accessible regions. Commercial agriculture, supplying the urban markets of western Europe and Constantinople with grain and meat, kept on spreading to new regions and gained weight and momentum throughout the seventeenth century in the plain and riverine lands of eastern Europe.

Landlocked regions like Transylvania and Hungary lagged behind because of difficulties in bringing their agricultural products to market. The survival of an archaic constitutional order in Hungary until the nineteenth century was related to this fact, for even professional bureaucrats could not squeeze blood from a turnip nor money from peasants who had no cash income.This made the middle Danubian plain such poor ground for the development of modern officialdom that it failed to take root in that land until after 1848–49, when river steamboats had already introduced new marketing possibilities.

On the other hand, in the Russian north older forms of commerce retained or perhaps increased their importance. Furs, pitch, lumber, fish, provided the populations of the forested zone with readily marketable products; and the rivers constituted ready-made highways as they had done from time immemorial. The fiscal basis for the Muscovite state thereby remained; and in due course was enhanced by the grain revenues of the south.

Direct government initiative was often needed for supplying an army (and navy) with the elaborate and ever changing equipment required for up-to-date warfare. Government arsenals, managed by officials and supplied with manpower and raw materials on a preferential basis through governmental decree, were familiar in Ottoman and Russian lands from the fifteenth century, if not earlier; they were only slightly less important in Austria, where a larger pool of artisan skills existed upon which government contractors could call for needed military supplies. Until after 1740, artisan and other technical skills remained in critically short supply in Russia. Turkey, on the other hand, possessed a numerous but tradition-bound artisan force. Their guilds were closely affiliated with the Janissary companies; and they had an effective means at their disposal to check any technological innovation that threatened their interest or piqued their pride. The Hapsburgs, with the technical and artisan resources of Germany, Italy, and Bohemia at hand, could afford a broader reliance upon an officially uncontrolled market for military supplies; and this, together with a constellation of unusually talented generals, gave the Hapsburg armies a real, if modest edge over their Ottoman and Russian counterparts in the years 1683–1718. Prior to this brief period of Austrian ascendency, the Ottoman armies and administrative machine took the offensive and won a number of important victories; afterward it was the Russians. An analysis of this ebb and flow, and of circumstances affecting its course, follows.

Renewed Ottoman Advance, 1650–1683. In 1645 the Turks attacked Crete, long a Venetian possession. The ensuing naval war did not go well for the Moslems; but once landed in Crete itself, Turkish troops quickly confined the Venetians to a single stronghold, Candia. Elsewhere, the Greek-speaking inhabitants were ready enough to welcome relief from Roman Catholic propaganda and Venetian taxes. The prolonged and often desultory siege of Candia lasted until 1669, when the Venetians at length yielded. Yet during and after this long war, a very substantial proportion of the island's inhabitants became Moslem, while retaining Greek speech and most of their Greek customs. No similar conversion from Christianity had occurred in the European territories conquered by Suleiman the Lawgiver a century earlier; but, significantly, conversions to Islam among Albanian and Montenegrin mountaineers of the western Balkans and among Bulgars of the Rhodope Mountains (known subsequently as Pomaks) also gathered momentum during the seventeenth century.

This renewed power of religious attraction into the Turkish-Moslem camp was a sign of far-reaching changes that took place in the internal structure of Ottoman government and in the religious policy of the state. Converts had contributed enormously to the growth of the Ottoman Empire in its early phases, and the check to conversion from Christianity which followed the establishment of a more rigorous Sunni orthodoxy in the early sixteenth century was correspondingly costly. By widening the psychological and legal gap between Moslem and Christian, orthodox rigor undermined the fabric of the state. Hence, in a thoroughly ironical fashion, the decay of strict Moslem learning that set in in the late seventeenth century was both a sign of cultural-intellectual enfeeblement and an opportunity for social-political renewal. The retreat of Sunni orthodoxy invited the never suppressed mystic heterodoxies of the fringes of Moslem society to resume a more public and unfettered operation; and this opened the door again to mass conversions from Christianity to Islam in Crete, the western Balkans, and the Rhodope Mountains.

Political events of the seventeenth century appear to have encouraged this sort of invigorating cultural decay. The harem intrigues, insurrectionary coups d'état, and praetorian presumptions on the part of the Janissaries of Constantinople, which had so disfigured Ottoman politics in the first decades of the seventeenth century, revived again in the face of naval failures against Venice. A Janissary mutiny, supported by a faction of the Moslem religious class, deposed and executed Sultan Ibrahim in 1648. In 1656 a new popular disturbance followed a Venetian victory in the Dardanelles — at the very gates of Constantinople. This crisis was resolved when a new grand vizier, Mehmed Köprülü, took office on condition that he be endowed with extraordinary autocratic authority. The sultan was then a minor, and the harem factions were ready in time of obvious emergency to submit, at least provisionally, to a reform administration such as that which Köprülü demanded full powers to institute.

Köprülü was already an old man when he took office as grand vizier. He died within five years (1661). Yet in this short time, his violent actions at home effectively repressed factional disorders, and under his whiplash the Turks succeeded in turning the tide of war. His son and successor, Ahmed Köprülü, continued the policies of his father with such success as to bring Turkish territorial conquests in Europe to their greatest extent in the year of his death, 1676.

How was such a revival of Ottoman power brought about?

The imperious personalities of the Köprülü grand viziers were certainly a main factor, for their commands and ruthless punishments were what galvanized thousands of official subordinates into action. Mehmed Köprülü was an Albanian who began his career as a scullion in the imperial palace. From such a humble beginning he rose by degrees, serving for many years as treasurer to the grand vizier in Constantinople before being intrusted with office in the provinces. He served successively as pasha of Damascus, Tripolis, and Jerusalem before unhappy involvement in the intrigues of the palace led him first to assignment to lesser posts and then to complete retirement. From this honorable retreat, the aged Mehmed Köprülü emerged to take supreme direction of the empire's affairs.[2]

[2] Joseph von Hammer, *Geschichte des osmanischen Reiches*, VI, 1–5. There seems to be no biography of this extraordinary man in any Western language.

Such a career almost precisely recapitulated the career of Mehmed Sökölli and many other servants of Ottoman greatness who had begun life as Christian peasant boys and ended as Turkish pashas. For although Mehmed Köprülü was born a Moslem (his father had migrated from Albania to Asia Minor), the poverty-stricken rural background from which he emerged and the succession of official posts he held corresponded exactly to the pattern established for the imperial slave family in the time of Suleiman and before.

The success of Köprülü's reform of Ottoman political life may have rested largely upon the fact that he was not the only Turkish official who had risen in this fashion from comparatively humble origin. Christian peasant boys were no longer admitted to the system, to be sure; but there was a modest supply of Moslem peasant boys who did enter the slave family and rose as far as their talents, their friends, and happenstance allowed.

Among such individuals, who constituted a particularly vigorous and effective element in the Ottoman administration, Albanians probably already played a conspicuous part. The mountaineers' warlike habits fitted them for military enterprise and accustomed them to an easy resort to force. Their pride and freedom as wild tribesmen encouraged self-assertion; but the incipient anarchy of Albanian life was mitigated by the peculiar sanctity accorded to an oath of friendship, or *besa*. The sanctity of the *besa* arose from the fact that in no other way could a blood feud be brought to an end.[3] But among Albanians who left their native mountains, the *besa* acquired a new meaning and function. For the Albanians treated the forms of agreement between strangers incidental to taking service in a wealthy man's household as equivalent to their traditional oath of peace and friendship. As a result, Albanian emigrants to the cities of the Ottoman Empire, when employed as servants, transferred to their employers the attitudes reserved in their homeland for sworn friends. The consequences were far-

[3] Cf. M. E. Durham, *Some Tribal Origins, Laws and Customs of the Balkans* (London: Allen & Unwin, 1928), pp. 282 ff.

reaching. An Albanian could be trusted not to betray his master under circumstances in which no other ethnic group of the Ottoman Empire would refrain from doing so. As a result, confidential but unskilled service as bodyguards or messengers eventually came to be almost Albanian monopolies. Any government officer would be glad, when he could, to have an Albanian subordinate whose loyalty he could trust.

Adequate data seems to be quite lacking as to whether the infiltration of Albanians into the Ottoman power structure preceded, accompanied, or merely followed Mehmed Köprülü's rise to supreme authority. It was, nevertheless, a leading feature of the eighteenth and early nineteenth centuries in Ottoman society and provided the urban-based Turks with an immensely valuable, vigorous, and comparatively dependable source of recruitment from the Balkan wild west. In this partial but still effective fashion, the old tradition of recruitment from below into the ruling strata of the empire continued or revived, and with it, some of the energy of Ottoman administration, so prominent aforetime, survived the corruptions and class interest introduced in the seventeenth century by the enhanced power of urban and landowning groups in the management of the empire.[4]

A new religious climate was closely linked with the Köprülü coup d'état. Struggles between dervish orders, whose vision of Islam was mystical and antinomian, and rigorous upholders of the Sunni law had preceded the elevation of Mehmed Köprülü to power. On the very first day of his tenure of office, he had to quell a public manifestation provoked by Sunni rigorists. The new grand vizier himself does not appear to have opted definitely for either of the opposing religious parties; but in checking efforts by the rigorists to

[4] Christian Albanians like Basil the Wolf, hospodar of Moldavia (1634–53), and the Ghika family, which repeatedly supplied hospodars for the thrones of the two Rumanian principalities between 1658 and 1859, also found unusual scope in Ottoman society. The culture of such successful social climbers became thoroughly Greek, just as the successful Moslem Albanians became Turkish. Cf. Georg Stadtmüller, "Die albanische Volkstumsgeschichte als Forschungsproblem," *Leipziger Vierteljahrschrift für Südosteuropa*, V (1941–42), 75–77.

suppress dervish latitudinarianism, he helped to give rein to a side of the Islamic tradition which had been officially held in check ever since the time of Selim the Grim and Suleiman the Lawgiver. These monarchs had been frightened by the outbreak of Shi'a heresy connected with the victories of Shah Ismail Safavi (1500–1524). Thereafter, the secular warfare between Ottoman sultans and the shahs of Persia never entirely escaped the character of a religious war pitting Sunni against Shi'a, legalists against mystics, rigorists against latitudinarians. But by the middle of the seventeenth century the Turks could afford to relax their guard against Shi'a heresy. First of all, the religious evolution of Safavid Persia had dulled the vibrancy of the original mystic vision and introduced a formidable Shi'a legalism to supplement and control what had once been an uncontrollable religious perfectionism. Even more reassuring to the Turks were Murad IV's victories (1630–38) against the Shah which pushed Ottoman frontiers safely across the Tigris once more. As a result, by about 1650, defense of Sunni legalism no longer seemed indissolubly bound up with the security of the Ottoman state. Hence, Mehmed Köprülü's refusal to persecute dervish mystics seemed a tolerable risk, especially in a time when all Moslem forces were needed to rally against the threat posed by a victorious Venetian fleet.

Yet mystics who walked familiarly with God and had special links with the Janissary corps to boot were troublesome subjects for any ruler to confront; and Mehmed Köprülü early decided that the only way to restore stability at home and prevent further riots and coups d'état in Constantinople was to resume the immemorial Ottoman tradition of an aggressive military policy. Shortage of ships meant that Crete could offer only a restricted theater of operations for the imperial land forces; and naval deficiencies could not at once be remedied. Accordingly, the grand vizier determined to engage his main military effort on the land fronts of the empire, while conducting a mere holding operation against the Venetians in Crete and in the Aegean.

Apart from the obvious military and political gains which

successful foreign conquest might bring, such a policy weakened the sharpness of religious collision between the rival parties in Constantinople. How could upholders of the Sacred Law assail freshly victorious Janissaries, even if they perversely chose to protect religious heterodoxy? And how could seers and mystics make trouble in Constantinople when their armed confederates were busy on the frontiers of the state, fighting the Christian enemy?

Furthermore, widened official toleration of the various forms of Islamic heterodoxy made conversion from Christianity to Islam once more a comparatively easy matter. If Islam assumed an uncompromisingly legalistic form, so that a convert was compelled to abjure all at once many of the customs and beliefs he had been brought up to honor, then it required a catastrophic personal experience such as that involved in enslavement by Tartar raiders and transportation to an entirely new social environment to bring about conversion from Christianity to Islam. But when Moslem missionaries appeared in the guise of Bektashi or other dervishes who taught that all religions were merely defective approximations to the truth, which lay in a private and ineffable vision of God, then whole communities of Christians could once again be inducted into Islam without expressly repudiating their Christian religious past or accustomed frame of daily life. It appears, therefore, that the ability of Islam to win large numbers of converts in such geographically diverse regions as Crete, Albania, Montenegro, and the Rhodope Mountains arose from the new scope for dervish activity which the religious policy of Köprülü and his successors allowed.

A second factor which perhaps determined the geographical distribution of these conversions was the degree to which Christian ecclesiastical organization already occupied the ground, ready to oppose dervish evangelism. In Crete, for example, the Orthodox hierarchy and priesthood had been systematically suppressed by the Venetians. This cleared a path for Islam, since when Venetian rule crumbled the Greeks of the island nearly all repudiated Roman Catholicism as an alien faith and badge of Venetian subjugation. In the Albanian and Montenegrin mountains, also, stable Christian ecclesiastical organization was absent, partly because here, as in Crete, Venetian Catholicism and Orthodoxy had long collided. Only after the venturesome Prince Danilo managed to secure consecration as bishop of Cetinje from the Orthodox Serbian patriarch of Karlowitz (1701) did he organize wholesale massacre of Moslem Montengrins (1702) and thus identify Montenegrin prowess with resistance to Islam and the Turks. I have no information about ecclesiastical conditions among the Bulgar-speaking population of the Rhodope Mountains who became Moslem; but the prevalence of pastoralism among Pomaks in later times suggests that they, too, had lacked stable attachment to any Christian religious establishment.

There were also economic and social advantages to be won by accepting Islam: above all exemption from the head tax. But this was not new in the seventeenth century and, by itself, can scarcely account for the renewed success of Moslem proselytism. The altered religious policy of the Ottoman government, which from the time of the Köprülüs began to allow a greater scope to latitudinarian dervishes, therefore appears to be the critical change that provoked this return to patterns upon which the early growth and initial strength of the Ottoman state had been founded.

Yet the dervishes won only limited success. With only trifling exceptions, the plowing peasants of the Balkans remained loyal to their traditional Christian faith. A stranger, preaching a doctrine identified with the faith of their Turkish rulers and oppressors, could have little appeal in village communities that were served in matters of religion by priests drawn from their own ranks who fully shared peasant outlook and sentiments in matters both sacred and secular.

If we consider Ottoman society as a whole, this meant that the critical social fissure which had opened in the early part of the seventeenth century between town and country could not be healed, even by reinvigorated Moslem missionary enterprise. It was only social extremes that met and entered into effective alliance. The barren mountains of Crete, Albania, and Southern Bulgaria, inhabited largely by pastoralists and tribally organized brigands, could and did forge a new link with the seraglio, with the apparatus of Ottoman government, and with urbanism. But the mass of the Balkan population remained aloof. Whole communities of mountaineers went over to Islam as a preliminary to entering upon a wide variety of urban occupations; but plowing peasants could not take the initial step without betraying their fellows—a move which only isolated individuals who had already broken away from their village community ever cared or dared to take. This limited the potentiality of the Köprülü revival to comparatively slender proportions, for the trickle of migration from the mountains could never become massive enough to transform the social structure of the Ottoman Empire. Nevertheless, a clear mountain stream did refresh the ruling clique mightily in the seventeenth century and continued to invigorate the Ottoman polity during the eighteenth and early nineteenth centuries.

In immediate, military terms, unmistakable indication of the enhanced power of the Turkish state was not long delayed. Mehmed Köprülü's first concern was to drive the Venetians from Tenedos, at the mouth of the Straits, where their ships cut direct sea communication between Constantinople and Crete. This he did in 1657 by combined land and naval operations; and Köprülü further secured Turkish access to the Aegean by recovering the island of Lemnos, which the Venetians had also occupied.

Next, the grand vizier turned attention to the northern frontier, where a complicated situation had arisen. In 1648, George II Rakoczi had succeeded his father on the throne of Transylvania. He promptly launched a more venturesome foreign policy, aimed at making his principality the center around which all the interstitial ground of Danubian and Pontic Europe might group itself into a new, great empire. At first, circumstances seemed unusually propitious for such an undertaking, for Transylvania's neighbors were all distracted by serious internal upheavals. Rakoczi's Turkish suzerains were paralyzed by coups d'état and the Venetian war; the Hapsburgs were still exhausted from the Thirty Years' War; and the Poles confronted disaster in the form of a tempestuous Cossack revolt which had broken out in 1648 under the leadership of Bogdan Khmelnitsky.

Rakoczi's first efforts were directed toward the Rumanian provinces, where judicious military intervention compelled both hospodars to become his vassals. Next, he allied himself with Sweden, Brandenburg, the Cossacks, and a dissident party of Poles to attack the king of Poland. Hoping, like his distinguished predecessor Stephen Bathory, to succeed to the Polish crown, Rakoczi invaded with all his forces in 1657. Rakoczi's initial success — in conjunction with the Swedes, he occupied Cracow and conquered Brest-Litovsk — persuaded the grand vizier that it was time to re-establish the familiar balance of power in eastern Europe by reasserting Turkish suzerainty. Köprülü therefore peremptorily ordered Rakoczi to withdraw. He refused, whereupon the Ottoman government commissioned the Tartars to attack their disobedient and contumacious vassal, the prince of Transylvania. Simultaneously, the coalition against Poland broke apart. Brandenburg changed sides, and the Russians and Danes attacked the Swedes, who withdrew their armies from central Poland to meet these new assaults. Even the Cossacks went home; and when the Poles rallied their forces, Rakoczi had no alternative but to retreat. His Polish enemies arranged that the tattered remnant of his army should fall into Tartar hands and suffer enslavement en masse. Rakoczi himself escaped, only to die in 1660 from a wound incurred while fighting against a Turkish army that had invaded Transylvania.

By 1662, a series of Turkish campaigns had both thoroughly devastated the principality and installed a dependably obedient prince named Michael Apafy (1661–90) on the Transylvanian throne. Simultaneously, Turkish authority over Moldavia and Wallachia was effectively reasserted by the appointment of hospodars native to the Phanar district of Constantinople. Phanariots could not easily afford disloyalty to the Turks, because they left so many personal and psychological hostages behind in the imperial capital. A swarm of hungry Greeks accompanied the new princes to their capitals and set busily to work collecting taxes, organizing commerce, establishing schools, and in other respects assimilating Rumanian society to the Greek style of urban culture that was developing so vigorously in the Ottoman capital under the shadow of the Turks. Turkish policy after 1658–60, therefore, by preferring phanariot princes, very much accelerated the process of cultural Hellenization of the Rumanian provinces which had begun in the seventeenth century.

The successes of Turkish arms in Transylvania, Wallachia, and Moldavia did not fail to attract the attention of the Hapsburg government. The Austrians even ventured a brief, half-hearted intervention in Transylvania against the Turkish protégé, Apafy; but friction between the imperial government and the Magyar diet over the question of who was to pay and quarter the troops needed to make intervention effective became so sharp that nothing but bad feeling resulted. Austria's intervention nevertheless gave Ahmed Köprülü, who succeeded his redoubtable father as grand vizier in 1661, an excuse for launching two full-scale campaigns against the Hapsburgs in 1663 and 1664. On the second occasion, the Austrian army, reinforced by various German and also by a French contingent, met and defeated the Turks at Saint Gotthard; but the peace of Vasvar, concluded immediately after this battle, actually conceded to the Turks a few frontier fortresses captured in the first year's campaign and recognized Apafy as prince of Transylvania.

Ahmed Köprülü next turned attention to Crete, where three years of hard fighting — papal, imperial, and, once again, French forces aided the Venetians — led to the capitulation of Candia and peace with Venice (1669). This substantial success in the south freed Turkish arms for further ventures in the north, where the grand vizier now confronted two very tempting opportunities.

In Hungary, discontent with the emperor's conduct of affairs reached an acute stage after the peace of Vasvar. Many Magyars felt they had been betrayed by Vienna; and a group of very highly placed magnates entered into a plot aimed at severing the relationship between the Kingdom of Hungary and the Hapsburgs. French and Turkish agents were closely involved; and when the imperial government arrested and executed some of the ringleaders (1671), others fled eastward to Transylvania and Turkish Hungary and from these refuges began to organize active guerilla operations against Hapsburg Hungary. Leopold's government reacted by suppressing the antiquated constitution of the kingdom (1673), subjecting Hapsburg Hungary to a special commission which set out to suppress all resistance, eliminate Protestantism, and erect a modern, absolutist, and centralized administration on Hungarian soil. The Magyar nobility was almost unanimously outraged by such reforms, and many began to believe that Turkish overlordship — with appropriate guaranties of local autonomy — would be preferable to Hapsburg absolutism.

Ahmed Köprülü, nevertheless, decided to forgo active military intervention on behalf of the Turcophile Magyars, because he saw even more inviting possibilities in Pontic Europe, where the confused and bitter struggles initiated in 1648 by the Cossack revolt against Polish lordship in the Ukraine had led, first, to the division of the Ukraine between Russia and Poland (treaty of Andrussovo, 1667), and then to a further rising against the regimes imposed by Moscow and Warsaw respectively. The leader of this second revolt was Peter Doroshenko, who in 1668 turned to the Turks, as the only third power available, and signed a treaty whereby the sultan took the entire Ukraine under his protection, guaranteeing the autocephaly of the Orthodox church and recognizing Doroshenko as hetman in return for a small tribute. Neither Poland nor Russia was in the least prepared to accept this turn of events; and in the eastern Ukraine, Doroshenko's authority was quickly overthrown, since his policy of collaboration with the Turks accorded ill with the Orthodox, crusading sentiments traditional among the Cossacks.[5]

In the Polish or western Ukraine, however, the tensions between Polish landlords and Orthodox peasants were sufficiently acute to give Doroshenko's Turcophile policy much stronger appeal. Accordingly, Turkish armies were despatched thither in 1672 to make good the sultan's claim to the Ukraine. Despite a serious defeat at the hands of the Polish hetman, John Sobieski, in 1673, annual Turkish campaigns swiftly wore down resistance; and in 1676 Sobieski, now king of Poland, was compelled to sign the treaty of Zuravno, whereby he surrendered all Polish claims to the Ukraine. According to this treaty, the disputed territory was to be divided between a section under direct Turkish administration (Podolia), a section independent of both powers (the Dnieper right bank above the rapids), and a section subject to Turkish suzerainty, but occupied by the Zaporozhian Cossacks and governed by their autonomous sech.

Shortly before the conclusion of the treaty of Zuravno, Hetman Doroshenko had abandoned the Turkish alliance by surrendering his capital, Chirigin, to a besieging Russian army. The Turks therefore had to continue the campaign against the Russians and their Cossack subject-allies if the gains of Zuravno were to be made good. Accordingly, during four successive years (1677–80) great Turkish armies marched into the Ukraine, wreaking extensive destruction, and winning indecisive victories. In the course of these struggles, Cossack opinion hardened against the Turks. Simultaneously, attachment to Russia was strengthened, for regular troops and professional generals from Moscow first tempered and then outweighed Cossack impetuosity and indiscipline in much the same fashion that the Turkish troops and com-

[5] Oddly enough, the Kievan prelates backed Doroshenko's Turcophile policy, for the Russians had shown their intention of making Kiev ecclesiastically subordinate to Moscow. This displeased the metropolitan of Kiev, for it challenged the whole conception of an independent, Orthodox, Ukrainian church (and liturgy).

manders dominated and disciplined their Tartar, Transylvanian, and Rumanian auxiliaries who took part in all of these campaigns.

Developments in Hungary, together with the growingly unprofitable character of the fighting in the Ukraine, persuaded the Turks to come to terms with the Russians in 1681. By the treaty of Bakshai-sarai (or Radzin) the grand vizier, Kara Mustapha, brother-in-law and successor to Ahmed Köprülü, surrendered Turkish claims to the west bank of the Dnieper and declared the entire region, both above and below the rapids, to be a no man's land, a buffer between Russia, Poland, and Turkey. Podolia, however, remained under Turkish rule; so the Turks had something to show for the great military effort they had expended during the decade 1672–81.

Turkish relations with the Crim Tartars became much closer as a consequence of the decade of northern war in the Ukraine. Year after year, Turkish and Tartar soldiers fought side by side; and Tartar khans and lesser commanders became fully accustomed to taking orders from Turkish commanders. Prolonged and large-scale campaigning may also have helped to swell the slave traffic upon which much of the commercial prosperity of the Crimea rested; but there seems to be no firm evidence to support such a surmise.

In general, the Crimean khans came to accept subordination to Constantinople willingly enough. It was no longer possible to play Russia off against Poland and both against the Turks, since the Polish partner had become too weak to count seriously in the power balance. Moreover, the expansive power of the Russian state, as evidenced by the absorption of the Cossacks hordes and the conquest of such once-mighty states as the khanates of Kazan and Astrakhan, was quite enough to convince the khans of the Crimea that they needed Ottoman support to stave off a similar fate. Hence rebellions and open defiance of Constantinople, such as had occurred sporadically in the sixteenth and early seventeenth centuries, ceased. Political differences and rivalries were instead fought out in the coulisses of the seraglio or in the tent of the grand vizier. The khans' pattern of appointment and dismissal from office therefore tended to assimilate itself to the pattern set earlier for Rumanian hospodars. To be sure, being Moslems, the khans were not tributary; but bribes were just as effective and nearly as indispensable in forwarding a khan's appointment as they were in securing the hospodarship of one of the Rumanian provinces. Simultaneously, the level of cultural refinement among the Crim Tartars probably rose. During the second half of the seventeenth century, local participation in the intellectual and artistic life of Islam as a whole became somewhat more intimate than before. At any rate, some of the khans were themselves poets and patrons of the arts, and local institutions of Moslem higher education also flourished.[6]

These changes all made the Tartars more fully civilized. All in all, the simultaneous transformations of Moldavia and Crim Tartary meant that in the second half of the seventeenth century the Ottoman style of civilization planted itself firmly on the north shore of the Black Sea.

Nevertheless, it remains true that the Ottoman armies and Islamic civilization suffered a serious defeat in the Ukraine between 1672 and 1681. For the Cossacks rejected Turkey. They preferred autocratic, bureaucratic Russia. Islam's missionary power, which had originally raised the Ottoman Empire to greatness and which had become sporadically apparent again during the seventeenth century in other theaters of prolonged guerrilla warfare — Crete, Albania, Montenegro — was scarcely visible in the Ukraine.[7] Since the days of Peter Sahaidachny (or before), the Cossacks had be-

[6] Cf. Joseph von Hammer, *Geschichte der Chane der Krim*, pp. 122–25, 184–86, 206–7.

[7] Conversion via enslavement continued; and some of the strength and energy of Tartar society in the Crimea certainly depended on the never interrupted influx of slave converts. This is illustrated by the story recounted in W. E. D. Allen, *The Ukraine*, p. 202, of how Ataman Sirko, the greatest frontier fighter of the day, having led a successful raid against the Crimea and liberated some 7,000 slaves, declared that any who wished to return to the Crimea might do so and saw nearly half start back — whom he then slaughtered so that they might not "settle in the Crimea and beget children and be damned to all eternity."

come too closely identified with the defense of Christianity and in particular of its Orthodox variety to be open to Moslem blandishments. Mass conversion of Christian frontiersmen was therefore not resumed in Pontic Europe in the seventeenth century, despite the fact that Turkish institutions allowed far wider local autonomy and were more attuned to the egalitarian authoritarianism of the Cossack hordes than were either the Polish or the Russian polities.

Instead of converts, the Turks produced desolation. Great areas of the western Ukraine were totally abandoned. Slave raids decimated the population; and many peasants fled eastward so that the lands across the Dnieper (under Russian suzerainty after 1654) underwent unusually rapid development. Moreover, these refugees from the ravages of war were more interested in effective protection than in Cossack freedom. As a result, landlords, whose efforts to reduce free men to serfdom had lent Khmelnitsky's revolt its weight and power, met little resistance when in the eastern regions a generation later they remorselessly recapitulated the social history of the western Ukraine. The absence of a religious division between landlord and tenant may have facilitated matters; Russian policy of granting empty lands to appropriate suppliants, who then sought settlers from among desperate and impoverished refugees fleeing from the ravages of the Turkish wars, also certainly assisted the evolution.

In the "old Ukraine," settlers had, generally speaking, outdistanced landlords and the establishment of regular territorial administration. Hence land grants by the Polish king and efforts by landlords to put their newly acquired lands to good commercial use were deeply and effectively resented by "Cossacks" who had preceded such enterprising gentlemen on the ground. When, however, in the "new Ukraine" east of the Dnieper, Russian administration and land grants outran the line of settlement, no comparable resentment could arise, since squatters' rights and property were not being destroyed by the landowners' efforts to forward commercial colonization.

At the same time, the taxation and compulsion required to

maintain the Russian armies and administration at a level capable of outrunning the limits of agricultural settlement in the Ukraine put very severe strain upon the older parts of the country. Riots and disturbances at the center in Moscow (1662), large-scale revolt at the periphery of Moscow's domain in the lower Volga region (Stenka Razin, 1669–71), and the bitter schism between Orthodox and Old Believers which achieved its most flamboyant and massive manifestations between 1667 and 1691 in the northern stretches of the country all reflected the extreme tension under which Russian society was then living.

Meanwhile, in Hungary the efforts of the Hapsburg administration to tax and garrison the land efficiently and to establish religious and administrative uniformity provoked a growing guerrilla. Magyar rebels and refugees regularly found support in Transylvania and among the pashas of Turkish Hungary. French gold together with French diplomacy likewise aided the Hungarian guerrilla cause. In 1678, the Hungarian rebels united behind a young and impetuous leader, Imre Tököli. But unfortunately for Tököli and his supporters, the cause of Hungarian independence simultaneously suffered a serious blow when the French lost interest in the enterprise, owing to the fact that the treaty of Nimwegen ended for a decade open conflict between the French king and the Austrian emperor. But the defection of Louis XIV's agents was soon made good by the Turks, who calculated that Magyar discontent with Hapsburg government had reached such a pitch that massive defection to Tököli's banners could be expected if only he had sufficient military support to make the gamble look promising.

The grand vizier, Kara Mustapha, was a man of restless ambition and welcomed the thought of imitating and surpassing the deeds of the great Suleiman in Hungary. Accordingly, he determined to break off the costly struggle against the Russians and Cossacks in the Ukraine in order to be free to turn Turkish armies against the emperor in

Hungary. In many respects, the situation resembled circumstances in the Ukraine a decade earlier, when Hetman Doroshenko and a numerically important faction among the Cossacks had invited Turkish aid. Tököli and his partisans now took the part of Doroshenko; and the Turks played exactly the same role as before, for after initial victories, their armies by spreading devastation alienated an overwhelming majority of the local population. The Turks' failure to gain Magyar support on a wide scale was very largely due to a timely reversal of Austrian policy. The pious Emperor Leopold I (1658–1705) canceled his plans for bringing modern, bureaucratic government to Hungary and in 1681 reinstated the ancient constitution of the land. Hence, by 1683, when the full strength of the Ottoman Empire was marshaled to enforce the claims of Imre Tököli to the crown of Hungary, most Magyars, instead of rallying with enthusiasm to Tököli's side, preferred to play a waiting game, opening their cities and fortresses to Tököli when his troops approached and then, a few months afterward, submitting with equal grace to the imperial and Polish forces which drove the Turks back from their second unsuccessful siege of Vienna.

After the dramatic failure before the walls of Vienna, July–September, 1683, political-military initiative in Danubian and Pontic Europe passed permanently from Ottoman hands. But before we turn our attention to the next period, when the Austrians took the center of the stage, two aspects of Ottoman society deserve notice, not so much because they had any obvious bearing upon the military fortunes of the empire, but because they are interesting and significant in themselves, and underline linkages running across the cultural boundaries between the Ottoman and Christian worlds.

a) First, the Köprülü revival of Ottoman bureaucratic and monarchical practice did not involve a complete suppression of the rival aristocratic-landlord principle. The old fief system survived, at least on paper. A part of the Ottoman armies of the Köprülü period was composed of old-fashioned Moslem cavalrymen who wintered in provincial towns and lived on the income of a landed estate as their predecessors had done since before the days of Suleiman the Lawgiver. But no prolonged and serious effort was made to restore the feudal cavalry by eliminating the innumerable irregularities which had arisen over time.[8]

As fief holding decayed, hereditary land ownership, under whatever legal guise it flourished, got new impetus from the widespread development of commercial agriculture in Ottoman lands. This development became particularly rapid about the middle of the seventeenth century, when the Köprülü revival began;[9] and one may even hazard the guess that the military efforts connected with the activities of the Köprülü viziers in Crete, Hungary, and the Ukraine hastened the emergence of, and was itself sustained by, the new style of rationalized, commercial agriculture producing for distant urban markets.

The relationship may be visualized as follows. Under Suleiman, and in backward regions of the Ottoman Empire in the seventeenth century as well, local subsistence agriculture supported Moslem fighting men by the simple device of bringing the warriors back to the land every winter, where they could rest and re-equip themselves on the basis of local resources. But in the seventeenth century, such cavalrymen, however brave, were already outmoded; the sinews of war were rapidly becoming an ever more elaborately equipped infantry and artillery. The Ottoman regime did not quite keep pace with the technical evolution of European warfare; the weight of old tradition and vested interests was too strong to permit the Janissaries, for example, to imitate European drill and battle tactics. Yet the Ottoman armed establishment did not entirely fail to respond to new conditions. The old-style feudal cavalry was allowed to decay because new and enlarged infantry armies, drawn mainly from the Moslem

[8] According to von Hammer, in the last year of Ahmed Köprülü's life an attempt was made to cancel improper fiefs and to recruit three thousand Christian boys into the army. But this archaism was not pursued thereafter (*Geschichte des osmanischen Reiches*, VI, 332).

[9] Richard Busch-Zantner, *Agrarverfassung, Gesellschaft und Siedlung in Südosteuropa* (Leipzig: Harrassowitz, 1938), pp. 84–89.

town populations of European Turkey and from the rural regions of Anatolia were available to lend weight to Turkish attack. And artillery parks that were far from despicable, even by the most advanced European standards, continued, as in Suleiman's day, to hold an honored place in the Ottoman armed establishment.

The support of such an enlarged, semi-professional armed force [10] was made possible by the expanding role of commercial agriculture in Ottoman society. Rural surpluses were carried comparatively long distances to cities — above all to Constantinople — where they became available to feed the civil and military establishment of the empire. More concentrated and more flexible power resulted from the commercial process: money income, always insufficient for the needs of the state, but for that very reason constantly being enlarged by a steady inflation of tax rates, bribe rates, and protection rates, could be turned this way or that, used to build a mosque, to stage a pompous festival, to equip an army, or to build a fleet, all at the will of a handful of men who directed Ottoman policy.

Precisely the same was of course true of absolute monarchies in the rest of Europe, where money income allowed the rulers to build standing armies and navies, pay professional administrators, and generally speaking, to increase the scope, range, and flexibility of their power. The principal difference lay in the wider social and psychological gulf in Ottoman society between the arts of rulership and those of commerce. The Turks consigned the capitalist, commercial

[10] Janissaries followed a trade, and in the major garrison cities of the Ottoman Empire merged into the Moslem artisanate so thoroughly that almost every artisan was also a Janissary. When armies were regularly exercised in the field, as occurred without fail under the Köprülüs, such troops soon acquired professional quality. Only when years of idleness eroded habits of discipline did they degenerate into vast, unwieldy mobs.

Tallies of Janissary numbers seem unreliable. In Suleiman's time, the Constantinople corps counted about 12,000 members; by 1683 it was five to six times as great. Cf. H. A. R. Gibb and Harold Bowen, *Islamic Society and the West*, Vol. I, Part 1 (London: Oxford University Press, 1950), pp. 173 ff. and Walter Livingstone Wright, Jr., *Ottoman Statecraft* (Princeton, N.J.: Princeton University Press, 1935), p. 40.

operation of their empire to subject peoples of a despised religion with a way of life consciously alien and implicitly opposed to the lazy violence and taciturn sensuality affected by the Moslem ruling clique.

The fiscal web that Jewish, Greek, Armenian, and "Frankish," i.e., west European, money men spun around Turkish warriors and legists was straitening despite its gossamer. Only through the operation of a complex financial machine could Constantinople be fed; only through its functioning could the Turkish armies be equipped; but the fact that the ruling cliques of the empire quite failed to understand how the system operated, and tended to believe that in a pinch sufficient application of violence could always be trusted to uncover the necessary cash, had the effect of exposing the financial structure of the empire to sporadic and cumulatively very damaging catastrophe. In the utter failure of mutual understanding between the masters of government and the commercial and monied interest lay the fundamental weakness of seventeenth-century Ottoman society when measured against the states and peoples of western Europe, where government and capital, force and money, tended to enter into a more equable alliance, based on shared values and presuppositions which were almost totally lacking in Turkey.

b) Second, chiliastic movements attained unusual prominence in Ottoman as well as in Russian lands during the second half of the seventeenth century. The key figure in the Ottoman Empire was Sabbatai Zevi, self-professed messiah, whose claims to that office excited wide attention, not only among the Jews of the empire itself, but also beyond Turkish borders in Poland and Italy.[11] Vivid expectation of the end of the world also found expression among Moslems: in the same year that Sabbatai Zevi had appointed to be the end of

[11] Sabbatai Zevi grew up in Smyrna, where his father served the English Levant Company in a humble capacity. It has been plausibly suggested that the young Jew may have received stimulation to his fantasy from Fifth Monarchy men in the Levant Company's service. Cf. Joseph Kastein, *The Messiah of Ismir: Sabbatia Zevi* (New York: Viking Press, 1931), pp. 29–34.

the world, 1666, a Kurd attracted considerable attention by claiming to be the long-awaited imam of Islam. Both these movements were brought under control when their leaders, having been arrested and carried off to Constantinople, confessed the error of their ways. Sabbatai Zevi, in fact, saved his life by becoming a Moslem; and some of his followers did likewise.

Beyond Ottoman borders, the contagion of excitement spread from the Jewish communities of Poland-Lithuania to the Old Believers of Russia, who readily saw the deeds of Antichrist in the acts of a tsardom which was wantonly tampering with the holy customs of the church and ruthlessly conscripting men and money. Self-immolation of whole communities and other extreme manifestations of religious excitement broke out in Russia, reaching a peak between 1667 and 1691 when official persecutions attempted vainly to compel the Old Believers to honor the revised rites of official Orthodoxy.

One may hazard the guess that these religious manifestations were in some fashion related to the widespread unsettlement of customary, local relationships created by the penetration of commercial agriculture and the increased dominance of urban centers. Sabbatai Zevi's movement coincided with what was probably a fairly widespread displacement of Jews by Greeks as the confidential go-betweens used by the Turks in their dealings with non-Moslems. In Suleiman's time, Jews had played the role of bankers and advisors to the sultan and grand vizier; from 1669, when Panagioti Nikosios returned from Crete, where he had triumphantly negotiated the Venetian capitulation of Candia and was rewarded with the newly created office of grand dragoman of the Porte,[12] these functions were reserved exclusively for Greeks. Thereafter, the Jewish communities of the Ottoman Empire lost most of their former influence. The urban Greeks, on the other hand, went from strength to strength,

[12] Cf. Joseph Gottwald, "Phanariotische Studien," *Leipziger Vierteljahrschrift für Südosteuropa*, V (1949), 9–11.

serving as pioneers of commercial activity in all the eastern and southern Balkans, and in extensive regions of Asia Minor as well. Tax farming, rent collection, money lending, retail and wholesale trade, ecclesiastical administration, professional medical service: these strategic social functions all tended to gravitate into the hands of the Greek urban community, whose most successful leaders governed Wallachia and Moldavia, presided over the ecumenical patriarchate, and handled most of the sultan's dealings with foreign governments.

After the repudiation of Cyril Loukaris' reforming notions (1637), Greek Orthodoxy had deliberately and consciously closed its mind against religious innovations. This may have helped to insulate the Balkan Christians from the messianic excitements that afflicted the Jews. The fact that the urban Christians saw new and enticing possibilities opening before them may have had even more to do with their apparent immunity from chiliastic contagion.

In Russia, however, a large proportion of the Orthodox peasantry, finding themselves hard-pressed by official exactions and usurpations, responded enthusiastically to flaming visions of the approaching end of the world. The sectarianism of the Old Believers, by deflecting popular discontents into politically passive channels, may, indeed, have served as a supremely important safety valve for the Russian state. Had the Russian peasants not indulged in ecstatic religious visions to such an extent, it seems at least possible that the example of direct action set by Stenka Razin in the seventeenth century and reaffirmed by Emilian Pugachev in the eighteenth might not have been confined to the Russian borderlands in the south and east. Similarly, one may hazard the guess that the truly extraordinary emancipation Peter the Great and his clique of boon companions enjoyed from all customary restraint upon their exercise of power over the Russian countryside may have been possible only because peasant discontent had taken the form of passive expectation of supernatural intervention in the affairs of the world—

an expectation so vivid as to make any merely human action to oppose Antichrist and his agents superfluous and, indeed, presumptuous.

The Reformation of the sixteenth century came to western Europe on the wings of a pervasive disruption of traditional social relationships that inaugurated the modern age. In the seventeenth century the no less deeply felt apocalyptic visions of Jewish artisans and Russian peasants in eastern Europe played a similar role in announcing a proto- or para-modern ordering of society and government in Turkey and Russia, i.e., an ordering related to the West, responding to the West — at least on the level of military technology — and yet not quite equal to the West, and consequently subject to persistent erosion, especially during the nineteenth century, when it became clear that the attractive power of the civilization of western European nations could not be matched by local Ottoman and Russian achievements. Moreover, the apocalyptic passivity inculcated by the eastern religious movements contrasted strongly with the more active political and social ethos cultivated by both Protestants and Catholics of western Europe, thus both reflecting and reformulating divergences of long standing between Latin and Orthodox Christendom.

Such speculation carries us far from the proper theme of this essay. We should instead return to the narrower bounds of Danubian and Pontic Europe to inquire how the period of Austrian ascendancy and expansion superseded Ottoman dominance of the region, so that from their high point on the outskirts of Vienna, in less than half a century the Turks withdrew south of the Danube and east of the Carpathians.

Austrian Ascendancy, 1683–1740. The army that drove the Turks from the walls of Vienna in 1683 was a composite force, in which Hapsburg and Polish troops played the primary roles, supplemented, however, by smaller detachments from many of the German states. Such an army had been difficult to assemble and even more cumbersome to put into the field. Prudence dictated postponement of any attack upon the formidable Turks until full strength had been attained. In other words, serious operations had to await the arrival of the tardiest contingents. Moreover, when field operations did at length get under way, conflicts between the commanders of each contingent reduced strategy to diplomacy and made rapid decision or boldly concerted maneuver impossible. Under such circumstances, the comparatively high level of technical competence German regiments had attained through the long tempering of the Thirty Years' War could be demonstrated only occasionally, briefly, tactically. The real superiority of German small units over the technically archaic Turkish, Polish, Magyar and all other eastern European armed forces was, in effect, canceled by defects in the Hapsburg high command.

During the fifteen years that followed the relief of Vienna in 1683, the Hapsburg government made good this defect and thereby unleashed a force with which the Turkish soldiery were not at first able to cope. This occurred less by design than by accident, as one confederate after another withdrew from active operations against the Turks. When only Austrian generals and troops remained in the field, unified command followed as a matter of course.

The army of 1683 dispersed almost immediately after its great victory. The Emperor Leopold and John III Sobieski of Poland found it difficult to divide credit for the victory before Vienna; and the Polish king had no wish to see Hungary subdued by the Hapsburgs; for such an event would merely facilitate Austrian intervention in Polish politics — an intervention that was already crippling enough. Hence Sobieski and his Poles went back home; and their further activity in the war against the Turks was restricted to operations in Moldavia aimed at staking out a Polish dominion to the southward that might compensate for their earlier relinquishment to Muscovy of important territories in White Russia and the Ukraine. Similarly, the lesser German states, having done their part to turn back the Turkish danger, recalled their troops from an enterprise which could only strengthen the Hapsburg house and, if too successful, might even create once more an imperial danger for local princely power. The Hapsburgs, after all, had never officially surrendered the ideal of extending their sovereignty over Germany, despite the Thirty Years' War.

Hence, the Emperor Leopold soon found himself with a major Turkish war on his hands and only his own troops with which to fight it. To be sure, Venice (1684) and Russia (1686) also declared war against the Turks; and the pope not only attempted to rally all Europe against the Moslems but contributed important sums of money to the war effort. But after 1683 each state conducted its own campaigns in theaters of war conveniently separated from one another; and of these, by the mutual decision of Vienna and Constantinople, the Hungarian theater of war remained by far the most important. Here both imperial governments continued to direct major military effort until 1697, when the Austrians under the command of Prince Eugene of Savoy annihilated a great Turkish army at Zenta and persuaded the Turks to begin negotiations for what they knew would be a disastrous and humiliating peace.

The balance of military forces in Hungary between 1683 and 1699, when the peace of Karlowitz was finally signed, fluctuated sharply, although after 1683 Austrian superiority in the field was never in doubt. To be sure, the Turks won some important victories, but only because after 1688 Austrian forces were withdrawn to fight the French in the War of the League of Augsburg. The rhythm of events is instructive, for it demonstrated both Turkish stubborness and the new-found Austrian superiority. After 1683, the Austrians had easy going for three years. The Turks could not oppose Hapsburg troops in the field because they had to assemble and equip a new imperial field army to replace losses they had suffered in the disaster of 1683. This took time; and in the meanwhile Austrian troops picked off Turkish garrisons one by one and thereby liberated most of Hungary from Moslem occupation. Then in 1687 the Turks launched their new army against the foe and met the Austrian veterans at Mohacz, the same battlefield on which Suleiman the Lawgiver had destroyed Hungarian chivalry one hundred and sixty-one years earlier. This time victory rested with the Christians, despite a vast Turkish numerical superiority.

The reaction in Constantinople was drastic, for the Turks had spared no effort to restore their shattered field army, and now a second disaster had ensued. The sultan was therefore deposed (1687), another Köprülü entered office as grand vizier (1689), and the construction of still a third Turkish army began. While this army was being assembled, the Austrians enjoyed another year of almost unopposed operations and were therefore able to capture Belgrade and Vidin on the Danube and to penetrate both Serbian and Bulgarian territory south of the river. Such successes encouraged the Serbian patriarch, Arsen Crnojević, to rally to the Austrian cause; and a not inconsiderable Serbian population followed his example.

Circumstances altered sharply when Austrian troops had to be withdrawn from the Turkish war for use against the French. In 1690, therefore, when the Turkish field army was once more ready for operations, it won easy victories. Everything south of the Danube was quickly recovered; and Turkish authority in Transylvania was again effectively asserted when Tököli became prince. In 1691 the Turks even met and defeated an Austrian army in the field; but the grand vizier, Mustapha Köprülü, was killed in this battle, and subsequent operations bogged down into a series of sieges in which neither side enjoyed any clear advantage.

The approaching end of the French war, however, allowed the Austrians to withdraw troops from Italy in 1697, and a new commander, Prince Eugene of Savoy, promptly assembled the scattered Austrian garrisons into a mobile field army with which he boldly attacked the numerically much superior Turkish army at Zenta after a remarkable series of marches and countermarches. The Turks were by now sufficiently disheartened to be ready for peace. If victory eluded them when the French had been engaging a major portion of the Hapsburg force, what chance had they now when all the Austrian troops could be concentrated against them?

Moreover, revoits in Mesopotamia and Arabia, the hardships of sustaining a major war effort for so many years, and the advice of English and Dutch ambassadors all urged peace. Turkish pride resisted loss of territory and definitive admission of a major defeat at Christian hands, yet the same pride made the only rational alternative even more unwelcome. For only if Turkish armies had been willing to abandon their own traditions and systematically imitate Western military technique could the Ottoman government really hope for victory. But this would have hurt Turkish *amour-propre* even more than the signature of a disgraceful peace. Hence at Karlowitz in 1699 the Turks agreed to cede all of Hungary to Austria except the Banat, and all of the Morea to Venice; they returned Podolia to Poland and concluded a truce with Russia whereby the port of Azov remained in Russian hands.

In the years that followed, the Turks made no serious effort to reorganize the traditional military establishment of their empire. Direct foreign stimulus was lacking. During the war the French had been eager to shower the Turks with military advice and had even sent small detachments of specially skilled troops to serve with the Turkish field forces in Hungary. But French military missions were emphatically out of favor at the Porte after 1697, for, by preparing peace at Ryswick, Louis XIV had freed enough Austrian troops for use against the Turks to precipitate the disaster of Zenta. No other European state wished to supplant the French in Constantinople and help the Turks to modernize their army.

Moreover, the governing cliques of Ottoman society looked with entire disfavor upon any tampering with Janissary privileges and traditions, however outmoded or unbattleworthy they might be. Popular riot and coup d'état, colored by religion and inspired by deep-seated xenophobia, clearly would result from any such policy; and no Peter the Great came to the Ottoman throne who was willing to confront such dangers in order to use the autocratic power of his office for revolutionary purposes. No mere grand vizier could work such a revolution, for he was always vulnerable to court intrigues which might persuade the sultan to depose him at any moment. The rigorous conservatism inculcated by Moslem education, which taught that success and failure in war, as in peace, depended upon Allah's inscrutable will and not upon mere cannon or any other weak instruments shaped by men's hands, made efforts at radical change, such as those Peter the Great was then bringing to Russia, both irrelevant and impious.

For these good and sufficient reasons — absolutely persuasive within the context of Turkish institutions and Moslem tradition — having lost four armies in the field one after the other, the Ottoman state yielded territory at Karlowitz in order to escape the still more painful loss of institutional and cultural autonomy.

The Hapsburg government faced no such agonizing choice. In the second half of the seventeenth century, baroque worldliness and Catholic piety had achieved a satisfactory modus vivendi in western and central Europe; and both technological ingenuity and persistent rationality in matters of government and war won remarkably wide scope as a result of the development of professional specialisms in every European country. The Hapsburg government therefore had only to adopt and adjust to local conditions the patterns of administration and war that had developed elsewhere, primarily in Italy and France.

This was not necessarily an easy task, for local custom and vested interests were often strong. But the struggle was straightforward: both sides knew what they wanted; and when the survival of the Hapsburg power cluster seemed really to be in danger, the local interests of provincial diets, towns, and noble jurisdictions regularly yielded. Hence it was the twin dangers assailing Leopold — the Turks from the east and the French from the west — that made Austria a great power, precisely because they offered sufficiently real and dramatic threats to the existing political order to persuade local interests within the Hapsburg Empire to give way and submit to paying the taxes necessary to create and maintain a first-class army. The costs were heavy, and finances always remained precarious. Whenever the immediate danger eased, resistance to centralization once more manifested itself. But each crisis strengthened the central regime within the hereditary lands. In addition, new territories in Italy and the Low Countries, brought under Hapsburg administration by the peace settlement following the War of the Spanish Succession (1701–13), added substantially to the money income available to the Hapsburg central authorities. Hence, after 1714 the Hapsburg emperor disposed of means for maintaining a formidable army on a permanent peacetime footing, as had conspicuously not been the case in 1683, when Leopold had first to assemble an allied and confederate force before taking the field against the Turks.

Major responsibility for organizing the Hapsburg army that thus became a permanent feature of the European balance of power rested on Prince Eugene (1663–1736). Eugene's early years had been spent at the court of Louis XIV, so that his notions of sound military administration and organization were derived, like those of every other European military man, from the model offered by France. As chairman of the Imperial War Council from 1703, Eugene superintended the introduction of uniform regimental organization for each unit of the Hapsburg army and attempted to make army service into a profession for officers and a career for soldiers. Regular pay, solicitous attention to supply, daily drill, severe but codified discipline, uniformity in dress and equipment, badges of rank, cantonment in barracks in peacetime, limited permission to plunder, promotion in rank based — at least in theory — upon demonstrated competence and seniority: all these and other familiar features of modern European army life were rapidly brought into juxtaposition during the years between 1683 and 1713. And because this was done, the Austrians could not only defeat the Turks in a single battle — as had been possible in 1664 or even earlier — but could defeat them regularly and end a war lasting decades with an armed force no less formidable than that with which the struggle had begun. This constituted a new level of administrative control over organized violence in Danubian Europe that carried everything before it, easily and overwhelmingly, until 1718, when, after a new round of war with the Turks, the Austrians secured further substantial territorial gains in Serbia, Oltenia, and the Banat (treaty of Passarowitz).

Nevertheless, Austrian administrative centralization and rationalization lagged substantially behind the French example. Each land owing allegiance to the Hapsburg house retained important local peculiarities, so that local diets, immunities, jurisdictions, and privileges continued to hamper the free and uniform exercise of central authority. This was particularly true in Hungary. The political settlement that emerged by 1723, when the Hungarian diet ratified the so called Pragmatic Sanction, gave unusually wide scope to the Magyar nobility, who emerged from the wars with an iron control of local politics and society that was even more absolute than before the Turkish conquest.

Two crisis points secured this eventual result. In 1687, after Austrian arms had cleared the Turks from most of Hungary, a Diet was summoned which not only repudiated Tököli's claims to the Hungarian crown, but recognized Leopold as king of Hungary by hereditary right — though the act expressly restricted the hereditary principle to the male line and reserved the right of free election in the event of the absence of a male heir. In addition, the legal right of rebellion against a king who infringed the constitutional laws of the kingdom was canceled. Otherwise, the Austrians and Magyars concurred in upholding the legal and constitutional provisions of the kingdom as codified in the *Tripartitum* of 1514. Hapsburg embarrassments with the French forbade any other policy that might threaten to alienate the Magyar nobility; for that truculent, old-fashioned, but still warlike community was capable of almost instantaneous armed revolt, if convinced that its rights and dignities were in danger of infringement at the hands of suspect German foreigners.

Nonetheless, the Austrian authorities took three measures in the following years that alienated Magyar sentiment, even though nothing that was done contravened the laws of the kingdom in any definite and unambiguous way. The first of these measures was the establishment of a special commission (Commissio Neo-acquistica) to adjudicate claims and award legal title to lands in the newly conquered portion of Hungary. Conflicting claims going back to pre-Turkish times, often ill-documented, could scarcely have been resolved in any other peaceable fashion; but clearly, too, such a commission had power to reward favorites and penalize opponents. Radical change was in fact brought to the Magyar higher aristocracy through the operation of this commission; for a handful of insiders secured title to enormous stretches of land, much of it initially almost uninhabited, while some older great families, particularly those who had records of opposing Hapsburg authority, were, not unnaturally, frozen out.

Second, the Austrians established a special military administration along the entire southern border of Hungary (1644–1702). Local arrangements were modeled on the much older Croatian *Militärgrenzen*; but administrative control was now lodged in Vienna, not with semi-independent provincial diets, as was still the case in Croatia. Serbian, Croatian, and in lesser numbers also Rumanian soldier-settlers were planted on these lands, organized into regiments, and exempted from ordinary taxation. In addition, a numerically substantial Serbian community was established in southern Hungary, where it enjoyed special autonomy under the administration of Orthodox bishops and the Serbian patriarch. When Austrian armies had retreated from Serbia in 1690–91 and the patriarch left his see at Peć, traveling north to Karlowitz with perhaps as many as 100,000 men, women, and children in his train, the migration had been thought of as temporary, pending an Austrian armed riposte into the heart of the Balkans. But when the riposte failed to materialize, the Serbs instead settled down north of the Danube under a privileged and semi-autonomous regime. To Magyar noblemen, these special regimes on Hungarian soil represented an alien infringement, all the more hateful because free peasants under arms constituted not only a counterweight to

Magyar noble military predominance in the kingdom, but also a socially dangerous example to the serfs upon whose labor the nobles' income depended.

In the third place, the Austrian authorities failed to reunite Transylvania with the rest of Hungary. Instead, an imperial diploma of 1691 guaranteed the preservation of local peculiarities — even to official toleration of Calvinists and Unitarians — and recognized the right of succession to the principality in the Apafy family. This diploma, which was issued at a time when the Turks had just installed Tököli as prince of Transylvania, and when Austrian armies were barely able to maintain themselves against the combined Turkish and Magyar-insurgent assault, was never fully adhered to. Michael Apafy's heir never actually ruled and soon (1697) abdicated. The Hapsburg king-emperor thereupon added Prince of Transylvania to his already lengthy array of titles. A special Transylvanian chancellery was set up in Vienna to administer the country; and the archaic Diet, long accustomed to consent to the will of a more or less autocratic prince, tamely concurred in Hapsburg rule from a distance. Objection came from Hungary proper, since the Magyar nobles recognized that Vienna's hold on Transylvania in the north, coupled with Vienna's special relation with the "Grenzers" of the southern border, meant that the Magyar noble community would find itself doubly outflanked in case of any really serious quarrel with the Hapsburgs.

Other irritants to good relations between Magyars and Austrians were not lacking. Rigorous enforcement of Catholic claims inflamed the not inconsiderable Protestant minority in Hungary. Demands for taxes and winter quarters for the armies which were engaged against the Turks were both difficult to refuse and dangerous to concede; for if a standing professional army loyal to the Hapsburgs and commanded by Germans were to be encamped on Hungarian soil, then indeed the traditional preponderance of the noble cavalryman in Hungarian society would lie perpetually at the mercy of an alien and fundamentally unsympathetic hand.

It is therefore not surprising that, soon after war was resumed between France and Austria in 1701, revolt broke out in Hungary, led this time by Francis Rakoczi, grandson of George II Rakoczi of Transylvania. At the very beginning, serfs and outlaws rallied to Rakoczi's banner, but very quickly French gold and the decision of a few Magyar noblemen to join the rebellion made the movement socially respectable. For a few months the rebels were everywhere successful and even planned a junction with French and Bavarian troops before the walls of Vienna in 1704. The battle of Blenheim, where Marlborough and Eugene beat the French and Bavarians, defeated this strategy. Immediately thereafter, regular Austrian troops were despatched to Hungary, so that military preponderance in Hungary itself no longer rested with Rakoczi. A persistent guerrilla lasted, nevertheless, until 1711, when by the peace of Szatmar the Hapsburg government offered a general amnesty to all rebels. Only a handful of irreconcilables refused the not ungenerous terms and took refuge in Turkey.

The defeated Magyars were, indeed, compelled at a Diet that met in 1715 to agree both to assess taxes upon their peasants for the support of the Austrian army and to admit units of that army to regular cantonment within the Kingdom of Hungary. Thereby the instrument of their suppression was legalized; and hope of real autonomy or effective participation in international high politics became clearly illusory.

Magyar nobles reacted in one of two ways. Some few accepted German dominance; and if they could afford it, began to live part of the year in Vienna, where they could participate in the court life and hope to play a role in the social and official affairs of the empire as a whole. Only large landholders, the magnates, could really afford this sort of life; and in a relatively short period of time, most such families became thoroughly Austrian in outlook and culture. They were often regarded by the Magyar stay-at-homes as renegades from real Magyardom.

A majority of the nobility stayed on their estates and concentrated upon strictly local politics and society. The county quarter sessions and courts remained entirely unchanged from the days of Verböczi. Here, if nowhere else, the Magyar nobleman was still master of all he surveyed. Legal conflict over land titles, which despite the decisions and awards of the special commission remained satisfyingly complicated and vague, rapidly became the major preoccupation of the Magyar nobles. Investigation of medieval charters and other legal documents in order to be able to lay claim to more land became an engrossing surrogate for earlier habits of violence and less sophisticated forms of self-aggrandizement. Encapsulated in this world of their own, the Magyar gentry condemned themselves to inhabit a cultural backwater. Suspicious of outsiders, resentful against real and imagined infringements of their ancestral constitution, disdainful of social inferiors, litigious and deliberately boorish when among equals, and scornful of social superiors who had allowed themselves to be seduced by the salons of Vienna, the typical Magyar noble became proudly vestigial, maintaining into the nineteenth century all that was salvageable of a style of life that had lost its *raison d'être* by the beginning of the eighteenth century.

Economic circumstances undoubtedly assisted the Magyar nobles in maintaining their truculence against the cosmopolitan European civilization of the eighteenth century. Between 1683 and 1711, the recurrent campaigns fought on Hungarian soil had increased the devastation and depopulation from which the country already suffered, with the result that wide territories of quite unoccupied land confronted the Austrian conquerors when they first penetrated southern Hungary. Resettlement began at once, and in some special regions, e.g., along the military borders and particularly in the Banat (recovered 1718), agricultural exploitation of an intrinsically rich soil got under way on a substantial scale even before 1740. But there were enormous problems of marketing agricultural surpluses, which could not really be solved without a far more energetic development of road and river transport than anyone was prepared to undertake. There was no adequate incentive for the large-scale investment which would have been needed to bring Hungarian grain to market in really large quantities. Vienna supplied itself from its immediate hinterland well enough; and there was only a very modest urban demand in the country itself, for the cities of Hungary remained very small and comparatively poverty-stricken. Even Transylvania, where town life had been long established, saw no vigorous urban development. The old Saxon towns of Transylvania tended, if anything, to decline in size and economic importance. Why this should have happened is hard to say. Perhaps unmitigated oligarchy and monopoly in the Transylvanian towns stifled enterprise, while taxes and rents, collected more carefully than in less bureaucratic times, so impoverished the peasantry as to leave little margin for purchases from town artisans. But hard data to support such surmise is not available.

What is clear is that trade and transport of goods to and through the prairies, swamps, and sand dunes of the Hungarian plain tended to divide between agents of the army commissariat — who controlled a considerable flotilla of river boats — and Balkan muleteers or peddlers who supplied the humble village folk with metal tools and other valuables, often on a barter basis. Until after 1740, livestock — mainly scrubby cattle that lived out-of-doors winter and summer — constituted the most important export product of the central parts of the Hungarian plain; wide stretches remained but very thinly inhabited; agriculture, where it was established, was still predominantly conducted as a subsistence operation; and the poverty-stricken serfs consumed very little that was not locally produced. Such an economy, controlled by economically unenterprising gentry, allowed the preservation of their archaic manners. Reciprocally, the nobles' archaic manners and narrowness of outlook perpetuated the economic backwardness of the land.

Thus Austrian forbearance in not pushing through bureaucratic centralization in Hungary, as had been briefly attempted between 1672 and 1681, meant that the newly acquired lands to the east were not smoothly incorporated into Austrian society, but remained separate and distinct, psy-

chologically alienated, and yet unable to express that alienation except by sulky retreat into an archaic localism. Only
after Maria Theresa came to the Austrian throne in 1740 did
the Magyar gentry begin to emerge from the sulky mood
brought on by the failure of Rakoczi's rebellion; and even
then, as we shall see in the next chapter, not whole-heartedly
nor for very long.

While Austria and Hungary were undergoing this evolution, the fate of the Turkish and Russian segments of Danubian and Pontic Europe was quite different. In Russia, there
was still plenty of room to the south or east. Restless individuals, resisting subordination to the landlords who had
effectively fastened their power upon the Russian Ukraine
in the decade of the 1670's, could migrate across the Don, as
in an earlier generation their counterparts had descended
the Dnieper. This probably provided a vital safety valve,
which, together with the concentration of peasant discontents upon eschatological expectations, in the end allowed
Russian autocracy, bureaucracy, and aristocracy to prevail.
Yet Russia's success in incorporating the population of the
Ukraine bodily into the social-administrative structure of
the Russian state was not assured until 1721, when the Great
Northern War came to an end, and the possibility of a Swed-
ish-Cossack-Tartar-Turkish coalition finally faded from the
realm of practical politics.

As in Hungary, military events played the decisive part in
setting the scene within which social evolution occurred.
First, and absolutely fundamental, was the fact that in 1698
Peter the Great, tsar and autocrat of all the Russias, reacted
with utter ruthlessness to a mutiny on the part of the old-
fashioned *"streltsy"* regiments he had inherited from his
predecessors. He completely destroyed the mutineers' units,
so that no armed and organized defenders of the Muscovite,
Orthodox, conservative past remained. He also executed a
large number of civilians suspected of complicity in the mutiny; and having thus disarmed and terrorized the opposition, Peter proceeded to devote himself to creating a new

Russian standing army, modeled on the latest and best in Western practice. Everything had to begin from scratch — or nearly so. New equipment and factories to supply it, new methods of training and drill masters to impose it, new concepts of tactics and officers to impart them; most of all, perhaps, a new concept of the corporate and personal ethos of the professional military, and men who might exemplify and impart the subtleties of this ethos which was only then emerging in Western armies: all these had at once to be created, imported, implanted. Monumental confusion was inevitable. The remarkable thing was how quickly Peter's military innovations took root and began to function effectively. Massive influx of foreign adventurers helped; so did the cowed passivity of millions of Russians, who after the suppression of the *streltsy* revolt quietly submitted even to what they most disapproved.

But the costs were very great. An efficient force could not be created immediately, despite Peter's best efforts. In 1697, the *streltsy* had been able to win important victories against the Turks, capturing the fortress of Azov. But when in 1700 the new guards regiments first took the field — to be sure, against a more formidable enemy, the Swedes — they met ignominious defeat. Fortunately for Peter, the Swedish king, Charles XII, had imperial interests in Poland and along the southern Baltic to defend; and this distracted him for some years from active operations against Peter's fledgling army. When in 1708 Charles XII was again ready to turn against the tsar, a more cautious Russian strategy and the seasoning of additional years' experience resulted in victory over the Swedes at Poltava (1709). This victory was the more important for Russia because Charles XII had invaded the Ukraine in expectation of rousing a revolt among the Cossacks. He did win the hetman, Ivan Mazepa, to his camp, and the Zaporozhian Sech joined Mazepa against Russia; but in the Ukraine as a whole, most Cossacks thought it better to wait and see. Hence Peter's victory ended the immediate prospect that the Cossacks might rally en masse to the side of Russia's enemies. Moreover, the principal seat of Cossack discontent and unruliness was destroyed immediately after the battle of Poltava; for Peter sent an army to punish the Zaporozhians, who fled for refuge to the Crimea, leaving their camp, the famous sech, to be captured and destroyed by the victorious Russian soldiers. Charles XII and Mazepa fled in the opposite direction and found refuge at Bender in a Turkish frontier fortress on the Dniester. Here Charles and Mazepa (after his death in 1709, Philip Orlik, Mazepa's elected successor) sought to weave a new anti-Russian coalition in which Turks, Cossacks, Tartars, and Swedes would all take part.

The refugees had sufficient success to provoke fresh hostilities between the Ottoman Empire and Russia in 1710, when the Turks took the initiative by declaring war. From the Turkish point of view, war against the Russians represented a return to the forward policy in the Ukraine which they had broken off in 1681 in order to launch the disastrous campaign against Vienna. The time seemed propitious: for in 1710 Austria was fully engaged in the War of the Spanish Succession, the Turks had had time to restore their armed establishment in its traditional mold, and the Crimean khan, among others, was insistent on action to forestall the nearer approach of Russian power.

From the Russian side, war in the south was a distraction from operations against the Swedes in the Baltic. Yet a campaign against the Turks seemed to offer glittering prizes, for if Russian armies could safely cross the deserted no man's land of the southern Ukraine and reach territory inhabited by Orthodox Christians, a general rebellion might ensue. Accordingly, Peter hastily organized a propaganda campaign intended to induce the Balkan Christians to rise in his support and entered into elaborate secret negotiations with the two hospodars of the Rumanian provinces. His army did indeed penetrate Moldavia via the Polish Ukraine and a detachment reached the Danube, but massive popular risings failed to occur — save in distant Montenegro — and Constantine Brancoveanu, the prudent hospodar of Wallachia, acting on the principle "first come, first served," allowed the advancing Turks to gain possession of the military stores and food he had assembled in anticipation of the Russian arrival. The result was disaster for Russian arms. Peter's army found itself surrounded on the Pruth River without supplies and with no means of retreat. Hasty negotiation ended in a treaty (1711) whereby the tsar surrendered Azov and some forts on the Dnieper and dismantled the fleet he had built on the Don. In addition, Peter promised not to interfere in Poland; and the signatories mutually agreed that Charles XII should be allowed to return to Sweden without hindrance.

On the whole, this was a very moderate penalty for the Russians to pay for their vulnerable military position on the Pruth; and charges that the Turkish negotiators had been bribed were soon bruited about in explanation. The charge was never proved, and an alternative explanation seems ready at hand. For the terms of the treaty of the Pruth restored to the Turks all they had ever possessed vis à vis the Russians in the Ukraine, whereas there were other frontiers where the losses of 1699 had not yet been made good. Why then spend the strength of the empire on deserts in the north, where the prospect of winning the Cossacks to obedience to the Porte seemed too remote to be worth considering? Instead, the Turkish armies should be used to recover the Morea from Venice and Hungary from the Austrians. So a loyal, conservatively minded Turkish official might be expected to reason, and this, indeed, was what the Turks set out to do. In 1714 they invaded the Morea and quickly overran the lands lost in 1699 to Venice. To be sure, the second item on the agenda, recovery of Hungary, was never realized; for in the war that broke out in 1714 the Austrians once more inflicted a series of crushing defeats upon the Turkish army, and as mentioned before, the peace of Passarowitz (1718), instead of restoring the old boundaries of the Ottoman state, handed additional important territories — Serbia, Oltenia, Banat — over to the Hapsburgs.

The successive setbacks of Karlowitz and Passarowitz stimulated a few Turks to wonder what the secrets of "Frankish" success might be. Modest but systematic efforts were inaugurated to study Western ways, and some steps to adjust Ottoman practices — especially in naval matters — to superior French models were taken. Galleys rowed by slaves ceased to be the core around which the Turkish navy was built, for example; and in 1727 the Turks permitted the establishment of a printing press in Constantinople, despite earlier religious prejudice against this device. Even these small beginnings did not fail to arouse popular displeasure; and when in 1730 the news came of a further defeat of Turkish arms, this time at the hands of a new-sprung Persian conqueror, Nadir Shah, revolution once more broke out in Constantinople.

Yet the new regime that came to power with Mahmud I (1730–54) did not turn its back upon Western-style reform. On the contrary, the new grand vizier decided to undertake the delicate task of tampering with the army and intrusted a French renegade, Count Alexandre de Bonneval,[13] with the task of remodeling the Ottoman artillery corps. This required the opening of a school to teach mathematics and the translation of a number of European technical treatises. For a brief while, the diplomatic situation was so threatening and the deficiencies of the traditional military establishment of the empire were so glaring that Bonneval and the reformers were able to operate unhindered.

Events moved very quickly. First, Russia and Persia made an alliance (1735) threatening the Turks' northeastern frontier. Even more serious was co-operation between Russia and Austria in Poland (War of the Polish Succession, 1733–35), which led logically to joint attack upon the Ottoman Empire, 1736–39. Yet the ensuing struggle turned out very differently from what the Russians and Austrians had expected. The Turks won a number of victories over the Austrians, whose armies, led by men brought up to imitate Prince Eugene's daring, took too many risks and got caught

[13] Bonneval (1675–1747) left the French army for the Austrian service in 1705, served with great distinction against the Turks and French under Prince Eugene before quarreling with him, then fled to Turkey and in 1729 accepted Islam to avoid extradition. He spent the rest of his life in Turkey.

by Turkish forces that had profited both from Bonneval's sketchy training and from his very emphatic advice. Russian victories along the northern coast of the Black Sea and in the Rumanian provinces led the Austrians to fear that their powerful northern ally might gain control of the mouth of the Danube, thus blocking Vienna's expansion downstream. For this the Austrians had no stomach, and the French were vehemently opposed to any further overturn of the balance of power in eastern Europe at the expense of their proteges, the Turks. Hence the Austrians determined to make peace, even at the cost of surrendering Oltenia and the territory south of the Danube which had been theirs since Passarowitz. Russian victories had been won only at the cost of heavy losses, as much from famine and disease as from Turkish and Tartar action. Hence, when Austria's intention to withdraw from the war became clear, the Russians decided that they could not afford the risk of continuing to fight alone. They therefore evacuated most of their recent conquests, and by the terms of the treaty of Belgrade, which ended the war, retained only Azov, whose fortifications were, however, to be dismantled and left ungarrisoned.

Thus with French diplomatic support, the Turks emerged from what had seemed a very tight corner at remarkably small cost to themselves. The prestige of their army had been restored, in their own eyes at least, by their victories over the Austrians, and Russian successes could be conveniently explained away as a result of the fact that the Turks had been unable to despatch their main field forces against them.

Under these circumstances, ironically, the reform party in Constantinople, which had been in good part responsible for these successes, rapidly lost ground. Why disturb traditional usages when existing institutions had again proven their worth? Why trust important matters to a Moslem whose piety was so suspect as that of Bonneval, who never even took the trouble to learn Turkish, and whose relations with the French ambassador were entirely too close and cordial to allow an undivided loyalty to the sultan? Why indeed?

Moreover, in the three decades that followed the signature

of the peace of Belgrade, unprecedented peace reigned un-
interruptedly across the European frontiers of the Ottoman
Empire. In view of this situation the urgency which had
briefly dictated serious effort toward military reforms evaporated. Instead, a rapid process of political and military devolution set in; and for the first time since the days of Murad
I (1359–89), the Ottoman Empire ceased to be a European
great power. The too easy victory of 1736–39 proved to be
more subversive of Ottoman power than earlier defeats had
been. In particular, reliance on French or other Western
diplomatic protection, so advantageous in 1739, hencefor-
ward offered Turkish officials an attractive alternative to the
painful reform at home which alone could have maintained
the empire as a great power in its own right.

Little need here be said about developments in the Rumanian provinces and the Ukraine between 1683 and 1740.
Commercial agriculture continued to spread. Military operations in the two regions were sufficiently modest in scale
and duration between 1683 and 1740 as not seriously to hin-
der agricultural advance. Indeed, the rival armies sometimes
provided markets for local products, thus actually hastening
commercial development.

The spread of commercial agriculture implied both the
advance of settlement and a further hardening of the lines
of social differentiation between serf and master; and among
the masters, acculturation to a more civilized style of life
made rapid progress throughout the period. These were
the years in which Phanariot culture reached its apogee in the
Rumanian provinces. Relatively lengthy reigns both reflected
and forwarded the stabilization of the new pseudo-Byzantine
way of life and code of manners that had developed so
ingeniously among the boyars, courtiers, merchants, tax collectors, clergy, and princes of Moldavia and Wallachia.

Constantinople's hold on the provinces was strengthened
after 1711, when the Turks ceased to appoint native born
princes to the two thrones. Thenceforward, the grand vizier
preferred men of the Phanar. Perhaps the Turks thought

such unwarlike types would be a little less likely to enter into intrigues with the Russians, as the last important native hospodar, Constantine Brancoveanu (ruled Wallachia, 1688–1714) had done. More important, the policy of appointing Greeks from Constantinople to office in the Rumanian provinces probably represented a victory for the "men of the pen" as against the "men of the sword" within the hierarchy of Ottoman officialdom.

The facts are not yet well established, but it is certainly true that a pervasive discrepancy of method and mode of operation between soldiers and bureaucrats had always been present in the Ottoman government. In the eighteenth century, bureaucrats, "men of the pen," became more influential, if only because every military undertaking now required money, money, and more money, together with increasingly elaborate procurement operations even after money had somehow been found. The soldiers, therefore, increasingly found themselves hog-tied by clerks and accountants who had mastered the mysteries of finance and army supply; and the Turkish bureaucrats, like their colleagues and counterparts in other contemporary European governments, tended to prefer diplomacy, calculation, and intrigue to raw force, when any alternative between these means offered itself. The long peace across Turkey's European frontier, 1739–68, was both sign and seal of this shifting balance within the Ottoman power structure. So, in all probability, was the firm establishment of the Phanariot regime after 1714.

The Phanariot princes, of course, were intimately connected with Turkish "men of the pen." A good many hospodars qualified for their office by serving first as dragomen of the Porte. This gave them a chance to form the multiple relations with key personalities at the top of the Ottoman administration to which, in fact, most of the hospodars ultimately owed their office. Plans such as those spun so busily around Charles XII during his stay at Bender, seeking under the distant aegis of the Turks to combine the military strength of all the various border peoples against Russia were no longer of interest to the Phanariot hospodars. Turks (and Crimean Tartars) who had supported this idea and urged Constantinople to follow a forward policy in the north (men of the sword, in all likelihood) were therefore tacitly repudiated by the appointment of such unwarlike princes to the hospodarships.

Thereafter, with a single-mindedness seldom equaled among European princes, the Phanariot hospodars based their power not on armed force, but on the subtle and not less harsh power of money. It was indeed remarkably rash for the Ottoman government to leave a border province as defenseless against attack as Wallachia and Moldavia became. But to arm the Rumanians would have been even more dangerous to Turkish power; and, as long as Poland remained weak and a protective zone of almost uninhabited land insulated Moldavia from Russia, in case of war in the provinces the Turks could count on a very real strategic advantage. Their own armies operating from a base in Constantinople across much traveled sea and river routes in relatively well-populated lands could arrive quickly on the scene and then maintain a far better system of supply than any invading Russian force could hope to do. The vulnerability of Russian armies in 1711 at the Pruth and again in 1739 proved the military viability, if not the entire wisdom, of the Turkish policy of leaving the two provinces without any effective military garrisons whatever.

The Ottoman policy of appointing Greeks to office in Rumania may also be viewed as part of a general alliance between the Turkish regime and the Greek urban classes that had begun to operate in the seventeenth century and now reached full flower. The Greeks used their partnership with the Turks to consolidate their authority over other Christian peoples of the Balkans. The Serbs, for example, lost control of the Patriarchate of Peć after 1691, when the Serbian incumbent trekked north to Karlowitz in the wake of retreating Austrian troops. A Greek prelate succeeded him; and thereafter a policy of subservience to Constantinople superseded earlier independence.

The system worked as well as it did because the Greek

community of the Ottoman Empire freely admitted new-comers who had acquired the language. All educated Christians, together with many artisans and others who pursued humble urban occupations, became Greek by acculturation, whatever their earlier ethnic identities may have been. Hence, a career open to talent, though talent of a special kind, adept at intrigue and profoundly fiscal in outlook, became characteristic of the Greek side of the Greco-Turkish clique that dominated Ottoman society during the eighteenth century.

Among the Tartars of the Crimea, a rather full acculturation to Ottoman civilization in its Moslem, Turkish, and specifically military rather than Christian and pseudo-Byzantine aspect was maintained or even strengthened. The Tartar khans and cavalry played a prominent part in the long wars in Hungary and the Balkans, 1683–99, soldering Tartar manpower to the Ottoman armed establishment more firmly than ever before. Yet the Tartar khans and their cavalrymen were militarily obsolete, though of course still occasionally useful in scouting, ravaging, or pursuing.

Thus the element in Ottoman society with which the Tartars tended to associate themselves as a result of the long wars was the military class, which was nearly as old-fashioned and ineffective against the Austrians as the Tartars themselves. The newer elements in Turkish society that were coming to the top — the men of the pen, relying rather on diplomacy and cunning than on naked armed force — had little use for the Tartars and in a pinch were prepared to jettison them, as events of the next generation proved.

Bureaucratization and urbanization certainly made some progress among the Tartars themselves; and the gap between the mode of life of the Nogais of the steppes, who adhered still to nomadism, and their suzerains, the Crim Tartars proper, tended to widen as a result. An evidence of this social change among the Tartars was the cessation of free-lance raiding against the Russian and Polish Ukraine. To be sure,

Russia's better frontier guard after the 1730's discouraged raiding, but the Polish frontier remained ill-defended, without provoking private military entrepreneurs to action. We may therefore safely assume that the tighter disciplines exercised by the khans and by prolonged service with Ottoman armies had the effect of concentrating the exercise of violence within Tartar society into fewer and fewer hands. In other words, bureaucratization of force made important advances in the Crimea as well as in all the other civilized societies of Danubian and Pontic Europe.

To the north, both the Russian and the Polish portions of the Ukraine saw steady and relatively very rapid incorporation of ex-frontier regions into the respective bodies social of the two states. The Russians retained a special administration in the Ukraine, but the office of hetman was not always filled. In 1722, for example, Peter put the Ukraine under a commission on which both Great Russians and Ukrainians were represented. Then in 1727 the hetmanship was revived, only to be again discontinued in 1735. In 1731 and following years, a regular defense line was built to guard the fringes of settlement against Tartar raiding and from that time this perennial scourge of Ukrainian peasant existence ceased to be important. Correspondingly, the military habits of Ukrainians decayed. Cossack regiments continued to exist, but the more active and enterprising warriors tended to drift away to further frontiers, east and south. Those who remained behind in many cases abandoned the military life, perhaps because economic factors operated against the survival of small-scale farming and a man who lost title to his land could no longer afford to equip himself as a Cossack warrior. Simultaneously, the fact that European standards of military discipline and deployment had made the old style of unregulated Cossack charge ineffective on the battlefield meant that the Russian government was not anxious to preserve the Cossack military manpower. On the contrary, official policy tended to favor engrossing landlords and land-grabbing nobles and distrusted the chronic restlessness of old-fashioned Cossacks and ex-Cossacks who could not quite close their ears to blandishments coming every once in a while from across the Turkish frontier. As a matter of fact, the remnant of the Zaporozhian Sech continued to eke out a miserable existence under Tartar protection until 1727, when most of the Cossack warriors who had fled Peter's wrath after the battle of Poltava returned and with Russian tacit consent again established their headquarters on islands of the Dnieper below the rapids. But this gesture did not restore Zaporozhian military or political importance. Instead, the old wild frontier style of life continued to fade rapidly away before the bureaucratized and rationalized organization of force that had been introduced into the Ukraine by Russian armies and administration.

By 1740 or thereabout, therefore, one may properly say that only very narrow interstitial areas remained unincorporated into one or other of the great agricultural empires that had long bordered upon Danubian and Pontic Europe. An almost uninhabited stretch of territory still separated the Russian Ukraine from the Crimean settlements and Turkish border forts at the mouths of the Dniester, Dnieper, and other strategic points. Very thinly populated regions also bordered the middle Danube, where they constituted the new frontier between Hapsburg and Ottoman empires. But these border areas were comparatively modest in extent; and the bureaucratic monarchies of Austria and Russia had already staked out claims to most of these uninhabited territories in such a fashion as to make it clear that only time was needed to bring in settlers and achieve at least an agricultural level of exploitation of the regions in question.

The Ottoman incorporation of the Rumanian provinces, the Crimea, and the coastal zone of the Black Sea was still unshaken in 1740; Russia's hold upon the Ukranian border lands was growing stronger every year; only in Hungary had the process of absorption into a more civilized pattern of life met with serious and systematic resistance. Thus, by a reversal of roles not perhaps unusual in history, the region which had been most developed tended to lag behind, partly for valid geographical reasons, but mainly because the heirs of Magyardom found it harder to surrender their past than did either Rumanian boyars or Ukrainian land grabbers.

CHAPTER FIVE

THE CLOSURE OF
THE FRONTIER

1740–1800

B Y 1740 THE supremacy of bureaucratic empire over any more local form of political organization had been definitively demonstrated in Danubian and Pontic Europe, and the frontiers between the three great empires abutting upon the region — Austria, Russia, and Turkey — had been sharply delimited. This political circumstance did not at once transform the social scene in the borderlands. But officials of both the Austrian and Russian governments felt that empty or almost empty lands along the borders of the state constituted both a danger (for such lands could not easily be defended) and an opportunity (for if populated by tax-paying subjects, new revenues would begin to flow into the government's ever hungry coffers). Hence systematic settlement under the aegis of state officials became a major concern of both governments. The success of these efforts was both prompt and solid, despite all the discrepancies between project and fulfilment, plan and reality, which always and everywhere plagued official enterprise.

The third great empire, the Ottoman, had other and more pressing concerns. In many parts of the state, insubordinate local officials had begun to usurp effective power, thus undermining the reality of the central authority. The establishment of planned new agricultural settlements in Ottoman society therefore remained a matter of private, local enterprise. New commercial farms often rested on a dubious legal basis, since title to the lands newly brought under systematic cultivation was often unclear, sometimes resting upon forcible usurpation, sometimes on judicious bribery, and sometimes on nothing more tangible than official indifference, ignorance, or inertia.

In such competition, therefore, it is not surprising to find that Russian and Austrian colonization far outstripped comparable Ottoman development. Moreover, the balance was tipped even further against the Turks by the fact that the central government was unable to retain its jurisdiction over

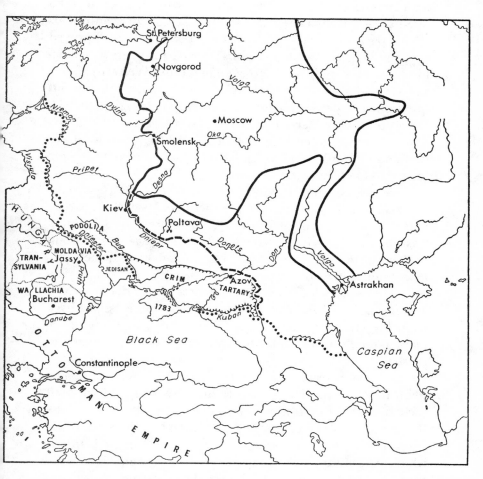

Boundaries of Muscovy *ca.* 1580

Russian Advance to 1689

Russian Advance to 1796

Borders of Crim Tartary in 1783

the Pontic borderlands which had been assigned to the Ottoman Empire by the peace of Belgrade. Instead, when in 1768
the Turks again declared war against Russia, after an unparalleled period of almost thirty years of peace, the event proved
that the Ottoman armed establishment had fallen so far behind the level attained by Russian (and other Western) armies
as to call the viability of the Ottoman Empire into serious
question. The peace of Kutchuk Kainardji (1774) pushed back
the Ottoman border to the Bug River[1] and declared the
Crimea "independent" of both empires — a juridical status
that endured only until 1783, when Russia annexed the peninsula and abolished the khanate.

Nevertheless, the shock of Ottoman failures in the Russo-
Turkish war of 1768–74, like the shock of Passarowitz earlier
in the century, provoked military reform among the Turks that
was not entirely without effect. When in 1787–88 war again
broke out, this time with both Austria and Russia, the Ottoman Empire did not simply collapse, leaving the Balkan peninsula to be partitioned like contemporary Poland, but instead
actually defeated Austrian forces and held the Russians back
from the vitals of their empire long enough to allow diplomatic complications centering around Prussia and France to
persuade first Austria (Sistova, 1791) and then Russia (Jassy,
1792) to make peace. By these treaties the Turks ceded some
small Bosnian frontier districts to the Austrians, and accepted
the Dniester as the frontier line between their empire and the
Russian. The Russian frontier thus came to adjoin Moldavia
without the cushion of agriculturally unoccupied steppe
which had always before separated the two empires. To be
sure, the eastern part of Moldavia (i.e., Bessarabia) was not
yet thickly inhabited, and settlement did not advance rapidly
under the Phanariot rule prevailing in that province. Nevertheless, it remains generally true that in all the regions west
of the Don River, the advance of the Russian political frontier and the successful colonization carried on by both Aus-

[1] In the following year Austrian diplomacy succeeded in annexing the
province of Bukovina from Turkey (i.e., severing it from Moldavia) as
compensation for Russian territorial gains.

trian and Russian officials in the second half of the eighteenth century successfully extirpated steppe nomadism, which had been a distinguishing feature of Danubian and Pontic Europe for more than 2,500 years. With this truly epoch-making change in social landscape this study of Danubian and Pontic Europe comes appropriately to a close, although the socio-political processes whereby agricultural settlement had advanced at the expense of nomadism were of course by no means exhausted. Steppe regions eastward all the way to Manchuria remained still to be tamed to the plow — a process, incidentally, not yet quite complete in 1964.

Before looking at each of the border regions separately, three preliminary observations seem worth making about the entire area.

1) Austria and Russia succeeded in making colonization and agricultural advance an economically self-sustaining operation. Costs to the government were sometimes substantial, yet the enhanced income secured from the newly settled lands after the lapse of relatively modest periods of time clearly compensated, and in Russia's case certainly more than compensated, for the initial costs of settlement and defense of the borderlands. The fiscally self-sustaining character of the process does much to explain its success. A hard-working, submissive peasantry, tax collectors under enough discipline to make them channel resources as directed by central authorities, and central authorities interested in using their power to forward settlement, were all required for the system to work.

The Ottoman Empire, to its misfortune, totally lacked the third of these requisites. Maximization of immediate tax yield for the support of the urban-based military-political ruling cliques was the only fiscal idea the Turks had. In addition, in some parts of the Ottoman Empire, tax collectors who were willing to put the resources they had wrung out of the local population at the disposal of the central government were lacking. Consequent shrinkages of Constantinople's tax income tended to be made good, so far as possible, by extracting more from the provinces that remained effectively subject to the imperial fiscal authority, i.e., the territories close to the capital, which were for the most part close enough to the Black Sea and Aegean coasts to be within effective sea transport range of Constantinople. Sometimes results were comparable to those in Austrian and Russian lands, i.e., the advance of commercial agriculture. In other cases, depopulation and flight from the land seems to have occurred.

In this, as in other, respects, the Ottoman Empire was archaic; for similar dilemmas (how find honest tax collectors? how escape economically destructive taxation?) had haunted Austrian and Muscovite bureaucracies in the seventeenth century and were, indeed, only precariously overcome in the eighteenth.

2) The army played a central role in the Austrian and Russian agricultural advance. First of all, the army carried state power into the empty lands ahead of settlement, thus giving officials the opportunity to superintend the establishment of new cultivators and set up rules to which the pioneers had more or less to conform. Second, a great many of the new settlers were military men, either discharged veterans or colonists assigned militia duty and thus subject to military rather than civilian official control. During the early phase, the identification between the army and the process of settlement was closest in Russia, where civil and military bureaucracies intertwined so intimately as to be practically indistinguishable. Austria established a sharper line between civil and military, with resulting conflicts that may have had some part in checking the process of Austrian expansion into the Balkans.

Once again, the Ottoman Empire found itself in a diametrically different and disastrously disadvantageous position by comparison with the two rival empires. For the Ottoman military establishment by the eighteenth century comprised two quite distinct elements, both of which were parasitic upon and unsympathetic toward the plowing peasantry. Urban artisan-soldiers, the Janissaries, and associated troops despised the life of rustic poverty to which the peasants of all eastern Europe were still condemned and valued their own social status and privileges in large part just because they separated them from rural idiocy, hardship, and helplessness. The second element in Ottoman armies — Albanian and Bosnian hillsmen and Tartar cavalrymen — were no less unsympathetic to farming populations, whom they regarded merely as potential victims of their prowess, usually without too careful a regard for whether the villagers in question were Ottoman taxpayers or not. Hence the operations of the Ottoman armies tended to discourage settlement rather than to advance it. As a matter of fact, peasants were prone to remove themselves beyond easy range even of garrison troops, so that Turkish frontier posts in both Danubian and Pontic Europe tended to develop agricultural vacuums in their rear, making maintenance of the garrison additionally difficult.

3) Rationalistic, secular attitudes accepting the advancement of state power as an end in itself and viewing population growth, agricultural advance, and technological improvement as self-evident goods inspired both the Russian and the Austrian officials who superintended the incorporation of the borderland into their respective agricultural societies. They even were prepared to embark upon wholesale and deliberate tinkering with inherited social and political institutions, so long as the proposed innovation seemed calculated to forward "progress" in any of its meanings or aspects.

This was a heady brew; and the opportunity to reorder the life of vast and potentially rich areas in accordance with their plans and in the light of their ideals was certainly a powerful factor in keeping the Austrian and Russian bureaucracies as loyal and efficient as in fact they were. Energetic and ambitious men could take satisfaction in seeing villages and towns emerge on what had been empty grasslands; and if self-interest could also often be served by judicious pre-emption of particularly promising pieces of property, this did not necessarily interfere with a simultaneous and perfectly honest pursuit of the common good, the interest of the state, and the progress of society and civilization.

This happy illustration of Adam Smith's providential harmony of interests developed most fully in Russia, where the agents of Catherine II's government in the Ukraine easily convinced themselves that "enlightened" ideas, derived in large part from France, did indeed explain all that was happening around them. Ideas, acts, and facts all seemed to combine harmoniously; and if old and outmoded superstitions persisted among the peasants, this merely demonstrated the intellectual superiority of the official (or landowner) — a useful prop to the legal and social privileges he also enjoyed.

In Austria, things were not quite so clear and straightforward. Catholicism and Hapsburg service had been deeply identified ever since the seventeenth century, and the two could never be totally dissociated even when, in the second half of the eighteenth century, a stream of "enlightened" recruits began to flow into the ranks of Austrian officialdom. The ambiguity thus implanted in the ideology of the Hapsburg bureaucracy became painfully explicit after Joseph II came to the throne in 1780 and demonstrated how recalcitrant Austrian institutions were to the sweet simplicities of reason and administrative convenience. When the Russians encountered comparably firm-set institutions among the Tartars of the Crimea, their brisk social engineering met with similar resistance. But here, too, Russian good fortune held, for Tartar resources were so restricted, when measured against the growing might of Russia, that Russian officials could afford to neglect and override irreconcilable Moslem opposition, as they had long been accustomed to neglect and override the opposition of ordinary Russian peasants. Neither the Crim Tartars nor the Old Believers had an alternative program of action to oppose to Russian enlightened despotism. Their ideas could therefore only appeal to passive, in-drawn personalities, a fact which assured Russian officials of the initiative in all dealings with such disaffected but ineffectual groups.

In Austria, on the contrary, Roman Catholicism, Magyar constitutionalism, and Belgian particularism (to mention only the most obvious divisive elements) offered elaborate and well-defended alternatives to bureaucratic *Gleichschaltung*. Only a great effort could have overriden such obstacles. The effort was never made over a long enough period and with a sufficient inner certainty to be victorious. Instead, shortly before his death, Joseph II yielded to the opposition he had aroused and retracted most of his reforms — leaving the Austrian bureaucracy divided between incompatible ideologies and unable to act freely in Hungary, where old constitutional forms were once more revived after Joseph's death.

The Ottoman Empire was in an even more disadvantageous position, for the secularist and rationalist ideals of enlightened despotism which inspired and strengthened Russian administration had a precisely opposite effect in Turkey, where official identification with Islam and true religion made secularism as suspect as Christianity itself. Yet Russian and Austrian successes, French theorists, and (after 1789) French actions too, all presented Ottoman officials with a challenge increasingly difficult to dodge. If Allah ruled the world, why did he award victory to Christian dogs, untrue even to their own faith? Within the frame of Moslem piety there was no intellectually satisfactory answer to this question, for from Islam's early days Allah's favor and success in battle had been closely linked.

The result, therefore, was that among a small but important educated class, secret doubts and inner uncertainty gained ground, yet were denied any straightforward overt expression by the fact that to remain a Turk at all a man had to remain Moslem; and the Sacred Law of Islam, massive and imposing, remained totally incompatible with the secularist rationalism of the European enlightenment. Cynical self-advancement was one response to secret doubts; renewed interest in the heterodox and antinomian forms of Islam which were clearly more hospitable to some of the new European ideas was another. But neither the one nor the other response to the challenge offered by secularist rationalism could invigorate the bureaucracy. On the contrary, a man dabbling in dervish lore was at least as subversive of administrative efficiency as was the private greed of the self-seeking cynic. The doubtful compromises possible within Austrian bureaucracy were here impossible. Head-on collision could only be escaped by systematically neglecting the new ideas swarming out of France, and many Ottoman officials doubtless were able to live out their lives in blissful and more or less deliberate ignorance.

Yet such an elementary defense against subversive ideas was barely tolerable in a state that desperately and increasingly required drastic military and administrative reform if it were to survive at all.

The decay of the Ottoman Empire, in short, set in sharply and decisively after the mid-eighteenth century. Moslem Turks no longer found it possible to do more than try to postpone disaster by resorting to an endless succession of emergency measures. They depended increasingly upon the working of the European balance of power to preserve their empire from destruction at Russian hands.

Thus ideological plasticity reinforced military and economic circumstances to give Russia a predominance in the disputed borderlands during the latter eighteenth century which was comparable to the predominance exercised by the Ottoman Empire in the sixteenth century at the beginning of this study of Danubian and Pontic Europe. But instead of destroying agricultural habitation in a border zone at the geographical limit of its power, as had occurred in the earlier time, Russian predominance was based upon the advancement of settlement into the zone which had been emptied (or kept empty) at the beginning of our story. Improved agricultural technique — in particular scientifically designed steel plowshares capable of turning a deep and tidy furrow even in virgin sod, played a part in this reversal; but the progress of commercial agriculture, making available tax money wherewith to maintain a bureaucracy and army, had far more to do with the change. And the commercial development of Danubian and Pontic Europe depended on markets — mainly in western Europe — as well as upon improvements in transportation facilities — river boats, harbors, ships, wagons, roads — and the invention of a social machinery to secure the systematic collection of grain and distribution of items needed by the peasant which he was unable to make for himself. These in turn depended on twin processes of pacification of the countryside and social differentiation. The whole added up, in short, to the successful incorporation of the Danubian and Pontic steppelands into the expanding European body social.

Let us now turn to a somewhat more detailed consideration of what happened in the Russian, Ottoman, and Austrian parts of the area.

The Russian zone. Between 1740 and 1764, the main attention and energies of the Russian government were directed westward rather than southward. Only when the Seven Years' War had been concluded (1763) was the imperial government free to take up afresh Peter the Great's project of wresting free access to the Black Sea from the Turks.

Nevertheless, official efforts to advance settlement in the Ukraine continued even in this period of relative inactivity. In 1752, for example, the Empress Elizabeth authorized a Serbian adventurer named Ivan Horvat, who had begun his career as an officer in an Austrian Grenzer regiment, to establish an autonomous military colony in the steppe lands between the Bug and Dnieper. Horvat originally proposed his scheme to the Russian ambassador in Vienna, holding forth the prospect of a substantial Serbian emigration from the Austrian to the Russian service. The project seemed promising in St. Petersburg, so Horvat was assigned lands sufficient to sustain four regiments of 4,000 men apiece, with their families, servants, and associated artisans, priests, and traders — all on the model of the long-established Austrian Grenzer regiments. Unfortunately for Horvat's plan, the Austrian authorities had just reorganized the administration of the Grenzer regiments in a fashion that eliminated most of the grievances that had arisen between Serbs and Austrians in the earlier part of the century.[2] Moreover, being just as conscious of the value of population as the Russians or any other mercantilists, they flatly forbade Serbs to emigrate to Russia and arrested some of Horvat's recruiting agents. He was therefore

[2] In 1747 the Grenzer regiments, having been reorganized to conform to the structure of regular regiments of the line, were fully incorporated into the Austrian army for the first time. Regular pay and other privileges went with this arrangement; and those whose names were inscribed on the regimental lists were therefore quite unwilling to migrate to Russia. Cf. Gunther Rothenberg, *The Austrian Military Border in Croatia, 1522–1747* (Urbana, Ill.: University of Illinois Press, 1960), pp. 111–23.

quite unable to find 16,000 soldier-settlers to fill the ranks of his four regiments.[3] Incessant quarrels attended the whole venture, for many Russians resented the privileges accorded foreigners. As a result, in 1765 Catherine II suppressed the autonomy of "New Serbia," as the region had been unofficially called; and the immigrants, who numbered several thousand families in all, dispersed or dissolved back into the general population.

This initial effort to attract foreigners under official regulation and direction therefore failed to accomplish very much. Yet other, older, and less pretentiously organized patterns of new settlement continued in operation under Elizabeth and were undoubtedly more important for the repeopling of the steppe than was Horvat's short-lived experiment. The Russian administration of the Ukraine, which was nominally subordinated to a hetman once more in 1750–64, continued to look favorably upon the land-grabbing activities of Cossack notables, Russian officials, and private adventurers of varied backgrounds. As a result, by 1764, when Catherine deposed the last hetman, there were almost no unassigned lands left under Russian administration.

Of course, the grant of title to empty acres did not automatically result in bringing in settlers and the commencement of cultivation, although the new proprietors certainly looked forward to such an outcome and were legally bound to bring in a number of cultivators proportional to the extent of land they had been granted. Precise statistics of this process of private colonization cannot easily be discovered. Migration from Polish as well as from Russian lands was sometimes organized by serf owners who wished to transfer labor power from their estates in the inhospitable north to rich new lands they had been allocated in the south. More often, serfs left their native villages by taking unauthorized flight from an unattractive tenure. Landlords of the steppe, desperately in search of man-

[3] In 1762, after ten years' operation, the regiments mustered about 25 per cent of their nominal strength, according to N. D. Polons'ka-Vasylenko, "The Settlement of the Southern Ukraine, 1750–1775," *Annals of the Ukrainian Academy of Arts and Sciences in the United States*, IV/V (1955), 112.

power, were not often inclined to look too closely at a prospective settler's past or to investigate his legal obligations to
some other master. Instead, competition for manpower meant
that landlords in the south offered new settlers better terms —
at least initially — than were common in the agriculturally
less fertile lands of central Russia. Substantial extralegal migration southward therefore helped to fill the empty spaces
and in doing so steadily extended the social framework and
administrative structure of the Russian homeland to ever
new areas.

Yet not all migrants were willing to take service with a new
master when complete freedom could be found a little further
to the south, in the portion of the Dnieper steppe assigned
by the treaty of Belgrade to Turkish suzerainty. There the
Turks offered hospitality to the remnant of the Zaporozhian
Sech, which had fled Peter's wrath after Poltava (1709). This
free Cossack community therefore attracted a stream of migrants from the north. The sech grew rather rapidly in numbers, and by 1768, at the beginning of the Russo-Turkish War,
had again attained a modest but real military importance.

The sech enjoyed an ambiguous political status in the
eighteenth century. Although inhabiting land assigned by
treaty to Turkey, the members of the Zaporozhian Sech had
sworn allegiance to the Empress Anna in 1734. Thereafter,
the Cossacks continued to maintain a distant attachment to the
Russian government, despite repeated frictions arising from
Cossack territorial claims and from their habit of lifting cattle
and seizing other valuables from pioneer agricultural settlements. Russian officialdom tended to look with considerable
distrust upon the unruly Zaporozhians, fearing that they
might renew their old seventeenth-century alliance with dis-
satisfied peasants living in the more settled parts of the
Ukraine. Tension between landlords and peasants — the one
seeking always to extract more unrequited services from their
serfs, the other trying to escape their obligations — was always
near the surface.

To the east, in the Don and lower Volga regions, the power
of landlords was even more precarious, as the great revolt led

by Emilian Pugachev (1773–75) showed. To the west, also, in the Polish Ukraine, endemic disorders had persisted since 1733, when widespread peasant risings against Catholics and Jews had accompanied (and embarrassed) Russian armed intervention in that country during the War of the Polish Succession. A particularly violent flare-up occurred in 1768. Russian troops that had been sent into Poland to support the cause of Stanislas Poniatowski were diverted from the pursuit of Polish noblemen to the suppression of Orthodox peasant insurgents, who had taken advantage of Russian intervention to massacre their Polish and Jewish oppressors under the inspiration of the cataclysmic visions of an abbot named Melchisidek and the leadership of an ex-Zaporozhian Cossack, Maxim Zaliznyak.

The Turks intruded into this inflamed and delicate situation with a declaration of war against the oppressor of Polish liberties, Russia. French diplomacy and long-standing Turkish grievances against the Russians precipitated this rashness. Yet before the failures of Turkish forces had become irreparable, the prospect of really checking the advance of the Russian columns seemed real. Indeed, if the Turks had been able to reconcile their indelible Islamism with an effective appeal to the discontented peasantry of the Ukraine, the outcome of the war might have been very different from what in fact it was. But an initial Tartar raid, renewed after long decades of inactivity, did not endear the Moslems to the Ukrainian peasantry; and the Zaporozhian Sech, which alone might have led a general revolt, instead rallied to the Russian banners. Its members, in fact, served with considerable distinction in several sieges and other incidents of the war.

After initial uncertainties had thus disappeared, Russia's problems lay less with Turkey than with Austria, Prussia, and the other European powers, who were reluctant to see any drastic disturbance of the balance of power in Russia's favor. Elaborate negotiations resulted in the first partition of Poland (1772), giving each of the three rival powers carefully matched accessions of territory and population; while Russia's gains at Turkey's expense were limited to comparatively modest territorial acquisitions: Azov at the mouth of the Don and the land between the Dnieper and Bug Rivers.

But the treaty of Kutchuk Kainardji (1774), which ended the Russo-Turkish War, in fact brought a far more fundamental transformation to Pontic Europe than the clauses dealing with Russia's territorial acquisitions suggest. Russian armies had thoroughly trounced the Turks, and for four years both the Crimea and the Rumanian provinces had been occupied by Russian troops. The fact that Austria, Prussia, and the other European powers had intervened to prevent the Russians from annexing outright the enormous territories thus brought under their military hegemony did not change the fact that Ottoman power had clearly crumpled. The region lay wide open, therefore, to a new Russian predominance.

Important provisions of the treaty of Kutchuk Kainardji hinted at the new balance of forces. The Russians, for example, were accorded free rights of navigation in the Black Sea; and commercial vessels operating under the Russian flag were guaranteed free passage through the straits. In addition, the treaty specified that Russian consuls were to be established in provincial cities of the Ottoman Empire and that a Russian church was to be erected in Constantinople. More vague, but by that very fact more threatening, was the clause in the treaty giving the Russians the right to make representations to Turkish officials on behalf of the Orthodox subject peoples of the Ottoman Empire. This clause was modeled on long-standing French rights of protection vis à vis Catholics in the Ottoman Empire; but because of the much greater number of Orthodox Christians under Turkish jurisdiction, it was far more subversive of Ottoman sovereignty.

However damaging to Turkey's former position in Pontic Europe, none of these clauses hurt Ottoman pride as much as those defining the status of the Crimea. For the first time, the Turks had to withdraw from a Moslem land. To be sure, Russian power was not explicitly substituted. Instead, the khanate with its associated Nogai tribes was declared to be fully independent, with the reservation that the religious establishment among the Tartars would continue to recognize the sultan as caliph. Such terms implied the separation of secular from religious authority, a notion totally alien to Islamic thought and tradition. Here lay ample ground for subsequent misunderstanding. Moreover, Russia's engagement to refrain from intervention in Crimean politics was clearly contingent upon having a "friendly" khan on the Crimean throne. If, as soon occurred, the Tartars allowed their cultural inclinations to attain political expression by elevating a pro-Turkish, anti-Russian ruler to the khanate, then the Russians were no longer willing to abide by the provisions of the treaty, any more than the Moslem Turks and Tartars were able or willing to recognize the sultan's "spiritual" authority in matters of religion and disclaim his political suzerainty in matters of state.

The psychological repercussions of the Russo-Turkish war of 1768–74 were profound. From the Turkish point of view, to be beaten so badly by Russians, who had but lately been tributary to the Crimean khans and belonged by their religious affiliation and past subjection to the class of despised Christian "rayah," was far more damaging to their self-esteem than any earlier defeats at the hands of the self-professed political head of Latin Christendom, the Hapsburg emperor of Austria, had been. Ottoman pride and self-confidence never in fact recovered from this blow. From the Russian side, the exhilaration of success against their secular enemy was correspondingly strong. The officials, army officers, and landowners who managed Russian society saw their victory over Turkey as the crown and completion of earlier victories over Sweden and Poland. The great effort inaugurated by Peter the Great had, indeed, been worth while; the costs of modernization had been richly recouped.

Buoyant confidence therefore sustained the Russian regime through the decades that followed as government officials and private landowners wrestled with the manifold tasks of settling the southern frontier lands, thereby confirming and extending the new power of the Russian state in the borderlands.

The central figure in this entire enterprise was Prince Gregory Potemkin, Catherine's lover and deputy for the south. He aimed at bringing the new lands within the framework of Russia's regular administrative, legal, and social institutions as quickly as possible. This meant, for example, suppression of the Zaporozhian Sech (1775), despite its distinguished military service in the war against the Turks. Some of the Zaporozhians were later reconstituted as Cossacks of the Black Sea, and in 1792 assigned lands east of the Sea of Azov in the valley of the Kuban River.

Nine years before this last vestige of the once mighty interstitial Zaporozhian polity had thus been laid permanently to rest, the Russians annexed the Crimea. This was scarcely a surprise, for as soon as Russian troops withdrew from the Crimea in accordance with the terms of the treaty of Kutchuk Kainardji, disputes and violent disagreements broke out between the Russians and Tartars about the meaning and limits of the khanate's new independence.

Russia's constant diplomatic and repeated military interventions failed to establish a friendly khan securely on the throne. Tartar sentiment and tradition were so strongly inimical to passive submission to a pro-Russian regime that nothing short of full-scale Russian administration and military occupation was in fact sufficient to prevent a pro-Turkish government from coming to power, which the Russians would not allow. Having the military means to enforce their will, they did so as soon as the European diplomatic line-up had altered in such a way as to make the move seem safe.[4]

The annexation of the Crimea and of the portion of the steppe dependent on that khanate lying between the Sea of Azov and the Dnieper River gave the Russians additional broad territories to settle and administer. Accordingly, three new provinces were carved out of the new lands: the govern-

[4] By 1783, Austria had made an alliance with Russia aimed at the partition of the Ottoman Empire. After Maria Theresa's death (1780) Joseph II decided that more was to be gained by co-operating with Russia than by opposing her.

ments of Kherson, Ekaterinoslav, and the region of the Tauris. The first two were administered as ordinary provinces of the Russian Empire. Russian law and institutions were extended to the new lands, with the result that local landowners, whatever their origins, became assimilated to the Russian nobility, whereas tenants rapidly became serfs. When, after another war against the Turks (1787–92), the steppe land between the Bug and Dniester was added to the Russian Empire, the process of settlement and assimilation of newly settled lands reached its geographical limit as far as the western steppe was concerned; for across the Dniester in Bessarabia, Moldavian peasants had already occupied a good proportion of the arable land. When the tsar did annex Bessarabia in 1812, the Russians no longer confronted virgin steppe lands, to be peopled and assimilated to the Russian style of society and civilization. Instead, they found the new province already occupied by peoples who had cultural traditions perceptibly and stubbornly different from the Russians'.

The Crimea of course confronted the Russians with the same phenomenon a generation earlier. The Tartars did not care to assimilate themselves into Russian society. Some Tartar chieftains were, indeed, accorded noble status by the Russian authorities, and there were a few individual quislings, both before and after 1783. But the rank and file would not abandon Islam and their past; nor could Tartar family systems, land law, class lines, and other legal and customary relationships be fitted into the Russian mold without ceasing to be Tartar.

One or the other party had to yield, and after 1783 it was quite clear that the Tartars were the weaker party. At first, the Russians were circumspect. They exempted their Tartar subjects from military service and from taxation. A dual administration was established, whereby the Russian military governor was assisted by a council, part Tartar, part Christian. Moslem law, as adjusted to Tartar custom and practice, was supposed to prevail whenever there was no conflict with the superior jurisdiction of Russian law and administration.

This initial compromise shifted rapidly in Russian favor during the following decade. A special Tartar regiment was raised in 1784 — mainly, perhaps, as a propaganda device to demonstrate how ex-enemies had been converted into faithful servants of the Russian empress. Taxation was introduced a decade later in 1794. More important was the influx of Russian and Greek settlers, matched by a massive Tartar emigration to Turkey. By the beginning of the nineteenth century, a very large proportion of the entire Tartar community, including most of the old upper classes, had departed from the Crimea and taken up lands made available to them in Turkey — for the most part south of the Danube mouth in the Dobrudja.[5] Tartars who remained behind tended to be the poorer, less educated, less enterprising portion of the community. Deprived of their traditional leaders, they were in no position to challenge Russia's new predominance. Instead, like the Magyar masters of the Hungarian plain after 1711, the former lords of the Pontic steppe lapsed after 1783 into a state of sulky and morose submission.

By 1796, therefore, when the Empress Catherine II died, the Russian flood had engulfed the once-formidable Tartar society, reducing the remnant to a culturally decapitated, economically impoverished and politically helpless enclave.[6] All the vast steppe region north of the Crimea and west of the Don had been occupied by landlords and settlers, and their political and social institutions had been effectively assimilated to those prevailing in the Russian empire as a whole. To be sure, the agricultural occupation of so vast

[5] One contemporary observer asserted that two-thirds of the Tartars had emigrated by 1802; a modern scholarly estimate arrived at the figure of 100,000 emigrants out of a population of 150,000. Cf. Boris Nolde, *La Formation de l'empire russe* (Paris: Institut d'études slaves, 1953), II, 193–94.

[6] The Tartar community survived until the latter stages of World War II, when Russian revenge for Tartar treason in welcoming the Germans took the form of uprooting the remnant of the community and dispersing it over the eastern vastness of the Soviet Union.

a domain was still thin in spots at the time of Catherine's death, and the higher manifestations of Russian culture were still absent or not very firmly rooted. Yet new towns had arisen (Kherson, 1778; Nikolaev, 1788; Odessa, 1794), and throve as administrative centers and grain ports; and with urban life the manifestations of higher culture — flavored by a distinctly cosmopolitan tincture owing to admixture of Greeks, Bulgars, Poles, Jews, and a few western Europeans — soon appeared. In short, civilization in the Russian style came in with a rush all along the northern Black Sea coast and hinterland.

Until the invention of steamships and railroads in the nineteenth century opened up such comparatively distant and landlocked regions as the American Middle West, the Argentine pampas, the Canadian prairies, and the Australian backlands to commercial farming, this Russian expansion remained unparalleled in the scale, scope, and rapidity with which it was carried through.[7] It still remains unparalleled in respect to the socio-political means that produced so massive an agricultural expansion; for it was not free labor using agricultural machinery on an ever more elaborate scale that

[7] Professor Arcadius Kahan has kindly drawn my attention to a recent population estimate by a Soviet scholar, based on official census figures, reproduced in the following table:

POPULATION INCREASES IN THE SOUTHERN PROVINCES OF RUSSIA
(In Thousands of Males)

	1724	1744	1762	1782	1795
Left Bank Ukraine	910	1,164	1,365	1,725	1,697
New Russia	n.a.	n.a.	n.a.	391	684
Tauris				52	130
Rest of New Russia	38	45	177	339	554
Right Bank Ukraine	n.a.	n.a.	n.a.	n.a.	1,738

Source: V. M. Kabuzan, *Narodonaselenie Rossii v XVIII–Pervoi Polovine XX Veka* (Moscow, 1963), p. 164.

These growth figures are the more remarkable in that simultaneously a substantial movement into the middle and lower Volga basin was taking place, as well as a trickle of settlement across the Urals into Siberia.

Calculation of net immigration as distinct from natural increase can only be very approximate. Professor Kahan has made the estimate that between 60,000 and 100,000 male immigrants helped to swell the population of the left bank Ukraine between 1724 and 1795. Females entirely escape the available statistical record.

broke the Ukrainian sod, as was later to happen in the American and Australian wheat lands overseas. Instead, the forced labor of serfdom, wielding sickle and scythe with human muscles and driving the plow with animal power, as men had done since early medieval times, was what tamed the Ukrainian plains.[8]

Hardship and ruthless collision between landlord and serf there certainly was, yet without such a differentiation of society and without the harsh entrepreneurship of Russian landlords, officials, and army officers, it seems sure that agricultural advance could not have been maintained at anything approaching the pace actually achieved. A locally self-sufficient peasantry, free, equal, and politically unorganized, could not have warded off nomad harassment any better in the eighteenth century than it had been able to do in the fifteenth and sixteenth. And to maintain a civil administration and a standing army capable of breaking nomad power on the western steppe required all or nearly all the panoply of the Russian imperial state. Overseas, in the United States, Canada, Argentina, and Australia, no such political overhead was needed because no militarily formidable enemies had to be overcome. Moreover, agricultural machinery soon permitted ordinary laborers and farmers to enjoy a standard of living and culture far higher than could conceivably have been attained by men who could produce far less grain per head while having to sell a large proportion of what they did raise to maintain their political and social masters, upon whom they depended for elemental military security and civil peace.

If these observations are true, then both the romantic idealization of the free Ukrainian life in which many Ukrainian nationalists of the nineteenth and twentieth centuries have indulged and the smugness of American and other Western critics who tend to decry the prevalence of

[8] Forced labor was of course far from absent from American agricultural expansion. Indeed, the legal compulsions and social inequalities between master and man that existed on the plantations of the New World usually exceeded the compulsions and inequalities of east European serfdom.

force and social inequality in the Russian and east European past seem equally beside the mark. What happened in Pontic Europe in the eighteenth century was an inescapable price of taming the steppe to agriculture. The truly enormous achievement of Russia's nobility and bureaucracy in superintending the process and taxing the result made Russia between 1762 and 1815 the arbiter of eastern Europe and allowed Russian might to outstrip Austrian and eclipse Ottoman power.

Mere geographic scale and numbers of population had much to do with this result, but important institutional frictions and failures in both the Ottoman and the Austrian empires from which Russia was comparatively free also played their part in determining this outcome. It remains, therefore, to look briefly at what happened in the Ottoman and Austrian zones between 1740 and 1795.

The Ottoman zone. As we saw in the preceding chapter, between about 1670 and 1740 the plains north of the lower Danube witnessed the emergence of a new and not unpromising cultural ideal and political regime, aiming at the recovery and preservation of a self-consciously Byzantine style of life and society. Such an ideal seemed to offer the courtiers and princes of the two Rumanian provinces the possibility of an autonomous cultural and political order that would be effectively independent of military-fiscal and cultural-intellectual pressures emanating from Ottoman Turks, Orthodox Russians, and "Franks" from the West, of whatever nationality or religion they might be.

After 1740 the autonomous development of this Phanariot regime was checked. Foreign pressures closed in; the cultural and psychological autonomy which the Phanariots had begun to construct for themselves withered. Restless uncertainty again prevailed, as it had in the decades before 1670; and the frenetic amoralism characteristic of men who have no stable cultural model and lack a recognized, workable code of conduct once more became apparent in the behavior of many Hellenized Orthodox Christians in Rumania and other parts of the eastern Balkans.

This phenomenon gave the Phanariot regime a bad name, which has lasted to the present, partly because both Greek and Rumanian patriots of the nineteenth century, from their opposing points of view, agreed in denouncing the Phanariots for failing to recognize transcendent national virtue in the linguistic habits of one or other of the groups of people whom they ruled. Under these circumstances, it is difficult to strike a just balance in trying to describe the Phanariot regime in its days of decadence and insecurity. The conventional denunciatory attack tends to generate an excessive apologetic on the part of anyone who does not share the indignations of those who have treated the Phanariots so unfairly. Yet the attempt should be made.

Politically and economically, the Phanariot regime of the Rumanian provinces successfully weathered the storms that arose with each round of war between the Ottoman Empire and its two Christian imperial rivals. Shorter reigns secured tighter control from Constantinople.[9] As foreign dangers became more acute, the Turks clearly operated on the principle that frequent changes of personnel at the top would prevent any one prince from building up a strong enough personal following to attempt rebellion against Ottoman suzerainty. Moreover, since the hospodarships were for sale in Constantinople, frequent changes meant frequent sale receipts, though it is not clear that the gifts and bribes dispensed in Constantinople by a ruler like Constantine Brancoveanu, who had survived for no less than twenty-six years on the Wallachian throne, 1688–1714, averaged any less per annum than the purchase prices paid in the latter

[9] In Wallachia between 1695 and 1740, ten princes held office, and during the same period fifteen rulers held sway in Moldavia. During the next forty-five years, however, twenty-one reigns in Wallachia and twenty-two in Moldavia were sandwiched in with two periods of foreign military occupation, by the Russians in 1769–74, and by both Austrians and Russians (variously in different parts of the two provinces) in 1787–92. Cf. table of ruling princes in Nicholas Iorga, *A History of Roumania, Land, People, Civilization* (London: T. Fisher Unwin, 1925), pp. 261–71.

part of the eighteenth century by men who knew they were purchasing only two or three years in office at best.

There is, indeed, good a priori reason to suppose that the net income Turkish officials secured from the princes of Wallachia and Moldavia did not much increase in the latter part of the eighteenth century despite the increased frequency with which office was sold. The price of office, after all, was a means whereby the balance of payments between Constantinople and the provinces might be adjusted, so that the city could command money to buy the agricultural surpluses of the lower Danube plains without exporting much in the way of artisan goods as an economic equivalent. Since this pattern of exchange underwent no great change in the eighteenth century and Constantinople's population did not grow and may even have shrunk, there was no basis in economic fact for any important increase in the scale of princely payments to Constantinople. If an eager candidate bid too high, he would be unable to recover his costs; and those who bid for his succession, knowing what had happened, would lower their offers accordingly. The very openness with which the Turks sold the hospodarships, therefore, created a more or less free market, where the real, cash value of office, ultimately defined by the cash value of economically unrequited Rumanian exports despatched to Constantinople, could be quite accurately determined by a process of trial and error.

Crisis of a different sort did, however, disturb the economic life of Wallachia in the 1740's. Austrian officials had been considerably shaken by the loss of important frontier provinces to the victorious Turks during the war of 1736–39. One response was to step up earlier efforts at settling the still uninhabited regions adjacent to the Ottoman frontier, where a flourishing agricultural population would make repetition of the crippling supply difficulties of 1736–39 much less likely. The nearest pool of agricultural population was in Wallachia, and Austrian authorities accorded immigrants from the principalities the same rights they had earlier assigned immigrant Serbs, admitting some to the status of

Grenzers and settling others as free peasants on imperial lands. Leakage across the Danube into what is now Bulgaria also took place; for no native aristocracy there tried to exact rents and services from the peasantry, as the boyars did in Wallachia.

The result of this constellation of circumstances was a substantial emigration.[10] The hospodars' revenues were endangered. Reform calculated to check the loss of population by protecting peasants from excessive exploitation and attracting settlers back into the provinces seemed necessary. Constantine Mavrocordato, during his third Wallachian reign,[11] 1744–48, tried to cope with this problem. He summoned a great meeting of boyars and announced to them that their demands for peasant labor would in future have to be severely cut back and limited by law. He also undertook important reforms of princely taxation and established favorable terms upon which returned emigrants would be allowed to settle on the land. Constantine Mavrocordato also either introduced or officially propagated the use of maize, which soon became the staple of the Rumanian peasantry's diet.

Of all these acts, the latter was undoubtedly the most influential. Mavrocordato's legal restrictions upon boyar oppression of the peasantry did not long remain effective, and his reforms of princely taxation did not even survive his own administration; for what had been designed as a quarterly rate of taxation came to be collected five, six, and presently twelve times a year! Nevertheless, the acute phase of agrarian unsettlement which struck Wallachia in the 1740's faded away quite rapidly after the middle of the century. It seems highly likely that the spread of maize cultivation was primarily responsible for this phenomenon. By the nineteenth cen-

[10] One contemporary Austrian asserted that three-quarters of the Wallachian peasants emigrated between 1741 and 1748. This seems certainly to be exaggerated, but attests the importance of the movement. Cf. R. W. Seton-Watson, *A History of the Roumanians* (Cambridge: Cambridge University Press, 1934), p. 141.

[11] Constantine Mavrocordato shuttled back and forth between the Wallachian and Moldavian thrones more often than any other single individual. He reigned no fewer than eleven times in all, across a period of thirty-nine years, between 1730 and 1769.

tury, it had become customary for the peasants of Wallachia and Moldavia to make corn meal mush the staple of their diet, while consigning practically all of the wheat they raised to export.

This pattern probably established itself very rapidly after maize was first introduced. On the one hand, the American crop produced abundantly in Rumanian soil and climate, and for a long time the urban populations of the Ottoman Empire refused to alter their food habits to make any use of the yellow grains. Hence the peasants were able to raise a food for themselves which was effectually exempt from the rapacity of tax and rent collectors, who had no use for the new crop. With such a suddenly expanded food supply, it seems probable that the Rumanian population began to increase with unexampled rapidity, allowing the peasantry to maintain or increase its numbers at home while sustaining a flow of emigrants into adjacent and hitherto almost unpopulated Russian and Austrian territories. Simultaneously, the attraction of the lands beyond the Ottoman frontier rapidly diminished as serfdom and normal imperial taxation were introduced into Austrian and Russian new lands.

It should be emphasized that this reconstruction of the course of Rumanian agricultural and demographic developments in the latter half of the eighteenth century remains largely hypothetical. What is sure is simply that the crisis of the 1740's failed to come to a head. Princely revenues, boyar rents, and peasant reserves for seed and food continued to divide the agricultural product of the country along customary lines that were not effectively regulated by public officials in accord with princely fiat, despite Constantine Mavrocordato's efforts to redefine these relations. Such stability even in the face of twice-repeated war and military occupation was probably due to the new security peasant life had attained by use of a food others despised.[12]

[12] Cf. the manner in which Irish peasants circumvented the Cromwellian settlement of Ireland by falling back upon another American crop, the potato, which allowed them to escape tithes and live cheaper, thereby undercutting English and Scottish immigrants who disdained to eat anything but wheat or oaten bread.

The political and economic history of the Rumanian provinces between 1740 and 1800 should therefore be considered a modest triumph for Ottoman and Phanariot conservatism, all the more striking in view of the increasing disparity between Turkish and Russian military strength. The same cannot, however, be said of the cultural history of the two provinces, for the Phanariot effort to surround the court life and higher culture of the two provinces with a deliberately revived stateliness of Byzantine splendor, thereby insulating themselves from both Turkish and Western challenges to their cultural autonomy, fell upon evil days as soon as French manners and political ideas began to knock insistently at the Phanariots' doors.

Constantine Mavrocordato was among the first of the Phanariot princes who had been educated to familiarity with French language and literature. His successors continued to command this sort of education, for the diplomatic service of the Ottoman Empire, in which the Phanariot princes were usually trained, now required mastery of French, the international language of European diplomacy. French tutors and nurses supplemented the labors of French secretaries, and beginning in 1776, a nine-year course of instruction in French was instituted in the higher school of Bucharest. As a result, a good many leading Phanariot families began to live not in two, but in three separate and distinct worlds at once: the real world of Ottoman intrigue and fiscality, where ruthlessness was the usual price of survival; the Byzantine world of the past, whose glories now tended to recede from the secular and concentrate more exclusively upon the ecclesiastical realm; and the new rationalist and secularist world of the French enlightenment, opened to leading Phanariots by their childhood inoculation with the French language.

To live in two worlds, the Ottoman and the Byzantine, was difficult enough, and it had required geographical separation

Maize played a somewhat similar role in many regions of the southern Balkans as well, where its cultivation was associated with the spread of commercial agriculture from the seventeenth century. Cf. Traian Stoianovich and Georges C. Haupt, "Le mäis arrive dans les Balkans," *Annals (Economics, Sociétés, Civilizations)*, XVII (1962), 84–93.

from Constantinople for the Byzantine ideal to attain any real expression in the late seventeenth and early eighteenth centuries. But to live simultaneously in three worlds was more than even the supple intellects of Phanariot princes and courtiers could ordinarily achieve. Consequently, the vividness of the dream of restored Byzantium faded without ever being formally repudiated.

At the same time, glib familiarity with the latest intellectual fashions of French salons could not escape an aura of unreality. Constantine Mavrocordato, indeed, justified his legislation on behalf of the Rumanian peasantry by referring to the natural rights of man, but this may have been no more than a convenient rhetorical flourish. Certainly no prince was so doctrinaire as to try to apply the ideas of radical French theorists to the governance of the Rumanian provinces; but in failing to make such an attempt, while continuing to indulge in the language of French political thought as a parlor exercise to demonstrate superior sophistication and perhaps as a device for attacking Turkish institutions without having to face responsibility for making practical improvements, the Phanariots and the princely circles in Constantinople, Bucharest, and Jassy surrendered intellectual seriousness. They became, indeed, an intelligentsia, analogous in most respects to the class of displaced spirits of nineteenth-century Russia who by flaunting systematic discrepancies between their words and deeds first brought the phenomenon (and the term) to the attention of western Europeans.

The psychological situation of Phanariot princes and courtiers in the latter decades of the eighteenth century was further complicated by the emergence of a "Dacian" or "Rumanian" alternative to the Byzantine ideal their predecessors had been able unambiguously to accept. The principal center of this idea lay across the Carpathians in Austrian territory, where Roman Catholic propaganda made considerable progress among Rumanian-speaking populations. Official Austrian support of Catholicism helped to forward the movement; so did the discovery that the Wallachian dialect was a Latin tongue, tied to Rome by the fact that its speakers were putatively descended either from Romanized Dacians or from the Roman legionaries Trajan had planted in his newly conquered province at the beginning of the second century A.D.[13]

It was not really until after the period of time with which we are here concerned that this "Rumanian" idea found any strong echo in Wallachia and Moldavia, yet the Russo-Austrian alliance against Turkey, concluded in 1781, could only be sustained by projecting a future "Dacia" that would serve as a buffer between the two Christian empires after the Ottoman state had been sheared of its outlying provinces and replaced in its heartlands by a revivified Byzantine Empire. This "Greek scheme" descended from plans for a general Orthodox rising in the Balkans in support of Peter the Great's campaigns against the Turks at the beginning of the century. It came to a climax in the tragicomedy of the "Philike Hetereia," whose plotting precipitated the Greek war of independence in 1821, an event which, instead of restoring Byzantine greatness, destroyed the Phanariot power utterly and forever. Such an upshot could not have been foreseen in the eighteenth century, when orthodox neo-Byzantinism, Catholic Daco-Rumanianism, and secularist Francophilism all competed for the attention and affection of the cultural leaders of Wallachia and Moldavia. From the resultant clangor, complicated by recurrent wars and military occupation, only moral confusion, ruthless self-seeking, and unscrupulous intrigue could be expected to emerge. The two provinces, in effect, found themselves once more awkwardly torn between rival and mutually incompatible cultural worlds, as they had been before, in the sixteenth-seventeenth centuries. Their ingenious effort to escape from this dilemma by constructing a Byzantine alternative had failed.

[13] This assertion in due course precipitated a counter Magyar school of historiography designed to prove that the Rumanians were recent intruders on Transylvanian and Hungarian soil. Hungarian and Transylvanian history has yet to recover from this essentially anachronistic projection of nineteenth-century national quarrels upon the past.

Even among the Crim Tartars, where Islam created an all but insuperable barrier against the penetration of Western culture, there were individuals who found it amusing to discuss the latest fashions of thought, watch experiments with electricity, and even to read translations of French literature. For example, Khan Krim Gerai, who held office from 1758–64 and again 1768–70, corresponded with Frederick the Great and for several months entertained Baron de Tott, a Hungarian adventurer in French service, showing considerable interest in what De Tott told him of Western ways. Yet when the Tartars commenced the war against Russia in 1768 with a destructive raid into "New Serbia" and the Polish Ukraine, their mode of operation — and the emphasis upon the capture of slaves — was completely traditional.[14] Clearly, the strange tales Baron de Tott and others had to tell about the West seemed merely titillating to their Tartar audiences, not matters for serious study, or calling for any adjustment in familiar institutions and habits.

Tartar reaction to the West remained entirely on this dilettante level until the Russians discovered a suitable puppet through whom to assert their influence in the Crimea: Shahin Girai, khan from 1777–83. But Shahin Girai's efforts to save Tartar independence by creating an army and navy on European lines never had a chance. He simply provoked the distrust of both Russians and Turks and precipitated a series of disturbances among the Tartars themselves which provided the excuse for the final Russian seizure of the Crimea.

Austrian sphere. The lands recovered by Hapsburg arms from Ottoman rule fell under two very different administrative systems. The geographically larger part had since 1712 been folded into the pre-existing constitutional regimes of Hungary, Croatia, or Transylvania; but along the Turkish border a belt of territory was retained under direct imperial administration. The social development of these two regions

[14] Cf. the vivid account of his experiences in François Baron de Tott, *Memoirs of Baron de Tott, Containing the State of the Turkish Empire and the Crimea during the Late War with Russia* (London: G. G. J. and J. Robinson, 1785) , I, 135 ff.

in the latter part of the eighteenth century diverged sharply. In the border areas, bureaucratic rationality and enterprise found almost unhampered scope. Imperial officials brought in settlers, built towns and villages *de novo* according to systematic plans, and created a new society of peasant farmers, all within little more than a decade. In the rest of Hungary, development was comparatively slow and unsystematic, depending more on the natural increase of the peasantry than on the initiative of noble landowners whose entrepreneurial energies in most cases concentrated on legal and political struggles to the exclusion of mere economics.

Austrian achievements in the border regions closely resembled the Russian achievements in the Ukraine, with the difference that a smaller geographical scale of operation allowed also a greater degree of bureaucratic precision. Austrian plans tended to be worked out in far greater detail and then translated into physical fact with a degree of faithfulness to plan which was never attained in the free-wheeling atmosphere of Potemkin's Ukraine, where plans exceeded reality as wildly as reality outstripped the dreams of earlier generations.

During the reign of Maria Theresa (1740–80), Austrian bureaucratic activity in the border regions fell into fairly distinct phases. From her accession until 1761, the problems of the Turkish borderlands were dealt with primarily by the War Council (*Hofkriegsrat*). Problems were handled on a more or less *ad hoc* and local basis. At the beginning of Maria Theresa's reign, the empress inherited a tangled and angry situation on the military frontiers, where conflicting jurisdiction between the *Hofkriegsrat* in Vienna and agents appointed by the estates of Inner Austria (which had long been specially connected with the Grenzers) had led to bitter quarrels. Proposals for centralizing jurisdiction in Vienna were finally put through in 1747; simultaneously the Grenzer regiments were reorganized to conform to the muster of the regiments of the line, and stricter rules separating the civil from the Grenzer population of the border were instituted.

The reorganized Grenzer regiments proved their military

value in the War of Austrian Succession (1740–48) and the Seven Years' War (1756–63), where their prowess as skirmishers sent out in advance of the line or posted on the flanks to harass the opposing army with enfilading fire presented the drillmasters of eighteenth-century armies with a tactical challenge they were not yet ready to accept.[15] Nevertheless, Austrian military authorities recognized their usefulness and regularly defended Grenzer privileges and territorial autonomy against Magyar criticism. As the Turkish threat faded and dissolved, however, it became difficult for the *Hofkriegsrat* to justify retention of wide belts of territory which had initially been placed under military jurisdiction. Thus in 1751, military administration was withdrawn from the lower Theiss Valley, where a skeletal Grenzer organization had been developed during the period when that river in its lower course had constituted the border with Turkey (1699–1718). In 1799, again, most of the Banat was divided into counties and administratively incorporated into the Kingdom of Hungary, leaving only a comparatively slender frontier zone under military jurisdiction and organized by Grenzer regiments.

Up until 1761, settlement of the frontier zone was the concern of the *Hofkriegsrat*, and recruitment was mainly local. Serbs, Rumanians, and other Orthodox populations were the most easily available and readiest to submit to the discipline of military command in return for land and exemption from ordinary taxation. No Magyar noble could accept a position in the ranks; no Magyar serf was legally free to enlist; hence new Grenzer settlements drew their manpower from across Ottoman frontiers, where freer and only semi-sessile styles of agricultural life prevailed. Some criminals were sent to the Banat from Vienna as settlers; but this was a small trickle, totaling only 3,130 persons between 1752 and 1768.[16]

Clearly, criminals and Orthodox immigrants whose tradi-

[15] Far away on the other flank of Europe's expansion, armed American backwoodsmen offered a similar challenge, as British regulars in both the French and Indian War and the War of American Independence discovered.

[16] Konrad Schünemann, *Osterreichs Bevölkerungspolitik unter Maria Theresia* (Berlin: Deutsche Rundschau, 1935), p. 78.

tional style of agriculture was of the slash-and-burn variety did not make very good material for the agricultural and economic development of the border regions. But by the second half of the eighteenth century, many officials in Vienna had come to believe that systematic development of economic resources and population was the secret of political and military strength and saw in the military borders a region where constitutional obstacles to their initiatives were minimal. Particularly during the Seven Years' War, when Austrian officials had a chance to see with their own eyes what the Prussians had been able to accomplish in Silesia in the short time since that province had been seized by Frederick the Great's armies, the determination to embark upon a more systematic, centralized program of economic development gained momentum among the high officials of the empire.

When the war ended (1763), this line of thought coalesced with administrative problems raised by the need to fit demobilized veterans, some of them partially disabled, into civil society again. A happy solution was to offer them land and initial subvention if they would pioneer the fertile but undeveloped regions of Banat and Bachka. This program was supplemented by efforts to recruit settlers from German lands outside Austrian borders. Transportation, land, initial capital, and tax exemption for a period of years were offered such immigrants. These inducements were such that between 1762 and 1772, when the program was in full operation, a total of about 11,000 German families were settled in the Banat under official, government aegis.[17] Others came from Lorraine, Belgium, Italy, and elsewhere, but the German immigration far outweighed all the other strands and sufficed to establish a fairly numerous "Swabian" population along the Danube from its junction with the Sava as far as the Iron Gates.

These settlers brought with them the techniques of west European high farming. New crops like potatoes and tobacco were introduced, the latter in particular offering a product which was light enough in proportion to its value to make transport, even by animal pack train, to distant urban markets

[17] K. Schünemann, *Osterreichs Bevölkerungspolitik*, p. 373.

a practicable proposition. Viticulture had previously been almost the sole form of commercial cropping known to Hungary; and on suitable soils, this, too, was skilfully pursued by the newcomers. In addition, effective methods for draining fields that in their natural state lay waterlogged for several months of the year were introduced from Holland and northwest Germany, where similar problems had long since been solved; and such improved implements as an experimentally designed moldboard plow capable of turning a furrow over neatly, even when confronted by tough-rooted native grasses of the steppe, made it possible for the newcomers to transform empty grasslands and fever-ridden swamps into smiling fields within a generation.

Their farmsteads and villages were laid out by surveyors on geometrically regular lines; houses duplicated the architecture of western Germany. Such outward distinguishing marks combined with the canny ethos of what soon became a prosperous, independent peasantry to set the newcomers off sharply from their neighbors, whether Magyar, Serb, or Rumanian.

Some gestures were made toward industrial and urban development, but Austrian officialdom refrained from any very active effort to establish industry in Hungary and the other eastern regions of the empire. Official inaction was matched by popular indifference. The "Swabian" and other immigrants were land hungry and land proud. They were little inclined to send their sons into artisan trades, preferring a professional or official career for those sons who could not inherit land. Hence the planned development of the frontier zone and its spontaneous aftermath agreed in stabilizing the economy at a not too intensive agricultural occupation of the soil. The new farms were comparatively large and were seldom subdivided, for in later generations the peasant owners became extremely conscious of the possession of land as a measure of economic and social status. Careful husbanding of family resources often made it possible to send surplus sons away to distant German schools or universities, while one son remained at home to inherit the whole farm. By this device, even a prolific family could escape the social disgrace of either subdividing the family land or sending sons into local towns as landless artisans. But, correspondingly, intensification of agricultural exploitation and the pace of local urban development were both reduced.

The effective ceiling of economic development in the Austrian borderlands was thus achieved rather quickly. By the close of Maria Theresa's reign, immigration practically ceased, for nearly all suitable land had been allocated to settlers. The real agricultural boom lasted therefore little more than a decade, but that sufficed to transform the landscape and transplant a German type of society to the southeasternmost frontier of the empire.

Nothing of the sort ever happened in the main part of the Danubian plain. In Hungary, Croatia, and Transylvania, ancient constitutional practices prevented the free exercise of bureaucratic initiative, and the economic initiative of the dominant noble and landowning class was sporadic and usually not very effective. The central problem was transport. Agricultural development and systematic settlement could only bring in tangible returns for a landowner if there were a ready market for the grain or other products of the soil. But central Hungary and Transylvania were separated from major urban markets by hopelessly expensive overland portages.

The map would suggest that the Danube and its affluents offered Hungary a ready-made transport network as good or better than that which made large-scale commercial agriculture feasible in the Ukraine and Poland. But this was not in fact the case until after elaborate and expensive navigational improvements had been made. The rivers of the Hungarian plain were flanked by extensive swamps, created by the ponding back of spring floods behind the natural levees that formed along the river courses. These swamps absolutely prevented access to the main stream during most of the year, at least for heavy goods. Moreover, the stream beds abounded in shifting sandbanks, log jams, and other hindrances to navigation; and many streams cut extremely circuitous meanders across the flat plain, so that cross-country progress required many times as many miles of river travel.

The only solution for these geographical difficulties was extensive canalization through artificial drainage and embankment. But such works required vast expenditures; and the Magyar nobles of the eighteenth century, even if they could conceive the physical possibility of taming the rivers that made their country what it was, were absolutely unwilling to pay the costs of any such program. In effect, the traditional claim of the Hungarian nobility to entire exemption from taxation prohibited large-scale public works of the sort required to create a river transport system in the central Hungarian plain.[18]

The result of this geographical-constitutional deadlock was that Hungarian wheat and other agricultural products could not be exported in any quantity to Vienna or to any other market. Livestock, being able to travel to market on its own legs, was a different matter. Cattle, horses, sheep, and pigs remained therefore the principal cash crop of the Hungarian plain. Agricultural development lagged correspondingly behind. Nevertheless, population increased, for the devastation of war and local violence, which had been chronic in Hungary for three hundred years, was sharply reduced after 1711; and populations whose demographic habits were attuned to survival under such precarious conditions could be expected to grow substantially when attrition through death by violence ceased to be statistically very important. But it was a poverty-stricken, oppressed, and economically unenterprising serf population that increased; a population of resentful men who knew that any labor they might undertake to increase the

[18] Road building, an obvious alternative to river improvement, confronted almost equally paralyzing difficulties, for the alluvial soils of the Alföld lacked rock and gravel. But without abundant application of these porous materials to the water-logged land surface of central Hungary, all-weather roads were impossible.

Hence, until well into the nineteenth century, overland travel was effectively restricted to horseback — or shank's mare.

produce of the soil would simply increase their noble masters' receipts.

Under these circumstances, it is not strange that Hungarian agriculture remained technically backward, and the Magyar social structure archaic. In 1777, for example, the towns of Hungary were recorded as containing only 31,000 industrially employed persons. Only five towns had a population of more than 20,000; and the largest, Debrecen, totaled a mere 30,000, of whom many were in fact cultivators, who preferred, in accordance with a very ancient Magyar custom,[19] to live in great village agglomerates, even if it meant having to travel long distances to their fields. A census of Hungary in 1787 arrived at a total population of almost 6.5 million; yet only 5,001 persons were listed as civil servants and members of the free professions. At the same time, one hundred and eight families owned about one-third of all the land of Hungary.[20]

Even at the end of the eighteenth century, therefore, Hungary exhibited a remarkably insulated, strongly medieval, strangely vestigial social and economic structure, which the progress of population did nothing to alter.

Among the nobility, changes pointing toward an eventual more perfect incorporation of the Hungarian body social into the familiar patterns of western European civilization were not entirely wanting in the latter part of the eighteenth century. Slowly but irresistibly, the psychological seduction whereby the Hapsburg court had weaned the magnates from narrow Magyardom in the earlier decades of the eighteenth century tended to seep down to the lesser nobility. Acculturation of the rude Magyar gentry to Viennese styles and sensibilities occurred mainly as a by-product of service in the imperial army. Honorific appointment to the Royal Hungarian Bodyguard was particularly effective. This corps, established by Maria Theresa, was recruited by annual ap-

[19] On this phenomenon, see A. N. J. den Hollander, "The Great Hungarian Plain: A European Frontier Area," *Comparative Studies in Society and History*, III (1960–61), 74–88, 155–69.
[20] These statistics come from C. A. Macartney, *Hungary: A Short History* (Edinburgh: Edinburgh University Press, 1962), pp. 98, 105, 111.

pointment of two young men from each county of Hungary, who were chosen by the local nobles at their periodic assemblies. The successful candidates then were posted to the court for a period of five years, after which they might take up regular service in the Hapsburg army or return home to the life of country gentlemen if they preferred.

The gradual process of acculturation that such experiences carried with them did something to relieve the sulky distrust with which the Magyar gentry had regarded Hapsburg power in the first decades of the eighteenth century. Sometimes, however, exposure to the great world had unexpected consequences. For a few of the young men of the Royal Bodyguard returned home imbued not with a spirit of loyalty to the Hapsburg regime, but with radical ideas that were subversive both of Hapsburg imperial and of traditional Magyar institutions. A handful of such idealistic malcontents started a literary circle as early as 1761, aiming at the purification and literary development of the Magyar tongue. The revived language they then used to disseminate radical and rationalist ideas derived primarily from the French *philosophes*.

At the other extreme, the old distrust of Hapsburg intentions was kept alive even during Maria Theresa's reign by her failure to conform to some of the constitutional prescriptions she had sworn to uphold. In her whole reign she only called three Diets (1741, 1751, 1764) and allowed the office of palatine to lapse after 1764. Moreover, such new enterprises as the colonization of southern and eastern Hungary, customs regulations, and educational reform were put into force by imperial decree. By a strict interpretation of Hungarian constitutional law, all such measures were not truly valid and binding since the Diet had not given consent. Much more important was legislation regulating and restricting the labor services that could legally be demanded of the peasants by their masters. The empress called the Diet in 1764 in the hope of persuading the nobles to give up their traditional exemption from taxation and accept official regulation of their rights over their serfs. When the Diet declined to accept such proposals, it was dissolved and the Empress never summoned another one. On prudential grounds she refrained from attempting to collect taxes from the recalcitrant nobility, but Maria Theresa did undertake regulation of noble-serf relations by resorting to the dubious legality of imperial decree — the so-called "Urbarium."

Such acts provided suspicious Magyar nobles with ample grounds for accusing the Hapsburgs of constitutional usurpation. The far more radical deeds of Joseph II (1780–90) confirmed their worst expectations and once again turned almost all the Magyar gentry into agitated enemies of the Hapsburgs.

Joseph's refusal to undergo the rituals of coronation and his decision that German should replace Latin as the language of administration offered emotionally vibrant symbols around which Magyar resistance rallied; but it was his intention — never carried through — of abolishing the old county organization and introducing centralized administrative districts controlled by officials appointed from Vienna, together with his judicial reforms depriving lords of jurisdiction over their peasants, that would have really revolutionalized the Hungarian social structure.

Joseph's intended revolution from above was, however, soon countered by revolution from below, and on two levels. Rumanian serfs raised bloody rebellion against their Magyar masters in 1784. Sympathetic tremors of unrest ran through most of Hungary, when Magyar and Slovak peasants began to believe distorted reports of the emperor's plans for trimming the power and privileges of the Magyar nobility. Simultaneously, among the nobles themselves, a different revolutionary spirit spread, aimed at radical preservation of their collective rights and privileges in the name, however, of such new-fangled notions as the rights of man, social contract, general will, and other imports fresh from France. These notions had recently been put into circulation by the radical literary circle founded by disenchanted graduates of the Royal Hungarian Bodyguard. The anomalous result was that during Joseph's short and troubled reign, in the minds of the Magyar gentry radical reaction and reactionary radicalism entered upon a perfect, if transitory, marriage. This meeting of extremes, presumed in the context of western Europe to be incompatible, recapitulated the sociological character assumed by Hungarian Protestantism in the sixteenth and seventeenth centuries and presaged the even more flamboyantly reactionary liberalism of Louis Kossuth (1848–50) and his heirs in the nineteenth.

After Joseph's death, his brother Leopold II (1790–92) was able to stave off open revolt by restoring the constitution, i.e., by accepting coronation as king of Hungary and agreeing to a law which guaranteed triennial Diets and required that all legislation be approved by the Diet before it could have legal force. When Francis II succeeded to the Hapsburg throne in 1792, he accepted Leopold's policy of professing at least an outward respect for the Hungarian constitution. His decision was made much easier by the fact the alliance between radicals and reactionaries in Hungary broke apart when a handful of youthful Magyar ideologues (perhaps stimulated by agents of the French republic) entered upon a "Jacobin" conspiracy which, being duly detected by the police, cost several of them their lives (1794).

The social implications of revolution in the French style had by this time become quite clear to the Magyar serf owners. They therefore emphatically repudiated the "Jacobinism" that had a few years before seemed so attractive and rallied around Hapsburg banners for the long war against France which began in 1792. Prolonged and frequently distinguished service in the Hapsburg armies during the ensuing two decades wedded thousands of Magyar noblemen to the Hapsburgs, just as Maria Theresa's wars had done in the eighteenth century, and in the process Europeanized them in a deeper and more intimate sense than their forefathers had ever previously been Europeanized.

Even when this process had been carried to its furthest point, strong traces of Hungary's peculiar past remained among the gentry, and the peasant serfs continued to inhabit a world apart. The same was true in Pontic Europe, where the European manners and intellectual culture of Ukrainian landowners and Odessa merchants did not suffice to bring the dark and deaf peasantry into the circle of European civilization in any but an imperfect — physical rather than psychological — sense.

The old frontier zone of southeastern Europe had, in short, not lost its own distinctive characteristics by 1800; and assimilation to the political, social, economic, and psychological conditions of western Europe was far from perfect. Yet the open frontier had disappeared. Empty land suitable for cultivation no longer dominated the landscape, and what remained untilled was nearly all assigned to private ownership and effectively enfolded into the territorial administration of one or other bureaucratic empire. The Rumanian provinces were in process of an awkward transition from Ottoman-Byzantine to Russo-Western cultural affiliations. But the only effective choice lay between two foreign models. The days of genuine autochthony, whether in economics, politics, or manners were long since past throughout the entire length of Danubian and Pontic Europe.

This, therefore, seems an appropriate point at which to break off our study, when the open frontier upon the steppe, which had been an enduring feature of European geography for more than 2,500 years, ceased to exist anywhere west of the Don; and before the irruption of the still uncivilized peasantries of southwestern Europe upon the political scene (a movement in which, incidentally, Ottoman territories led the way) gave Danubian and Pontic Europe of the nineteenth and twentieth centuries its own distinctive historical character.

T
BIBLIOGRAPHICAL ESSAY

HOUGH A majority of books treating the history of Danubian and Pontic Europe ask questions different from those raised in the foregoing essay, and therefore only incidentally cast light on matters specially interesting to me, there are a few works that contributed fundamentally to my understanding and pointed my investigations in the direction they took. Accidents such as the order in which I happened to read particular works have something to do with their relative importance for this essay. Thus, for example, Albert H. Lybyer, *The Government of the Ottoman Empire in the Time of Suleiman the Magnificent* (Cambridge, Mass.: Harvard University Press, 1913) constituted a fundamental frame within which my understanding of Ottoman history gradually formed. Yet it was with a sense of release from a constricting schema that I read Norman Itzkowitz' "Eighteenth-Century Ottoman Realities," *Studia Islamica*, XVI (1962) 73–94, which takes brusque issue with Lybyer's schematic analysis of Turkish institutions. Unfortunately, Stanford J. Shaw's bold and illuminating essay, "The Ottoman View of the Balkans," published in Charles and Barbara Jelavich (eds.), *The Balkans in Transition: Essays on the Development of Balkan Life and Politics since the 18th century* (Berkeley: University of California Press, 1963), pp. 56–80, reached me only as the typescript of this essay was being readied for the printer. His analysis of Ottoman society seems generally to be consonant with my less expert notions, even though he uses a quite different set of terms.

Three major landmarks lay between my encounter with these works: Paul Witteck, *The Rise of the Ottoman Empire* (London: Royal Asiatic Society, 1938), a masterpiece of compression; H. A. R Gibb and Harold Bowen, *Islamic Society and the West, I: Islamic Society in the Eighteenth Century*, Parts 1 and 2 (London: Oxford University Press, 1950, 1957), a storehouse of data, not always perfectly put together; and the monumental, vast, and imposing classic, Joseph Freiherr von Hammer-Purgstall, *Geschichte des osmanischen Reiches* (10 vols.; Pesth: C. A. Hartleben Verlag, 1827–35), whose antique bulk had long frightened me off. In fact, however, Von Hammer turns out to be suprisingly interesting. His lengthy paraphrases of Turkish chronicles and other sources are interspersed with some very shrewd and persuasive observations on the nature of Turkish institutions and society; and his remorseless presentation of what happened in all available detail allows someone with questions of his own in mind to scoop up data and illustrative episodes by the bucketful.

Works less central for my understanding of Ottoman history, but vigorously contributory nonetheless, include: Richard Busch-Zanter, *Agrarverfassung, Gesellschaft und Siedlung in Südosteuropa, unter besonderer Berücksichtigkeit der Türkenherrschaft* (Leipzig: Otto Harrassowitz, 1938); Halil Inalchik, "Land Problems in Turkish History," *The Muslim World*, XLV (1955), 221–28; Walter L. Wright, *Ottoman Statecraft: A Book of Counsel for Viziers and Governors* (Princeton, N.J.: Princeton University Press, 1935); Theodor Menzel, "Das Korps der Janitscharen," *Beiträge zur Kenntnis des Orients*, I (1902–3), 47–94; Traian Stoianovich, "The Conquering Balkan Orthodox Merchant," *Journal of Economic History*, XX (1960), 234–313; Traian Stoianovich, "Land Tenure and Related Sectors of the Balkan Economy," *Journal of Economic History*, XIII (1953), 398–411; Franz Babinger, *Mehmet der Eroberer und seine Zeit* (Munich: F. Bruckmann, 1953); L. S. Stavrianos, *The Balkans since 1453* (New York: Rinehart & Co., 1958); and Nikolai Jorga, *Geschichte des osmanischen Reiches* (5 vols.; Gotha: E. A. Perthes, 1908–13). The other famous, massive history of the Ottoman Empire, Johann Wilhelm Zinkeisen, *Geschichte des osmanischen Reiches in Europa* (7 vols.; Hamburg: F. Perthes, 1840; Gotha: F. Perthes, 1854–63), I have yet to explore; but casual leafing through some of its pages did not suggest that Zinkeisen had much to add to what could be gleaned from Hammer-Purgstall's and Jorga's already multitudinous pages.

Anyone approaching the area afresh would do well to start off with four books I happened to read rather late in the game: Dorothy Vaughn, *Europe and the Turk: A Pattern of Alliances, 1350–1800* (Liverpool: Liverpool University Press, 1954), an admirable diplomatic history, marred only slightly by a few disproportionate excursuses; B. H. Sumner, *Peter the Great and the Ottoman Empire* (Oxford: Basil Blackwell, 1949), a learned, perceptive little essay; Georg Stadtmüller, *Geschichte Südosteuropas* (Munich: R. Oldenbourg, 1950), a good, brief survey; and the magistral work of Fernand Braudel, *La Méditerranée et le monde méditerranéan à l'époque de Philippe II*[e] (Paris: Librairie Armand Colin, 1949), which, however, allows the currents of the Dardanelles to exclude the Black Sea from its purview.

The numerous books dealing with Hapsburg history as a whole nearly all fasten their gaze so intently upon relations westward as to leave but little attention for the eastern frontier. Hugo Hantsch, *Geschichte Oesterreichs* (2 vols.; Graz: Verlag Styria, 1947), and the monument to the English alliance with Austria against Napoleon, William Coxe, *History of the House of Austria 1278–1792* (first published in 1807, and republished in the edition I used at the time of the Crimean War) [3 vols.; London: H. G. Bohn, 1854–64], were the books I used for refreshing my memory as to names, dates, and events. Special mention should be made of the little monograph, Gunther Erich Rothenberg, *The Austrian Military Border in Croatia, 1522–1747* (Illinois Studies in the Social Sciences, Vol. XLVIII [Urbana: University of Illinois Press, 1960], which provided much useful information about the Grenzers.

Russian historiography remains a great reservoir that I have barely sampled. Boris Nolde, *La Formation de l'empire russe: études, notes et documents* (2 vols.; Paris: Institut d'études slaves, 1953), was by far the most useful book I encountered. Nolde's second volume deals with the incorporation of the Ukraine and Crimea into Russia and achieves an irenic detachment from the clash of nationalisms which so often disfigures Ukrainian history. In addition, B. H. Sumner, *Survey of Russian History* (London: Gerald Ducksworth & Co., 1944), has some perceptive things to say about the frontier in Russian history; and George Vernadsky, *Russia at the Dawn of the Modern Age* (New Haven, Conn.: Yale University Press, 1959), though he treats of events only to 1530, discusses conditions in the west Russian lands, then under Polish sovereignty, in terms applicable also to considerably later times. Two articles were helpful in confirming and extending my notions about the nature of the Russian nobility: Mark Raeff, "Staatsdienst, Aussenpolitik, Ideologien: die Rolle der Institutionen in der geistigen Entwicklung des russischen Adels im 18. Jahrhundert," *Jahrbücher für Geschichte Osteuropas*, VII (1959), 147–81; and Karl-Heinz Ruffmann, "Russischer Adel als Sondertypus der europäischen Adelswelt," *ibid.*, IX (1961), 161–78. Both are penetrating, learned, and persuasive.

Three books dealing specifically with the Ukraine I found particularly good. W. E. D. Allen, *The Ukraine; A History* (Cambridge University Press, 1940), is a fine piece of work upon which I relied both for the narrative of events and for many insights into social changes that lay behind them. Gunter Stökl, *Die Entstehung des Kossakentums* (*Veröffentlichungen des Osteuropa-Instituts, München*, Vol. III [Munich: Isar Verlag, 1953]), and N. D. Połonska-Vasylenko, *The Settlement of the Southern Ukraine, 1750 till 1775* (*Annals of the Ukrainian Academy of Arts and Sciences in the United States*, Vol. IV/V, No. 4) were both very useful to me, although the latter is marred by its persistently outraged Ukrainian national feeling. I stumbled upon Claude J. Nordmann, *Charles XII et l'Ukraine de Mazepa* (Paris: R. Pichon and R. Durand-Anzias, 1958) only after writing this book, but admired what I there saw.

Of all the polities touched upon in this essay, the Crim Tartars have fared by far the worst in Western historiography. The indefatigable Freiherr Joseph von Hammer-Purgstall compiled his *Geschichte der Chane der Krim unter osmanischer Herrschaft* (Vienna: K. und K. Hof- und Staatsdruckerei, 1856) from Turkish and other chronicles. Henry

H. Howorth, *History of the Mongols from the 9th to the 19th Century* (4 vols.; London: Longmans, Green & Co., 1876–1927), devotes a chapter of nearly two hundred pages in Part II, "The So-Called Tartars of Russia and Central Asia," to the Crimean khans, using approximately the same sources as Hammer-Purgstall had used before him. Aside from these two bald paraphrases of local chronicles, travelers' accounts (see below), and the useful essay by Nicholaus Ernst, "Die ersten Einfälle der Krymtartaren in Südrussland," *Zeitschrift für Osteuropäische Geschichte*, III (1913), 1–59, there seems to be nothing worth mentioning in any language available to me. A modest effort by anyone able to read both Turkish and Russian ought here to reap real reward. The Crimean Tartars are certainly worth a modern study, and materials are not lacking.

For the history of the Rumanian provinces, N. Jorga, *Geschichte des rumänischen Volkes in Rahmen seiner Staatsbildungen* (2 vols.; Gotha: F. A. Perthes, 1904–5) is both fuller and less disfigured by patriotism than his later works, N. Iorga, *Histoire des Roumains de Transylvanie et de Hongrie* (2 vols.; Bucharest: Imprimerie Gutenberg, 1915–16); and N. Iorga, *A History of Roumania, Land, People, Civilization* (London: T. Fisher Unwin, 1925). R. W. Seton–Watson, *A History of the Roumanians from Roman Times to the Completion of Unity* (Cambridge: Cambridge University Press, 1934), is worth mentioning only to warn English-speaking readers of its deficiencies for the period with which this essay is concerned. Seton-Watson presents the most trifling explanations of, e.g., Phanariot corruption, and ladles out an uncritical, näive Rumanian patriotism at second hand. Three articles were far more helpful than any books in stimulating me to reappraise traditional disdain for the Phanariot period of Rumanian history, to wit: L. Sainéan, "Le régime et la société en Rumanie pendant le règne des Phanariotes, 1711–1821," *Revue internationale de sociologie*, X (1902), 717–48, which offers a vivid account full of picturesque details that recreate vanished splendors and the artificial atmosphere of court ritual; Joseph Gottwald,

"Phanariotische Studien," *Leipziger Vierteljahrsschrift für Südosteuropa,* V (1941), 1–58, which struck me as an ill-digested collection of bits of information, inspired, however, with a general sympathy for the Phanariots which has otherwise been almost entirely lacking in modern historiography; and N. Jorga, "Le déspotisme éclairé dans les pays Roumains au XVIIIe siècle, *"Bulletin of the International Committee of Historical Sciences,* IX (1937), 110–15, which despite its brevity offers important information I met nowhere else. Two other books deserve mention as superior presentations of rival national views upon the history of the Rumanians in Transylvania, where Magyar and Rumanian patriotisms have clashed particularly strongly: Alexandru Dimitrie Xénopol, *Histoire des Roumains de la Dacie trajane, depuis les origines jusqu'à l'union des principautés en 1859,* (2 vols.; Paris: E. Leroux, 1896), whose title is itself a manifesto; and the collection of essays, written from the Magyar point of view, Ladislaus Galdi and Ladislaus Makkai, *Geschichte der Rumänen* (Budapest: Ostmitteleuropäische Bibliothek, 1942). Finally, the sumptuous collective work of Communist historians, A. Otetea *et al.* (eds.), *Istoria Rominiei* (Bucharest: Editura Academiei Republicii Populare Romine, n.d.) contains much of interest even to someone who can only stumble through the Rumanian language by pretending it is Latinate French. The illustrations of Rumanian-Phanariot architecture alone are worth many pages of text.

Although the state of historiography dealing with Crim Tartars, the Ukraine, and the Rumanian provinces may be disappointing to anyone accustomed to the national histories of western Europe, the state of Hungarian and Polish historiography is even worse, if only because there is so much more of it, nearly all sadly distorted by narrow-minded nationalistic polemic. Since this essay touched only marginally upon Polish history, I made only a limited exploration of available materials, and found nothing I could admire. W. F. Reddaway, *et al.* (eds.), *The Cambridge History of Poland* (2 vols.; Cambridge: Cambridge University Press, 1941) is a very uneven collection of essays, compiled under the shadow of World War II, and Oscar Halecki, *A History of Poland* (new ed.; New York: Roy Publishers, 1956), were what I used for sampling Polish patriotism as applied to history. In addition, a second-rate monograph, Jan Rutkowski, *Histoire économique de la Pologne avant les partages* (Paris: H. Champion, 1927), provided some interesting data.

Hungarian historiography does not seem in quite such parlous state — perhaps because I have investigated its resources more thoroughly. Two recent slender volumes in English offer comparatively sophisticated, though still distinctly patriotic, accounts of the entire span of Hungarian history: Denis Sinor, *History of Hungary* (London: George Allen & Unwin, 1959); and Charles Aylmer Macartney, *Hungary: A Short History* (Edinburgh: Edinburgh University Press, 1962). Of these, Macartney's book is distinctly the better, being only mildly apologetic for Magyardom. Behind these recent essays there lies a small but solid tradition of scholarship able to rise above the immediate national controversies. Three books I found particularly useful: Henry Marczali, *Ungarische Verfassungsgeschichte* (Tübingen: J. C. B. Mohr, 1910), a lapidary work distilling generations of Magyar legalism into a precise, exact, and dispassionate account; Henry Marczali, *Hungary in the Eighteenth Century* (Cambridge: Cambridge University Press, 1910), which includes a fine survey of the state of the kingdom at the accession of Joseph II and achieves a tone of aloof majesty; and Franz Salamon, *Ungarn im Zeitalter der Türkenherrschaft* (Leipzig: Haessel, 1887), containing much information, mainly from the sixteenth century, imperfectly digested but admirably precise. A far more arid book is Albert Lefaivre, *Les Magyars pendant la domination ottomane en Hongrie, 1526–1722* (2 vols.; Paris: Librairie Perrin & Cie., 1902). I saw only the first volume of this work, which combined meticulous political narrative with intense Catholic piety and naïve anti-Turk sentimentality.

Transylvanian history has a semi-independent existence, just as the principality itself once had. Two books are really very good in bringing social, cultural, and economic conditions into relation with the complications of Transylvanian and Hungarian politics: Maja Depner, *Das Fürstentum Siebenbürgen im Kampf gegen Hapsburg. Untersuchungen über die Politik Siebenbürgens während des Dreissigjahrigen Krieges* (Stuttgart: W. Kohlhammer, 1938); and Ladislas Makkai, *Histoire de Translyvanie (Bibliothèque de la revue d'histoire comparée*, Vol. V [Paris: Presses universitaires, 1946]).

In addition, I discovered five articles that dealt in one way or another with intercultural exchanges within the Hungarian plain. With one exception, none of them added much to my thought, though they did confirm the fact that others are beginning to think along approximately similar lines. Trifling but interesting, with bits of information new to me, were: Robert Gragger, "Türkisch-ungarische Kulturbeziehungen in Literaturdenkmäler aus Ungarns Türkenzeit," *Ungarische Bibliothek* (Herausgegeben vom Ungarischen Institut an der Universität Berlin, erste Reihe [Berlin: Walter de Gruyter & Co., 1927); Charles d'Eszlary, "Les mussulmans hongrois du Moyen Âge," *Ibla, Revue d'instituts des belles-lettres arabes* (Tunis), XIX (1956) 375–86; Charles d'Eszlary, "L'administration et la vie dans la Hongrie occupée par les Turcs au cours des 16ᵉ et 17ᵉ siècles," *ibid.*, XX (1957) 351–68; and A. N. J. Hollander, "The Great Hungarian Plain: A European Frontier Area," *Comparative Studies in Society and History*, III (1960–61), 74–88. Far more valuable was the splendid, penetrating analysis of Magyar intellectual and social history offered by Peter F. Sugar, "The Influence of the Enlightenment and the French Revolution in 18th-Century Hungary," *Journal of Central European Affairs*, XVII (1958), 331–55.

Religious history of Danubian and Pontic Europe is, in some ways, better treated than political-national histories of the region, perhaps because the clashes between rival faiths lost some of their erstwhile sharpness as secular nationalisms arose to supplant older religious lines of demarcation. Moreover, relations with Rome, Geneva, Wittenberg, Stamboul are taken for granted, so that the religious history of the region, as it were automatically, becomes a story of cross-cultural competitions, not a paean of praise for a more or less arbitrarily isolated compartment called a nation. The books I found most informative and useful were: Frederick W. Hasluck, *Christianity and Islam under the Sultans* (2 vols.; Oxford: Clarendon Press, 1929); John Kingsley Birge, *The Bektashi Order of Dervishes* (London: Luzac & Co., 1937); Laszlo Hadrovics, *Le Peuple serbe et son église sous la domination turque* (Paris: Presses universitaires, 1947); Ernst Benz, *Wittenberg und Byzanz, zur Begegnung und Auseinandersetzung der Reformation und der östlich-orthodoxen Kirche* (Marburg: Elwert-Gräfe and Unzer Verlag, 1949); Michaly Bucsay, *Geschichte des Protestantismus in Ungarn* (Stuttgart: Evangelisches Verlagswerk, 1959); Grete Mecenseffy, *Geschichte des Protestantismus in Oesterreich* (Graz-Cologne: Herman Bohlaus, 1956). I discovered no good treatment of the Counter Reformation as a whole in our region. This is a theme deserving a good book. Two popularizations were also helpful: George A. Hadjiantoniou, *Protestant Patriarch: The Life of Cyril Loukaris, 1572–1638* (Richmond, Va.: John Knox Press, 1961), which is a laudatory apology; and Joseph Kastein, *The Messiah of Ismir: Sabbatai Zevi* (New York: Viking Press, 1931), which lacks the apparatus of scholarship, but appears to be well informed and reliable as well as interesting. Theodore H. Papadopoullos, *Studies and Documents relating to the History of the Greek Church and People under Turkish Domination* (Brussels: Bibliotheca Graeca Aevi Posterioris, 1952) is exactly what the title states — not a book but fragments for a book. Western languages appear to lack any serious study of the history and development of the ecumenical patriarchate or of the Greek Orthodox church in our period. Standard works on the Eastern church all appear to assume an unchanging, immobile reality throughout Turkish times — a myth Papadopoullos effectively explodes.

Generally speaking, I did not attempt to rest this essay directly on primary sources. A limited number of source collections have been published, which I list merely to encourage any student thinking of his Ph.D. dissertation to have a look: Henry Marczali, *Enchiridion Fontum Historiae Hungarorum* (Budapest: Societatis Athenaei, 1902); Roderich Gooss, *Österreichische Staatsverträge: Fürstentum Siebenbürgen, 1526–1690* (Vienna: A. Halzhausen, 1911); Joseph, Graf Kemeny, *Notitia Historico-Diplomatica Archivi et Literalium Capituli Albensis Transilvaniae* (Cibinii: W. H. Thierry, 1836). The handsome and admirable collection of Gabriel Noradounghian, *Recueil d'actes internationaux de l'empire ottomane* (4 vols.; Paris: F. Pichon, 1897–1903), is also relevant.

Travelers' accounts constitute another and for my purposes often a more instructive sort of source material, although the usual problems of credibility are acute when Western adventurers are regaling Western audiences with the wonders of the East. Important travelers' books I consulted include: Baron de Tott, *Memoirs concerning the State of the Turkish Empire and the Crimea* (2 vols.; London: G. G. J. & J. Robinson, 1785), a most vivid and entertaining story, generally credible despite a bit of naïve boasting; Mary Holderness, *New Russia: Journey from Riga to the Crimea by Way of Kiev with Some Account of the Colonization, Manners, and Customs of the Colonists of New Russia, to Which Are Added Notes relating to the Crim Tartars* (London: Sherwood Jones & Co., 1823), a pleasant monument to the observant powers of a venturesome Englishwoman; and the learned polymath's report, translated from the German original as P. S. Pallas, *Travels through the Southern Provinces of the Russian Empire in the Years 1793–94* (2 vols., 2nd ed.; London: J. Stockdale, 1812). By comparison, earlier travelers' reports are not very helpful, e.g., *Russia seu Moscovia itemque Tartaria, Commentario Topographico atque Politico Illustratae* (Leyden: Elzevier, 1630); George Sandys, *A Relation of a Journey Begun in An. Dom. 1610* (2d ed.; London: W. Barrett, 1621); Chevalier Pierre, Conseiller du roi, *Histoire de la guerre des Cossaques contre Pologne, avec un discours de leurs origines, païs, moeurs, gouvernment et religion, et un autre des Tartares precopites* (Paris: C. Barbin, 1663); Guillaume, Sieur de Beauplan, *A Description of Ukraine,* translated and reprinted in Awnsham Churchill, *A Collection of Voyages and Travels* (London: A. & J. Churchill, 1704–1732), I, 571–610. The well-known and deservedly famous reports by Busbecq and Sir Thomas Roe are in a class by themselves. I used reprints: E. S. Forster (trans.), *The Turkish Letters of Ogier Ghislain de Busbecq* (Oxford: Oxford University Press, 1927); and Thomas Roe, *Negotiations in His Embassy to the Ottoman Porte . . . 1621–28* (London: S. Richardson, 1740).

Not all garrulous travelers were Westerners. Evilya Effendi, *Narrative of Travels in Europe, Asia and Africa* (London: Oriental Translation Fund of Great Britain and Ireland, 1846–50), offers miscellaneous sidelights on the confrontation of cultures as it struck an intelligent Turk in the seventeenth century. Richard F. Kreutel and Otto Speis, *Leben und Abenteur des Dolmetschers Osman Aga* (Bonn: Orientalisches Seminar der Universität Bonn, 1954), is an account of the experiences of a Turk captured by the Austrians in 1688. The same scholar also published a Turkish diary of the siege of Vienna, Richard F. Kreutel, *Kara Mustapha vor Wien* (Graz: Verlag Styria, 1955). Interesting sidelights on the last prominent Magyar to opt for the Ottoman alliance may be had by glancing through Coloman Thaly (ed.), *Lettres de Turquie (1730–39) et notices de César de Saussure, gentilhomme de la cour de S.H.S. le prince François Rakoczi II* (Budapest: Academie Hongroise des Sciences, 1909).

Old histories and chronicles constitute another type of source. Especially interesting to me was the sumptuously published book, Grégoire Urechi, *Chronique de Moldavie depuis de milieu du XIVᵉ siècle jusqu'à l'an 1594* (Paris: Ernest Leroux, 1878). Francesco Sansovino (ed.), *Dell'historia universale dell'origine et imperio dei Turchi* (Venice: F. Rampazetto, 1564); and the better known Richard Knolles, *The Generall Historie of the Turkes* (London: Adam Islip, 1621) are also worth looking at.

More specialized treatises and books that proved somewhat less useful for this essay have mostly been acknowledged in the footnotes. A few of them nevertheless deserve comment here. Two books that purport to deal with relations between Germans and Eastern peoples are both disappointing: Stephen Fischer-Galati, *Ottoman Imperialism and German Protestantism* (Cambridge, Mass.: Harvard University Press, 1959); and Fritz Valjavec, *Geschichte der deutschen Kulturbeziehungen zu Südosteuropa, II: Reformation und Gegenreformation* (Munich: R. Oldenburg, 1955). The Nazi period produced two relatively slender works which are nevertheless quite useful for the information they assemble: Konrad Schünemann, *Österreichs Bevölkerungspolitik unter Maria Theresia* (Berlin: Deutsche Rundschau, 1935), and Rupert von Schumacher, *Des Reiches Hofzaun: Geschichte der deutschen Militärgrenze im Südosten* (Darmstadt: Ludwig Kickler, 1940). Rather less persuasive is F. Thierfelder, *Ursprung und Wirkung der französischen Kultureinflüsse in Südosteuropa* (Berlin: Duncker and Humblot, 1943). By comparison, both pre- and post-Nazi German scholarship, as applied to comparatively restricted themes, stands out very favorably: Hans Halm, *Habsburgischen Osthandel im 18. Jahrhundert* (*Veröffentlichungen des Osteuropa Instituts, München* [Munich: Isar Verlag, 1954]), for example, or the older, admirable monographs by Wilhelm Fraknoi, *Matthias Corvinus, König von Ungarn, 1458–1490* (Freiburg im Breisgau: Herder'sche Verlagshandlung, 1891): and Wilhelm Fraknoi, *Ungarn vor der Schlacht bei Mohacz, 1524–26* (Budapest: Lauffer, 1886).

Three brief but admirable works deal with topics that lie on the fringes of our subject: Berthold Spuler, *Les Mongols dans l'histoire* (Paris: Payot, 1961), which summarizes in brief compass what is known about the entire sweep of Mongol history, including a very short chapter on the Crimean and other Tartar hordes of Russia; Georg Stadtmüller, "Die albanische Volkstumgeschichte als Forschungsproblem," *Leipziger Vierteljahrsschrift für Südosteuropa*, V (1941–42), 58–80, which raises the right questions without answering any of them; and L. S. Stavrianos, "Antecedents to the Balkan Revolutions of the 19th Century," *Journal of Modern History*, XXIX (1957), 335–48, which offers a stimulating, though not quite consistent (I think) interpretation of the economic and social changes that helped precipitate the Greek and Serbian revolutions.

The very careful work of Oswald Prentiss Backus, *Motives of West Russian Nobles in Deserting Lithuania for Moscow, 1337–1514* (Lawrence: University of Kansas Press, 1957), offers an interesting insight into the interrelations of aristocracy and autocracy, though it deals with a region beyond the limits properly of concern in this essay. At the other extreme, I cannot forebear mentioning F. F. Seeley, "Russia and the Slave Trade," *Slavonic Review* XXIII (1945), 126–36 —a totally unscholarly presentation of a pregnant idea, un supported unfortunately by information or research.

Any honest bibliographical essay should conclude with titles of books that look promising but which have not, in fact, been seen. The whole corpus of Turkish, Slavic, Magyar learning remains outside my purview for linguistic reasons. Due either to limitations of time or to faulty citations, I have also failed to locate H. Schumann, "Die Hetmanstaat," *Jahrbücher für Geschichte Osteuropas*, I (1936) 499– 548; N. Jorga, *La Revolution française et le sud-est de l'Europe* (Bucharest, 1934); Gustav Gründish, *Die siebenbürgische Unternehmung der Fugger, 1528–31* (Bucharest: 1941); H. Hahn, *Österreich und Neurussland, I: Donauschiffsfahrt und -handel nach dem Südosten, 1718–1780* (Breslau, 1943); N. Ernst, *Beziehungen Moskaus zu den Tartaren der Krym unter Ivan III and Vasilij III*, Berliner Dissertation, 1911; A. Vandal, *Le pasha Bonneval* (Paris: 1855); Peyssonel, *Traité sur la commerce de la Mer Noire* (Paris: 1787); J. Raicevich, *Osservazioni storiche naturali, e politiche intorno la Valachie e Moldavia* (Naples: G. Raimondi, 1788); Joseph Marshall, *Travels through Holland . . . Russia, the Ukraine and Poland in the Years 1768, 1769 and 1770* (3 vols.; London: J. Almon, 1772–76). No doubt many more did not even come to my attention.

INDEX

tion), 57, 58, 65, 68, 70, 71, 73,
95, 126, 128, 128 n., 129, 130,
145, 148, 166, 167, 174, 176,
177, 178, 182, 186, 187, 188,
189, 190, 202, 211, 215, 221
Burghers (*see* Townsmen)
Busbecq, Ogier Ghislain de, 232
Busch-Zantner, Richard, 38 n., 149
n., 223
Byzantinism, 21, 35, 38, 47, 104,
106, 107, 107 n., 108, 108 n.,
173, 176, 202, 207, 208, 209

Caesarism, 71
Caliph of Islam, 196
Calugareni, battle of, 94
Calvinism, 36, 44, 66, 72, 93, 99,
100, 100 n., 110, 163
Cambridge University, 123 n.
Canada, 200, 201
Canals, 54, 55 n., 216
Candia, 131, 132, 141, 152
Caribbean Sea, 155 n.
Carinthia, 33 n.
Carniola, 33 n.
Carpathians, 2, 3, 5, 10, 11, 34, 44,
47, 101, 109, 118, 154, 208
Caspian Sea, 54, 55 n.
Catherine II, empress of Russia,
187, 192, 197, 199, 200
Catholics, 12, 29 n., 36, 66, 67, 68,
69, 71, 72, 73, 78, 80, 81, 82,
84, 85, 86, 89, 92, 93, 97, 98,
100, 109, 110, 115, 132, 137,
138, 154, 159, 163, 188, 194,
195, 208, 209
Cavalry, 13, 18, 20, 23, 32, 38, 42,
44, 47, 56, 60, 63, 78, 86, 96,
99, 128, 128 n., 129, 148, 149,
163, 176, 187
Centralization, 32, 33, 34, 35, 37,
38, 39, 66, 68, 70, 72, 73, 77,
97, 99, 126, 128, 142, 160, 161,
182, 185, 213, 219
Cetinje, 138
Charles V, Holy Roman Emperor
(r. 1519–55), 35, 66
Charles XII, king of Sweden, 168,
169, 170, 174
Cherkassy, 114

Chiliasm (*see* Millenarianism)
Chirigin, 143
Christendom, Christian Europe, 9,
38, 38 n., 39, 55 n., 58, 196
Christians, Christianity, v, 8, 24,
28, 31, 33 n., 35, 36, 40, 40 n.,
42, 44, 46, 49, 50, 55, 55 n.,
56, 58, 62, 79 n., 107, 112,
120, 132, 134, 135 n., 137, 138,
146, 148, 149 n., 153, 154, 156,
157, 158, 169, 175, 176, 189,
195, 198, 203, 209
Church Slavonic, 109
Churchill, Awnsham, 232
Cimmerians, 6
Civilization (*see also* Culture), 8,
13, 32, 71, 72, 76, 90, 113,
115, 115 n., 122, 126, 145, 154,
165, 173, 176, 178, 187, 198,
200, 217, 221
Colonization (*see* Settlement)
Commerce (*see* Trade)
Commercial agriculture, 49, 101,
103, 105, 106, 113, 130, 149,
150, 152, 173, 182, 186, 190,
200, 214, 215, 216
Commissio Neo-acquisitica, 162
Commoners (*see* Peasantry; Townsmen)
Conquests, 8, 9, 10, 36, 40 n., 133,
137, 162
Constantinople, 14, 21, 22, 23 n.,
24, 25, 26, 28, 30, 35, 41, 42,
42 n., 43, 43 n., 47, 48, 49, 50,
54, 55 n., 61, 63, 65, 88, 90,
101 n., 102, 103, 103 n., 104,
107, 109, 110, 116, 118, 119,
130, 132, 133, 136, 137, 139,
140, 141, 144, 150, 151, 152,
157, 158, 171, 172, 173, 174,
175, 185, 186, 195, 203, 204,
208
Constitution
of Croatia, 210, 215
of Hungary (*see also* Tripartitum*), 18, 20, 45, 72, 94, 95,
96, 97, 98, 130, 142, 148,
161, 165, 188, 189, 210, 215,
216, 218, 219, 220

of Poland, 79, 80
of Sweden, 82 n.
of Transylvania, 210, 215
Consuls, 195
Cossacks, 14, 49, 50, 58, 77, 78, 81,
   82, 83, 87, 89, 91, 94, 102, 111–
   23, 128 n., 140, 142, 143, 145,
   146, 147, 148, 167, 168, 169,
   170, 177, 178, 192, 193, 194,
   197
   Registered, 112, 117, 118, 121,
      122
   Unregistered, 112, 122
Counter Reformation, 58, 72, 84,
   85, 92, 99, 109
County government (Hungary), 18,
   44, 164, 218, 219
Coups d'état, 102, 132, 135, 136,
   140, 158
Coxe, William, 224
Cracow, 140
Crete, 109, 131, 132, 136, 137, 138,
   139, 141, 145, 149, 152
Crimea, Crim Tartars, 2, 12, 13, 14,
   22, 23, 24, 25, 25 n., 26, 28,
   29 n., 46, 47, 48, 49, 50, 54, 58,
   76, 77, 78, 83, 88, 90, 94, (111–
   23), 128 n., 137, 140, 144, 145,
   145 n., 167, 169, 172, 175, 176,
   177, 178, 184, 187, 188, 194,
   195, 196, 197, 198, 199, 199 n.,
   199 n., 210
Crnojevic, Arsen, 157
Croatia, Croats, 43, 91, 162, 210,
   215
Culture (see also Civilization), 9,
   11, 13, 34, 36, 37, 49, 57, 62,
   77, 81, 84, 85, 86, 88, 90, 101,
   105, 105 n., 106, 107, 108, 108
   n., 132, 141, 145, 165, 173,
   196, 198, 199, 200, 201, 202,
   207, 209, 210, 221
Custom (see Traditionalism)
Cyprus, 55, 55 n., 56

Dacia, 208, 209
Damascus, 133
Danilo, prince of Montenegro, 138
Danube River, 2, 3, 26, 33 n., 41,
   48, 49, 54, 119, 154, 157, 169,
   172, 178, 199, 202, 204, 205,
   213
Danubian Europe, v, vi, 2, 3, 4,
   5, 6, 8, 14, 18, 23 n., 28, 33 n.,
   50, 51, 55, 58, 59, 75, 87–123,
   126, 129, 139, 148, 154, 167,
   177, 178, 182, 185, 187, 190,
   215, 221
Dardanelles (see also Straits), 3, 133
David, Franz, 93, 93 n.
Debrecen, 217
den Hollander, A. N. J., 44 n.,
   217 n.
Denmark, Danes, 77, 78, 140
Depner, Maja, 101 n., 229
Dervishes, 31, 35, 135, 136, 137,
   138, 189
Diet,
   Hungarian, 17, 18, 45, 72, 95,
      96, 141, 161, 164, 218, 220
   Polish, 78, 79, 80, 82, 84, 92,
      116, 121
   Transylvanian, 37, 96, 163
Diplomacy, 24, 25, 26, 89, 95, 96,
   147, 155, 172, 173, 174, 176,
   184, 184 n., 194, 197, 207
Disease, 8, 9, 29, 38, 172
Dnieper River, 114, 118, 143, 144,
   146, 167, 170, 178, 191, 193,
   195, 197
Dniester River, 26, 119, 169, 178,
   184, 198
Dobrudja, 199
Don River, 54, 120 n., 167, 170,
   184, 193, 195, 199, 221
Doroshenko, Peter, 123 n., 142,
   143, 143 n., 148
Dragoman of the Porte, 152, 174
Durham, M. E., 134
Dutchmen, 86, 130, 158

Eastern Europe, 27, 88, 91, 98, 101,
   110, 112, 128, 129, 130, 154,
   155, 172, 186, 201 n., 202, 221
Ecclesiastical organization, 67, 76,
   137, 138, 143 n., 153, 207
Economics, 4, 20, 27, 29, 29 n., 32,
   38 n., 49, 60, 88, 107, 108,
   110, 111, 130, 138, 165, 166,
   177, 186, 190, 199, 203, 204,

240   INDEX

Mesopotamia, 158
Mester, Nikolaus, 101 n.
Michael the Brave, prince of Wallachia (r. 1593–1601), 88, 94, 102, 103, 106, 107, 117
Michael Romanovv, tsar of Russia, 81, 83, 84
Militärgrenzen (*see also* Grenzers), 162
Military class, 16, 18, 20, 33, 34, 38 n., 56, 57, 176
Military forces (*see* Army; Artillery; Cavalry; Infantry; Navy)
Military operations (*see* War)
Military organization, 114, 128, 160, 168, 186, 190, 191, 191 n., 192 n., 211, 212, 213
Military power, 6, 10, 11, 13, 24, 25, 26, 32, 33, 35, 43, 48, 49, 55, 57, 71, 72, 74, 79, 80, 88, 89, 92, 102, 108, 110, 111, 121, 129, 130, 131, 133, 140, 147, 148, 156, 174, 175, 184, 195, 203 n., 207, 209
Military service, 17, 198
Military tactics, 128, 128 n., 132, 149, 168, 212
Millenarianism, 93, 152, 153, 154, 167, 194
Mingli-girai, Tartar khan, 24, 25
Mining, 3, 10, 11
Mohacz, battle of, 6, 18, 42, 45, 46, 156
Mohammed the Conqueror (*see* Mehmed)
Moldavia, 11, 12, 14, 16, 21, 24, 25 n., 47, 48, 49, 58, 77, 88, 91, 100, 101–11, 117, 135 n., 140, 141, 145, 153, 155, 169, 173, 174, 175, 184, 184 n., 198, 203 n., 204, 205 n., 206, 209
Monarchy, 58, 59, 126, 128, 129, 150
  Austrian, 68, 70, 73, 74, 91, 95, 97, 98, 103, 147, 178, 196
  Crimean, 144, 145, 176, 177, 184, 196
  Hungarian, 16, 17, 18, 20, 37, 45, 97, 148, 161

  Polish, 34, 75, 78, 79, 80, 83, 92, 112, 116, 118, 121, 140, 146
  Rumanian, 48, 102, 140, 145, 174, 203, 204, 205, 205 n.
  Russian, 75, 81, 82 n., 86, 91, 112, 121, 152, 178
  Swedish, 77, 82 n.
  Transylvanian, 90, 95, 96
  Turkish, 27, 28, 30, 31, 32, 34, 37, 38, 40, 41, 42, 44, 45, 57, 59, 60, 61, 64, 70, 102, 148, 152, 153, 157, 158, 196
Money (*see* Economics; Finance)
Mongols, v, 8
Montenegro, Montengrins, 132, 137, 138, 145, 169
Moravia, 16
Morea (Peloponnesus), 158, 170
Moscow, 14, 49, 77, 82, 111, 116, 147
Moslems (*see* Islam)
Mountaineers, 134, 139, 187
Movila princes (of Moldavia), 102
Murad I, Ottoman sultan (r. 1359–89), 173
Murad IV (r. 1623–40), 61, 63, 64, 65, 136
Muscovy (*see* Russia)
Mutinies (*see also* Rebellions), 133, 167
Mysticism, 31, 132, 135, 136, 137

Nadir Shah, 171
Nationalism, v, 76, 81 n., 98, 115, 122, 201, 203
Naval operations, 24, 55, 55 n., 118, 119, 131, 132, 139, 171
Navy, 59, 128, 129, 131, 133, 136, 139, 150, 166, 170, 190, 210
Negroes, 28
New Russia, 200 n.
New Serbia, 192, 210
Nicholsburg, treaty of (1622), 97
Nikolaev, 200
Nikosios, Panagioti, 152
Nimwegen, treaty of, 147
Nistor, J., 111 n.
Nobility, 38 n., 39, 59, 101 n.
  Austrian, 68, 69, 71, 73, 74, 126
  Bohemian, 97